CRITICAL INSIGHTS

Inequality

CRITICAL INSIGHTS

Inequality

Editor
Kimberly Drake
Scripps College, California

SALEM PRESS
A Division of EBSCO Information Services, Inc.
Ipswich, Massachusetts

GREY HOUSE PUBLISHING

Publisher's Cataloging-In-Publication Data
(Prepared by The Donohue Group, Inc.)

Names: Drake, Kimberly, 1965- editor.
Title: Inequality / editor, Kimberly Drake, Scripps College, California.
Other Titles: Critical insights.
Description: [First edition]. | Ipswich, Massachusetts : Salem Press, a division
    of EBSCO Information Services, Inc. ; Amenia, NY : Grey
    House Publishing, [2018] | Includes bibliographical references
    and index.
Identifiers: ISBN 9781682176900 (hardcover)
Subjects: LCSH: Equality in literature. | Marginality, Social, in literature. |
    Segregation in literature.
Classification: LCC PN3352.E68 I54 2018 | DDC 809.933556--dc23

First Printing

Contents

About This Volume, Kimberly Drake   vii

Introduction: "Deprived of the Same Privilege": On Inequality,
Kimberly Drake   xv

Critical Contexts

Caste: The Engine That Runs (ruins) India, Lucky Issar
     Essay Discusses: Arundhati Roy's novels *The God of Small Things* and
     The Ministry of Utmost Happiness   3

Punishment, Spirituality, and Materialism in the Anti-Utopia, Roger Chapman
     Essay Discusses: Fyodor Dostoyevsky's novels *Poor Folk*, *Notes from the Dead*
     House, *Winter Notes on Summer Impressions*, *Notes from the Underground*, and
     Crime and Punishment   19

Leveling the Playing Field: Cultural Relativism and Inequality, Adam T. Bogar
     Essay Discusses: Kurt Vonnegut's novel *The Sirens of Titan* and short story
     "Harrison Bergeron"   35

Structural Inequality, Labor Exploitation, and the Foundation of America,
Jericho Williams
     Essay Discusses: Solomon Northup's slave narrative *Twelve Years a Slave* and
     Frederick Douglass' slave narrative *My Bondage and My Freedom*   47

Critical Readings

Racial Classifications and Crossing the Color Line, Almas Khan
     Essay Discusses: Nella Larsen's novel *Passing*   63

Ideological Control and Human Nature in the Dystopian Society,
Boyarkina Iren
     Essay Discusses: George Orwell's novel *1984*   78

The "Closet" and Marginalized Identities, Sonia Mae Brown
     Essay Discusses: James Baldwin's story "The Outing" and novel *Giovanni's Room*   94

White Femininity and the Black Female Gaze: Internalized Oppression,
Julie Prebel
     Essay Discusses: Toni Morrison's novel *The Bluest Eye*   108

Not Just Any Ol' Injun: The (Re)Appropriation and Alteration of
    Native American Stereotypes, Robyn Johnson
    Essay Discusses: Louise Erdrich's novel *Tracks*   124

Tracking Wolves: A Metaphor for Cross-border Inequality, Peter Arnds
    Essay Discusses: Cormac McCarthy's novel *The Crossing*   144

Historical Trauma and the Haunting of "Comfort Women," Ji Nang Kim
    Essay Discusses: Nora Okja Keller's novel *Comfort Woman* and
    Yong Soon Min's Art Works   158

Dwelling in Time: The Representation of Poverty on Film, Andrew Bingham
    Essay Discusses: Pedro Costa's film series *Letters from Fontainhas*   174

Immigrants, Nationalism, and Xenophobia in London, Önder Çakırtaş
    Essay Discusses: Anders Lustgarten's play *A Day at the Racists*   189

Resources

Additional Works on the Theme   205
Bibliography   209
About the Editor   221
Contributors   223
Index   229

About This Volume

Kimberly Drake

In this volume, we explore some key texts in what one of the chapter authors, Jericho Williams, has called a "subgenre" of American literature: the literature of inequality. Much of early U.S. literature could fit into this category in a variety of ways. The settler colonies[1] transformed themselves into a nation through rebellion against systemic tyranny, yet paid for this war through enslavement and the appropriation of American Indian land, perpetuating forms of inequality with which they were familiar. Enslavement is one example of labor exploitation, which has taken many other forms over the centuries, including indentured servitude, apprenticeships, sweatshops, prostitution, migrant or seasonal labor, and prison labor. While individuals have survived or escaped these systems, they are usually permanently marked by them and viewed thereafter as being unequal.

Segregation and borders are other ways that those in power continue to use to maintain control over spaces and resources on the land. When, over one hundred years ago, W. E. B. Du Bois described the primary problem of the twentieth century as the "problem of the color line" in *The Souls of Black Folk*, he refers to both mechanisms of inequality used by the settler colonists: in the idea of "color" as racial inequality and the "line" as a border used to control access to spaces. As the twenty-first century gets underway, we are still struggling with race, borders, and the control of the minds and bodies of those without power.

The chapters in this volume examine works that focus on people who have been exploited, colonized, and "disappeared" as the result of various systems of inequality in the U.S. and elsewhere. These works focus primarily on the effects of or the resistance to inequality and to the violence that often accompanies it. Individual chapters look at particular nuances of inequality, such as the various ways that marginalized people resist or unlearn the indoctrination about their own inferiority, or develop a voice within conditions that seek to silence them. Some of the characters in these texts appropriate the tools used to oppress them: they strategically inhabit racial stereotypes, or they disguise themselves so as to "pass" as white, or they keep their sexuality hidden in the "closet" and use that confining space as a shelter.

Other chapters study texts that attempt to confront inequality or to imagine solutions to it. Some of these texts portray the damage done by forms of violent inequality not only to the victims of violence and their ancestors, but to those who inflict violence upon them, and even to entire nations or cultures. A number of texts take the opposite path, imagining solutions to the problem of inequality or portraying societies in which oppression does not exist. For a number of authors writing about such utopian societies, however, a fully egalitarian society does not seem possible in the face of what the authors see as flaws in human nature, the desire for power over others, or the inability to see difference among humans without attempting to categorize and control it. None of the texts discussed in this volume could imagine a fully functional egalitarian society that did not try to eliminate difference or restrict individual liberty, despite the fact that all of their authors were known to be working against particular forms of inequality.

Perhaps because of the centrality of inequality in the history of the U.S., most chapters here focus on texts written by U.S. authors, but some focus on literature and film from countries outside the US, countries that similarly struggle with imbedded traditions of inequality. The texts discussed here include many very well-known works of literature, including some that are considered representative of their particular literary form (such as the slave narrative, or the dystopian novel), as well as texts that might be less familiar to readers. All of the texts here discuss issues and ideologies that will be familiar to readers, however, as touching on some aspect of inequality and resistance to forms of oppression.

My own introductory chapter discusses the meaning of the terms "inequality" and "inequity" and their connection to the concepts of "the norm." The very definition of "inequality" suggests that any form of bodily or behavioral difference from a norm must automatically fall into a hierarchy of power, in which those most different from the norm are considered the most socially inferior. The chapter foregrounds the way that various people accept this hierarchy as "natural," even people who are resisting social oppression.

Lucky Issar's chapter, entitled "Caste: The Engine That Runs (ruins) India," contextualizes and historicizes class and gender-based injustices in two novels by Arundhati Roy, whose Man Booker prize-winning novel *The God of Small Things* was a best-seller and made Roy the most famous novelist in India. The first of the Critical Contexts chapters, it locates the genesis of class and gender-based inequalities in the Indian caste-system– a divinely ordained system, delineated in ancient Hindu texts, of ranked hereditary classes of people who must follow the appropriate lifestyles and social behaviors for their caste. Issar examines how Roy connects the plots of her novels to the historical construction of caste, ultimately revealing that the exploitation of those at the bottom of the hierarchy damages those at the top.

In "Punishment, Spirituality, and Materialism in the Anti-Utopia," the Critical Reception chapter, Roger Chapman discusses how Russian novelist Dostoyevsky's class privilege and political activism shaped his literary work as well as how his writing career and the reception of his work influenced his life. After some literary success, Dostoyevsky began to act on the socialistic ideas he had embraced in his youth; his political activism, however, nearly got him executed, and a last-minute reprieve commuted his sentence to hard labor in Siberia. During his years of imprisonment and penal exile, Dostoyevsky underwent a reexamination of his political beliefs, and although he still condemned class inequality, he did so by embracing traditional Russian Orthodox spirituality, something he connected to the poorest people in his society. In subsequent writings, such as *Winter Notes on Summer Impressions, Notes from the Underground, Crime and Punishment, The Devils*, and other works, he offered a condemning critique of western ideologies, such as socialism, that he believed were in opposition to the good of humankind.

In his Critical Lens chapter, "Leveling the Playing Field: Cultural Relativism and Inequality," Adam T. Bogar explores class inequality in the literary work of Kurt Vonnegut through the lens of a particular theory from the discipline of anthropology, a discipline in which Vonnegut was very interested. Beginning with an analysis of how American writer Vonnegut developed an interest in anthropology and political thought, Bogar analyzes Vonnegut's 1959 novel *The Sirens of Titan* and his 1961 short story "Harrison Bergeron" as well as a selection of his non-fiction. Noting that Vonnegut's fiction portrayed the hardships suffered by the poorest members of society empathetically, Bogar suggests that Vonnegut's interest in anthropology led him to a rejection of the idea that we should create egalitarian societies through cultural relativism, an idea influencing anthropologists during Vonnegut's college years. Cultural relativism suggested to Vonnegut an artificial and destructive leveling of difference.

In the Comparative Analysis chapter, "Structural Inequality, Labor Exploitation, and the Foundation of America," Jericho Williams argues that the two slave narratives he studies should hold a central place in what he considers an American literary subgenre, the literature of inequality. Williams discusses two of the three most influential works of antislavery literature in history, and *Twelve Years a Slave* continued its influence when it was made into an Academy Award-winning film in 2013. In his chapter, Williams compares them not to each other but to the majority of the texts in the slave narrative tradition. Written by authors who had experienced slavery but also years of life in freedom, these two slave narratives display a nuanced understanding of the ways that slavery-era capitalism fostered the dehumanization of African Americans, facilitated the impoverishment of lower class whites, and jeopardized an entire nation.

The Critical Readings chapters focus more generally on literary interpretations of works on inequality, organized chronologically. In "Racial Classifications and Crossing the Color Line," Almas Khan examines Larsen's portrayal of African Americans "passing" for white during a period of legalized racial segregation. Inclusion in or exclusion from privileged spaces functions in the text as a metaphor for communal and national recognition (or lack thereof). Privileged spaces in *Passing* range from swaths of cities to individual homes, and characters' interactions in these spaces illustrates how African Americans living under Jim Crow could subvert spatial restrictions intended to reinforce their status as second-class citizens, but often at a profound personal cost.

In "Ideological Control and Human Nature in the Dystopian Society," Boyarkina Iren finds that George Orwell's *1984*, while showcasing inequality in a dystopian totalitarian society, also critiques socialism as being another kind of totalitarian society, one that abandons the ideals of liberty and equality. Orwell's well-known novel depicts a rigidly stratified society in which control of inhabitants is maintained through a greatly reduced lexicon, widespread indoctrination and rewriting of history, and various kinds of surveillance. Through the chilling dystopia set up in *1984*, Orwell provides a thorough explanation of the mechanisms of inequality in human society (including our own societies) from its origins to the present day, one of those mechanisms being the kind of ideological control of consciousness that the dystopian society in the novel accomplishes. Ultimately, however, Orwell portrays egalitarian socialism as impossible because of the ruling class's desire for power and its ability to control consciousness in this way.

Focusing on works by noted author James Baldwin, Sonia Mae Brown examines the way that the "closet" functions in the lives of queer individuals but also marginalized individuals more broadly. Her chapter, "The "Closet" and Marginalized Identities," explores Baldwin's use of the closet both as a space of containment and a place of transformation, a protected space of becoming in which one can construct a particular sexuality. Baldwin's discussions of the closet engage larger discussions of identity and spatial dynamics, similar to those in discussions of "passing" and borders.

In "White Femininity and the Black Female Gaze: Internalized Oppression," Julie Prebel focuses on Morrison's rendering of the ways white standards of beauty are internalized by the novel's protagonists. In particular, as shown through the novel's focus on the racial stigmas associated with appearance and beauty, Morrison highlights how white society's contempt for blackness can have devastating effects on African Americans, Pecola Breedlove in particular. Pecola represents both to the reader and to other characters in the novel the manifestation of the history of violence and oppression both she and her community experience. However, the novel also showcases various subtle acts of rebellion against white supremacy by black women who reject white standards of beauty and white-centered values.

In her essay "Not Just Any Ol' Injun: The (Re)Appropriation and Alteration of Native American Stereotypes," Robyn Johnson also investigates subtle acts of rebellion by marginalized protagonists. Johnson focuses on Erdrich's appropriation and manipulation of the Native American stereotypes, the Savage and Noble Savage, in the era of post-colonial and decolonialized literature. While Erdrich tackles the serious issues of racism and poverty, what makes *Tracks* (1988) a unique resistance to colonialism is Erdrich's innovative use of gender; she applies the masculine stereotypes to Pauline and Fleur, the two main female characters. Through this choice, Erdrich establishes that Native stereotypes are not innate, but created through social actions and perceptions of both the white and Native communities, and she suggests that embracing inappropriate stereotypes can give control of the narrative back to Native people.

Peter Arnds explores Cormac McCarthy's use of a wolf as a metaphor for human forms of inequality connected to nations and borders in his chapter "Tracking Wolves: A Metaphor for Cross-border Inequality." As McCarthy argues, wolves have served cultures around the world and through the ages as a metaphor for wicked or immoral human behavior. In his novel *The Crossing* (1994), McCarthy's sixteen-year old male protagonist recognizes a common bond between himself and the pregnant wolf that trespasses across the border from Mexico into the US and is hunted by farmers as vermin. McCarthy's she-wolf is a metaphor on multiple levels, expressive of social injustice, ethnic violence, and the treatment of indigenous peoples, but this is also a story that deserves renewed attention in light of contemporary politics regarding both migrants and the environment.

Ji Nang Kim's chapter focuses on wartime sexual slavery and the ways that these repressed histories are spoken and reinhabited in "Historical Trauma and the Haunting of 'Comfort Women.'" Juxtaposing Keller's novel to Min's sculptural installations on sexual slaves for Japanese imperial armies during World War II, this chapter examines the portrayal of ghosts as emblems of inherited trauma that revisit present-day society in attempts to find justice. Keller's and Min's reconstructions of traumas provide an alternative paradigm for justice focusing on women's silencing and discovery of voice, one that challenges not only patriarchy and violence in Japanese colonialism, but also in Korean nationalism.

Andrew Bingham's chapter "Dwelling in Time: The Representation of Poverty on Film" focuses on Costa's documentary films and their portrayal of severely impoverished people in Lisbon. Bingham focuses on the struggles of Costa, a widely acclaimed Portugese filmmaker, to discover the most fitting representational form for his film, an issue that is of paramount importance to those using art to work against inequality. Costa works to maintain an ethical standard for how to depict impoverished people and environments to an audience which almost inevitably comes from a more privileged socio-economic reality, and which brings with it stereotypes about the subjects of Costa's film.

Finally, in "Immigrants, Nationalism, and Xenophobia in London," Önder Çakırtaş picks up again on the issue of immigration, which he notes is becoming one of the most important problems we face today. Immigrants are in the unique situation of being shaped by the society to which they have migrated, while simultaneously influencing and perhaps changing the social, cultural, psychological and economic structure of that society. That's exactly what Lustgarten's play offers in its examination of the way white working-class Londoners define their sense of "Britishness" and national identity. With direct relevance to recent political events in the UK and the US, this play depicts the ways that the politically progressive members of the white working class are becoming conservative around the issue of immigration. Çakırtaş traces this transformation while insisting that Lustgarten empathetically portrays the struggle of these characters to get the attention of their government, which has abandoned them.

The chapters in this volume thus explore examples of inequality that are unique to the current moment, such as those in Lustgarten's play, as well as those that have continued in a fairly consistent manner for centuries, such as issues related to bodies (gender, race, ability, sexuality) and to geographic and domestic spaces (borders, closets). All of the texts studied here were attempting to intervene in the problem of social inequality not only by educating their readers or audiences but by enabling them to identify with those whose lives have been damaged or cut short by violent forms of oppression. While many societies around the world are working to confront their histories of oppression due in part to interventions like these, a close look at the chapters in this volume will remind us that this work is far from over.

Note

1. "Settler colonialism" is the particular form of colonialism practiced in the United States (and elsewhere, such as Canada and Australia). Colonialism is characterized by the attempt of one nation to conquer people in another area and exploit the resources of that area for itself, thus establishing domination over the colonized people. However, "unlike other types of colonialism in which the goal is to maintain colonial structures," in settler colonization, the settlers come not to manage and control the indigenous people of the conquered land, but to replace them; they work to establish "a supreme and unchallenged settler state and people," eliminating "the challenges posed to settler sovereignty by indigenous peoples' claims to land by eliminating indigenous peoples themselves and asserting false narratives and structures of settler belonging" (Global Social Theory).

Introduction: "Deprived of the Same Privilege": On Inequality

Kimberly Drake

> Inequality is as dear to the American heart as liberty itself.
> (William Dean Howells 565)

The Oxford English Dictionary defines "inequality" as "difference in size, degree, circumstances, etc.; lack of equality." By resting the definition on the idea of "difference," this definition suggests that difference is always infused by power relations, highlighting the notion embedded in the meaning of "inequality" that equality can only be found in sameness. We can see this notion more clearly in the archaic definition of "inequality" in the OED: the "lack of smoothness or regularity in a surface." Such a lack of "regularity" can only be the result of difference among the "surface's" component parts. But in real life, we don't need to be the same to be equal. Perhaps because of this kind of confusion, recently the term "inequity" has been preferred over "inequality" by those attempting to theorize the causes and/or effects of hierarchies in various areas. Inequity, defined by the OED as "lack of fairness or justice," resists suggesting that difference inevitably leads to inequality. It allows for the idea that individuals may experience injustice or unfairness without regard to their similarity or difference to other people. Why am I spending so much time on definitions? Because as Sensoy and DiAngelo put it, "Language is not a neutral transmitter of a universal, objective, or fixed reality. Rather, language is the way we *construct* reality, the framework we use to give meaning to our experiences and perceptions within a given society" (70). Because it often gives archaic meanings and initial usages in context, the Oxford English Dictionary helps us see how our ideas have been constructed through language over time.

What we can see in the definitions of "inequality" and "inequity," then, is that our society suggests a "fair" and "just" way of treating people that may be tied to their closeness to or distance from some standard of "regularity." Let's take a look at how "equality" was constructed in some texts in earlier periods of the US to examine the extent to which the authors relied on concepts of similarity or normativity. Let's start with *Narrative of the Life of Frederick Douglass, an American Slave* (1845), a kind of memoir written by a man who had recently escaped slavery. In the first paragraph of the first chapter, Douglass states that as a child, he was not allowed to know his birthday. He notes, "the white children could tell their ages. I could not tell why I ought to be deprived of the same privilege" (Douglass 12). In this sentence, Douglass recognizes his difference from the other children, a difference in skin color, but he "cannot tell" why this difference should translate into a lack of "privilege." This statement begins the dismantling of the ideology of African inferiority that slaveholders used to justify American slavery, one that continues throughout Douglass's narrative, which demonstrates throughout that Douglass himself is the intellectual and physical equal of any white man.

To highlight this dismantling process, Douglass often uses the chiasmus[1] in his depictions and discussions of equality and difference, notably, in the scene in which Sophia Auld, the wife of Douglass's master Hugh Auld, has begun to teach him how to read. Sophia Auld is new to being a slaveholder, and her impulse shows her belief that the young Douglass and her own son Thomas should have equal access to the tools of literacy. However, when Hugh Auld realizes that his wife is teaching their slave to read, he lectures her in a "decided manner" about the "evil consequences" of this action. Overhearing Auld's tirade, Douglass realizes that he can "rely with the utmost confidence on the results which, [Auld] said, would flow from teaching me to read," which would be to "forever unfit him to be a slave" (29). He recognizes the premise of Mr. Auld's argument, which is that Douglass is capable of literacy and thus potentially equal in intelligence to little Thomas or any other white person; if he weren't capable of literacy and thus of learning to read texts that would make him unhappy and unfit for slavery, Auld would not have had to correct his wife in this particular manner. Douglass subsequently comes to understand that

> What [Hugh Auld] most dreaded, that I most desired. What he most loved, that I most hated. That which to him was a great evil, to be carefully shunned, was to me a great good, to be diligently sought; and the argument which he so warmly urged, against my learning to read, only served to inspire me with a desire and determination to learn. In learning to read, I owe almost as much to the bitter opposition of my master, as to the kindly aid of my mistress. I acknowledge the benefit of both. (29-30)

Through his chiasmatic inversions of all of Auld's beliefs, Douglass underlines his sense of his equality to Hugh Auld, one that causes him to trust Auld's perception of the results of reading—freedom— while also recognizing that Auld's pro-slavery beliefs give him a different interpretation of such an outcome. Douglass understands the full implications of Auld's argument and resolves to act in direct yet symmetrical opposition to it. Achieving a literacy equal to that of Auld will, Douglass believes, automatically render the system of slavery impotent to stop him from achieving liberty. Thus the most significant difference between himself and Auld is not skin color or race, but only Douglass's legal status as a slave; the system of slavery has created racial inequality.

Nearly six decades earlier, Thomas Jefferson makes a convoluted and contradictory argument about gender equality in Query 6, a section of his *Notes on the State of Virginia* (1781); we see in this section how he draws on the idea of equality but works to manipulate its meaning so as to avoid disturbing contradictions in social ideologies in the US. Despite its misleading subtitle, "A notice of the mines and other subterraneous riches; its trees, plants, fruits, &c.," Query 6 in Jefferson's text contains a section on "Animals." In this section, Jefferson argues for the health, substantial size, and excellent quality of the indigenous species of North America, rebutting the argument put forth by Count de Buffon that climatic conditions in that region are unhealthy and cause degeneration in indigenous species; he is doing so because he wants European

---

support for the very new United States in the form of investment and immigration. Buffon has claimed that "the animals common both to the old and new world" are "smaller in the latter," and that "those which have been domesticated in both" have "degenerated in America" due to "colds and moisture" (Jefferson 994). Having discussed this phenomenon in animals both "aboriginal" and "transplanted," M. de Buffon has gone on to apply his argument to humans, compelling Jefferson to defend the indigenous North American man so as to maintain his overall argument that the resources in North America are equal to or superior to those in Europe. Jefferson defends the innate equality of the North American Indian, who is "neither more defective in ardor, nor more impotent with his female, than the white reduced to the same diet and exercise" (995). In other words, the North American man possesses the same degree of sexual potency as the European man, if they are in the same state of physical health. In fact, he states explicitly that if we were to gather more "facts" about indigenous North American people and make "allowance" for "those circumstances of their situation which call for a display of particular talents only," we "shall probably find that they are formed in mind as well as in body, on the same module with the 'Homo sapiens Europaeus'" (996). This seems to match Douglass' overall point: any apparent inequality of the races can be attributed to a clear set of external forces that have obscured the intrinsic equality of American Indian and European men in a range of categories.

However, at the end of a long passage apparently intended to praise the bravery, honor, sensibility, and rhetorical capabilities, among others, of American Indian men, Jefferson does make one major concession, about gender: "The women are submitted to unjust drudgery," he states. He believes this to be "the case with every barbarous people," in which cultures, the "stronger sex" always "imposes on the weaker" (995). Jefferson means that North American Indian men use physical force to make their wives do more physical labor than Jefferson believes to be "just" or natural, and the result is that European men are physically stronger than American Indian men, and American Indian women are physically stronger (but less fertile) than European women. The implication that American Indian women might possess roughly the same physical strength as American Indian men is not "equality" to Jefferson, but rather the result of a barbaric and unnatural lifestyle; in such societies, he thinks, women and men are not working in the ways and to the extent that their sex naturally dictates. Jefferson argues that it is "civilization alone which replaces women in the enjoyment of their *natural equality*" (my emphasis), by which he means that civilized men don't "impose" undue physical labor on women because in civilized societies, we "respect those rights in others which we value in ourselves" (995). In other words, European women have more social privilege relative to men than do American Indian women to American Indian men; this apparently allows them to refuse "unnatural" amounts of labor.

Although Jefferson seems to suggest that in his era, women and men had the same "rights," he was known for his logical mind and must have known that that was not true legally, so I suggest he means that women and men have by "nature" distinctive physical and mental capabilities and social spheres that in civilized societies, they have the "right" to pursue and inhabit. Of course, the notion that American women (especially those who were in the working class or enslaved) had the social status to refuse "drudgery" requires Jefferson to ignore entire areas of society; similarly, the idea that European American men are physically stronger than American Indian men requires him to ignore wealthy slaveholding intellectuals like himself, who used slave labor for all physical work. More importantly for the current discussion of "equality," however, is that Jefferson uses "equality" to refer not to the outcomes of men's and women's conditions (e.g., strength) but to their ability to determine their unequal paths through life. Because his premise is that women and men are naturally both different and unequal in their capabilities and the outcomes of their endeavors, he uses "equality" to refer only to their freedom to choose the "natural" path and to resist the unnatural one. He makes systemic gender and racial oppression[2] invisible here because, like most oppression, it is "built into the society as a whole and becomes automatic, normalized, and taken for granted" (Sensoy and DiAngelo 61-62). This normalization of politically constructed difference (such as those among genders and races) as "natural" has continued on with little abatement in the years since Jefferson wrote his *Notes*, despite legal changes produced by activist authors such as Douglass.

Over two centuries after Jefferson's *Notes*, we continue to live in a world characterized by profound inequality, one that has continued to naturalize inequality in various areas of society. Nor do we seem to be making consistent progress in this area, as seen by the growing gap between the most wealthy in the world and the rest of its inhabitants. In the past few decades, most countries have experienced what the most recent Oxfam International report calls "high and rising inequality" ("Reward" 7). Wealth for the top 1 percent, who received 82 percent of "all the growth in global wealth in the last year," has continued to skyrocket, whereas the bottom 50 percent of the global population saw no increase in their wealth ("Reward" 8). And as noted by Guy Ryder, Director-General of the International Labour Organization, the Oxfam International report also confirms that "a majority of people want to live in far more equal societies," something that has finally been recognized by many world leaders; the "Sustainable Development Goals" of the UN 2030 Agenda include a reduction of "inequality within and among countries" and "inclusive economic growth, full and productive employment and decent work for all" (qtd. in "Reward" 6). Even Alan Greenspan, "an ardent advocate of free markets," has admitted that inequality is a "fundamental threat to the system," stating that one "cannot have the benefits of capitalist market growth without the support of . . . virtually all of the people; and if you have an increasing sense that the rewards of capitalism are being distributed unjustly, the system will not stand" (Komlos). Greenspan's comment suggests that in his mind, economic inequality has gone too far only because it appears to most people to be the result of "unjust" distribution.

Greenspan knows that capitalism is built on economic inequality and manufactures it; he would defend it by saying that usually, capitalism's "rewards" are "distributed justly." He believes that wealth is the deserved result of "merit" and hard work and that the poor are responsible for their condition, ideas that have long been naturalized not just in the US but in the West in general. I once asked a group of students to explain the Great Depression, and one promptly answered, "it was a time when the market crashed and too many people were poor, so something had to be done about it." Her explanation implies her belief in an acceptable number of people in poverty in her society because, to her, all individuals in the US have equal opportunity to succeed in society. She couldn't see that neoliberal state-sponsored policies, such as "privatization, trade liberalization, coercive debt loads, the elimination of unions, and the taxation of income rather than wealth," pull wealth upward into the pockets of those who own corporations and/or land or who otherwise already possess wealth; at the same time, these policies "drastically decreas[e] the funding available for public services that benefit those groups disproportionately exposed to poverty" and destroy or damage "services like education, public housing, food assistance, and health care," redirecting those funds to "ever-expanding criminalization and imprisonment systems that recapture those abandoned to poverty" (Gordon). As a result, 70 percent of those born below the "middle rung" of the "income ladder" never rise higher than that, and only 4 percent make it into the "top" quintile of income ("American Middle").

These policies impact women and non-white, non-cisgender, able-bodied people far more negatively than they do white men, and the effect is compounded for those who experience discrimination intersectionally, across two or more aspects of identity.[3] Globally, "more men than women own land, shares and other capital assets," are paid more for the same jobs as women, and occupy "most of the better paid, higher status jobs" ("Reward" 13). Gender disparity stems from ideological causes, as "social norms" and beliefs around the world "devalue the status and abilities of women, justify violence and discrimination against them, and dictate which jobs they can and cannot expect to hold" (13), and many women in various nations subscribe to all or part of these ideologies. Even more devalued and discriminated against by way of these ideologies and norms (as well as by some laws[4]) that determine how bodies should look and how people in particular bodies should behave are transgender, queer, and disabled people, who are far more likely to become impoverished because of employment discrimination and other kinds of violence.

In terms of race, there is a huge disparity in wealth. Among black and Latinx people in the US, disparities in annual household wealth compared to whites are already large (by an order of magnitude), but they became larger during the recession of 2007–2010; white household wealth did decrease during the recession, but it has increased steadily since then, while black and Latino household wealth has continued to decrease since 2007 (Wolff). Yet most people don't want to see or accept the fact that people who aren't able-bodied, white, cisgender males do not have the same opportunities or the same acceptance as able-bodied white cisgender males. As James Gee notes, "Americans tend to be very focused on the individual, and thus often miss the fact that the individual is simply the meeting point of many, sometimes conflicting, socially and historically defined discourses," his term "discourses" referring to belief systems about identity-based characteristics (145). Those who tend to be furthest from socially accepted norms about human bodies, beliefs, and behaviors tend to have the hardest time navigating social institutions.

Apart from the fact that social and economic institutions are currently set up to maintain the economic power of the wealthy and the privilege of the white, cisgender, able-bodied, middle-class, people as a group tend to accept the status quo and fear any change to their current economic and social systems. Apparently, many also delude themselves about their own circumstances. When asked by Pew researchers in 2014 to disclose their economic class, the vast majority of people (about 90 percent) labeled themselves middle class. In this same period, the middle class was actually made of about 50 percent of the population, with 29 percent being lower class ("American Middle").[5] We could attribute this to people's shame at being labeled "lower class," or we could also attribute it to hope—the hope that even later in life, one's fortune might be made. Hiding one's economic status can be a symptom of cognitive dissonance, in which two conflicting beliefs or ideas about oneself cause stress that can be resolved by denying the less acceptable belief or idea. System justification theory provides one explanation for the embracing of the status quo by members of socially marginalized groups. As Jost notes, "system justification theory emphasizes the 'palliative function of ideology,' whereby individuals feel better and reduce guilt and discomfort by rationalizing the status quo" and perceiving "the system as legitimate and stable" (15).

James Baldwin explains this kind of rationalization in a different way in discussing the reactions of African Americans to experiences of racial injustice. He describes "two ideas" that are "in opposition" in their minds: the idea of "the acceptance totally without rancor, of life as it is, and men as they are" (and racial injustices as they are), and the conflicting idea "that one must never, in one's own life, accept these injustices as commonplace but must fight them with all one's strength" (Baldwin 114-115). The tension between these two ideas suggests the tremendous difficulty of embracing both of them completely, but simply "accepting" one's life and the people around one without anger doesn't mean that one must deny or repress the reality of racial injustice. While over the decades, African Americans and other socially marginalized groups have fought for "equal power" with all their strength, others in those same groups have decided to "accept life as it is" while still believing in the need for others to fight.

Protests for equality over the years have brought much more awareness to social inequalities, but they have not always had the desired results. While in the twentieth century, the US did at one point or another see serious reductions in the most blatant aspects of economic and social inequality, such as civil rights, many of those reductions were later reversed, and many are in the process of being reversed right now. However, even in the past five years, increasing numbers of protests are taking place in the US and elsewhere. In Brazil, Lebanon, Greece, Ireland, and South Africa, among others, people lacking essential resources have taken to the streets to demand change from their governments. Beginning with Occupy Wall Street (2011), the US in recent years has seen various kinds of protests of inequality, including but not limited to Black Lives Matter (2013), Ferguson (2014), and Baltimore (2015) protests about deadly police racism, Colin Kaepernick's "Take a Knee" protests in 2016 over racial injustice, Dakota Access Pipeline protests (2016), coordinated prison strikes and protests (fall 2016), Women's Marches (2017–2018), Day Without Latinos and other immigration-related protests (2017), protests over Trump's transgender military ban (2017), and the 2017–2018 outing and firing of high-profile sexual harassers. Frances McDormand's recommendation of "inclusion riders" in her 2018 Oscar Best Actress acceptance speech, intended to reduce inequality on movie sets, is an individual protest that was nevertheless broadcast to 26.5 million viewers and garnered immediate support on social media. (About a month earlier, outside the Oscar nominees' luncheon, a group of people staged a protest of the underrepresentation of Latinx people in the film industry.)

Some of these protests are having or will have immediate and measurable effects, but for others, the effects are less clear. It is difficult to tell what causes social change. This is in part because protests are often aimed not only at changing policy or the punishment of particular oppressors, but to changing the minds and beliefs of the majority of people. People do this kind of egalitarian work through protesting and pushing for changes to laws, policies, and institutions, but they also work for social change through media and the arts. They write, they perform, they craft tweets, they create works of art that capture the imaginations of viewers and cause them to rethink their views. Exposure to these ideas can seep into enough minds to create cultural change; people come to understand "what it means to be white, black, Hispanic, male, female, heterosexual, homosexual, rural, or urban" due in part to "the way those social categories are defined and interpreted in popular media" (Stewart).

And there is plenty of exposure. More than two thirds (71 percent) of the US/Canada population—or 246 million people—went to the cinema at least once in 2016 ("Theatrical"), and according to the Bureau of Labor Statistics, in 2017, 96 percent of people fifteen and over watched television for 2.7 hours per day. As Duncan Stewart notes, "movies and TV have power to construct the 'normal' aesthetic of American society more than any other form of media" (Stewart).

Before there was electronic media, this cultural work was done by performances, lectures, newspapers, and, beginning in the eighteenth century, novels. Novels allow hours of time in which a reader is immersed in another world, imaginatively seeing that world through the mind of one or more characters; reading a novel can thus expose readers to cultures, ideas, and people unfamiliar to them, or to familiar subjects depicted in a completely different way. Novels were, therefore, thought to be dangerously influential, causing early publishers to impose moral guidelines on the content of novels to make sure that readers wouldn't be corrupted by harmful ideas that pushed too far against the social status quo.[6] At the same time, the novel arose as part of the project of middle-class hegemony (or ideological domination); novels were written for and read by the growing middle class, people with the leisure to spend hours reading. Protagonists of novels, then, were also frequently middle class, and "the plot and character development" of the novel tends to "pull toward the normative," emphasizing the "universal quality of the central character whose normativity encourages us to identify with him or her" (Davis 9). To help readers navigate the world in the novel, the author reproduces the "normative signs"—ideas, beliefs, objects, behaviors—familiar to the reader; this "paradoxically help[s] the reader to read those signs in the world as well as the text" (Davis 9). The novel, then, can be a good vehicle for egalitarian social change if it asks readers to identify with "the Other" and get comfortable being that person while reading the novel—but for that to work, the novel must build in many normative elements. This is obviously also true of most forms of visual media, with even more financial investment riding on them.

One way that members of marginalized groups can attempt to create use the "normalizing" effects of novels and visual media is to feature characters who are marginalized living their lives with little to no reference to their differences from the mainstream, and to foreground those characters' unique experiences of naturalized inequality and social norms. This can mitigate the symbolic violence of exclusion that has been common in books, films, and television designed for mainstream consumption, in which marginalized peoples are stereotyped, killed off, or ignored in plots and storylines. However, to do this, one needs the time and inclination to write and/or the financial resources to create such representations; one then needs to convince those in charge of various industries (publishing, television, filmmaking) that despite its featuring of a nontraditional protagonist, this unique representation will produce a profit. This explains why we are only seeing more accurate and nonstereotyped representations of marginalized people in the last few decades.

Playwright and novelist Susan Nussbaum was able to make such an intervention. She became a wheelchair user and starting doing disability activism at age twenty-four; describing her initial days of identifying as disabled, she says,

> all I knew about being disabled I learned from reading books and watching movies, and that scared the shit out of me. Tiny Tim was long-suffering and angelic and was cured at the end. Quasimodo was a monster who . . . was killed at the end, but it was for the best . . . Ahab was a bitter amputee . . . Laura Wingfield had a limp, so no man would ever love her. This imagery fresh in my mind, my own future seemed to hold little promise. (Nussbaum 301)

Nussbaum decided she wanted to resist the symbolic violence in most representations of disabled people. She began writing plays (she had been in acting school before her accident but was unable to enter most theaters after becoming a wheelchair user), and then wrote her first novel, *Good Kings Bad Kings*, about a group of people living and working in a nursing home for disabled young people without the resources or support to live at home. One goal of Nussbaum's novel is to portray the disabled young people as being recognizable to readers, not too unlike any group of young people or teenagers. She acknowledges their differences, which include mental, physical, emotional, and cognitive disabilities and diseases, without using those differences to justify their lack of social equality. Instead, like Douglass does, she blames their lack of social equality on the discriminatory treatment of people with disabilities inside the nursing home, which is connected to and contiguous with the social and physical aspects of our society that are not accessible to people with disabilities.

Nussbaum and other disability rights and justice activists want us to acknowledge that the human body and the human mind—disability justice scholar Margaret Price uses the term "bodymind" because the body and mind really cannot be separated—have always been varied, and "disability is the most universal of human conditions" (Garland-Thomson 2001, McRuer 2006). Human minds do not work the same way, and most people who reach what we call "old age" will experience some form of disability. Yet our built environment only functions for human beings with a particular kind of body; our social conventions and institutions demand certain abilities and modes of behavior. The reason for this is connected to the constructions of norms, which have functioned as constructs of the ideal human against which all other humans are measured (and often found wanting) in terms not only of physical or mental ability but also race, gender, wealth, heritage, and sexuality.

During what is called the Enlightenment era in Europe (1685 to 1815), the ideologies of logic and empiricism began to dominate culture. As disability studies scholar Nirmala Erevelles notes, Enlightenment intellectuals began "setting up the European, bourgeois, heterosexual, healthy, male body as the . . . standard against which to compare 'other' bodies" (30). A particular kind of body eventually became "species-typical and therefore essential and fully human" (Campbell 5, qtd. in Erevelles 33). This "typical" body was categorized "scientifically," which allows a convincing "rational" justification for treating non-typical people unjustly.

The concept of an ideal "body" was further developed in the mid-nineteenth century when the words "normal" (1598) and "norm" (1821) began to be widely used after "a burst of interest in statistics" (Davis 2). The field of statistics (or numerical data analysis) was developed in the Enlightenment. We might think of statistics as a neutral tool that we can use to describe populations. But in fact, as Dean Spade argues, "administrative systems that classify people actually invent and produce meaning for the categories they administer" (32). In other words, they never just describe, but also define and alter. An important consequence "of the idea of the norm is that it divides the total population into standard and nonstandard subpopulations" (32). The next step logically is "to attempt to norm the nonstandard," and statisticians became obsessed with the elimination" of nonstandard people (Davis 2-3). Almost all of the first statisticians supported "eugenics," which is the idea that we should control human reproduction (often through forcible sterilization) so as to produce the "fittest" people. (Eugenics was used by the Nazis to justify first sterilizing and then killing disabled people—T4 was the name of that plan.) People who deviated "from the norm" started to be regarded "as contributing to the disease of the nation" (Davis 7). Norms thus produce two classes of people: those who are "normal" and who are eligible to receive all of the security that comes with inclusion into a community and those who are "deviant" or "abnormal" and are excluded from the community and thus vulnerable (Spade 24). Using norms, those in power can more easily construct a standard for equality, in which it appears that most people are roughly equal because they are "normal," and those who are "abnormal" are unequal because of something intrinsic to themselves, not because of conditions in their society.

Once disability was linked "scientifically" with disease and depravity, it became a tool for stigmatizing groups of people. "Discrimination against [marginalized] groups" has been justified for centuries "by attributing disability to them" (Baynton 17). For example, "nonwhite races were routinely . . . depicted as evolutionary . . . throwbacks" (19) and aspects of their blood and bodies were described as "abnormal"; "women" of every race "were said to be" more abnormal and "less evolved than the men" of those races, with less blood going through their brains, for example (23). In response, many members of these groups worked hard to prove that they were not disabled, rather than challenging the idea that disability is a catastrophe. Disability justice activist Mia Mingus comments on this kind of logic: "for many people, even just the idea that we can understand disability as 'not wrong' is a huge shift in thinking" (Mingus). Let's make it clear—when marginalized groups argue that they should not be considered "disabled," they represent disability as catastrophic failure. Logically, this is calling for the eradication—the genocide—of disabled people—to not let disabled people be born at all. Disability scholars work against this entrenched idea by insisting that disability is not an objective consequence of a particular body or mind but a "product of social relations" to be solved "not though medical intervention" or genocide but through "social change and political transformation" (Kafer 6). Since some form of disability awaits most of us, Robert McRuer asks us to consider this provocative question: "'What might it mean to welcome the disability to come, to desire it?" (McRuer qtd. in Erevelles 27). Under what conditions and in what kind of society would disability be desirable?

This question can be asked about any form of socially marginalized identity. How would society have to be transformed in order for a person with a significant difference from social norms to be seen as desirable, as a model citizen? We might imagine such a society to be one in which differences from statistical and social norms did not automatically signify inferiority, in which people cherished uniqueness, welcomed change, and resisted conventionality and homogenizing. Such a society would be one of equity but not one of sameness. As Sara Ahmed argues, it would also be one in which the idea of "equality" is not, as it has become in some corporations and in educational institutions, "another performance indicator" in the "disciplinary regimes, whose ends might not be consistent with equality understood as a social aim or aspiration" (85). "Equality" is not achieved when an administrator checks off a box indicating racial diversity among students or employees, but when all people can feel comfortable in both their differences from and their similarities to others because those difference and similarities do not result in social hierarchies, exclusion from opportunities and necessities, and/or consolidations of power.

Notes

1. A "chiasmus" is a literary figure in which a sequence of concepts (often using the same words) are arranged and then repeated in reverse order, for emphasis.

2. As noted by Sensoy and DiAngelo, the term "oppression" refers to a "set of policies, practices, traditions, norms, definitions, and explanations (discourses), which function to systematically exploit one social group to the benefit of another social group. . . . oppression is different from prejudice and discrimination in that prejudice and discrimination describe dynamics that occur on the individual level and in which all individuals participate. In contrast, oppression occurs when one group's prejudice is back by legal authority and historical, social, and institutional power" (Sensoy and DiAngelo 61-62).

3. Intersectionality has been defined as the notion that "identity cannot be fully understood via a single lens such as gender, race, or class along what legal scholar Kimberlé Crenshaw (1989) called a 'single axis framework.' Everyone, in fact, has a race, a gender, a class, a set of abilities, and a sexuality, among other elements of identity, and we can't easily isolate the effects of gender from those of ability or sexuality. These aspects of our identities must be "understood in their interdependence on one another; identity is multidimensional" (Sensoy and DiAngelo 175).

4. For example, laws pertaining to bathrooms and to gender on identity documents; violating these laws can put a transperson into the criminal justice system, which upon their release will reduce their ability to survive in society.

5. I want to thank Professor Nathalie Rachlin of Scripps College for directing me to this connection in her lecture on class in Core I at Scripps College.

6. See Cathy Davidson for further discussion of this.

Works Cited

Ahmed, Sara. *On Being Included: Racism and Diversity in Institutional Life*. Duke UP 2012.

"The American Middle Class is Losing Ground." *Pew Research Center*, 9 Dec. 2015, www.pewsocialtrends.org/2015/12/09/the-american-middle-class-is-losing-ground/. Accessed 29 Mar. 2018.

Baynton, Douglas C. "Disability and the Justification of Inequality in American History." *Disability Studies Reader*, 4th ed., pp. 17-33.

Baldwin, James. *Notes of a Native Son*. 1955. Beacon Press, 2012.

Davidson, Cathy. *Revolution and the Word: The Rise of the Novel in America*. Oxford UP 2004.

Davis, Lennard. "Introduction: Normality, Power, and Culture." *Disability Studies Reader*, vol. 4, Routledge, 2013, pp. 1-16.

Douglass, Frederick. *Narrative of the Life of Frederick Douglass, an American Slave, Written by Himself*. Edited by William L. Andrews, Norton, 1997.

Erevelles, Nirmala. *Disability and Difference in Global Contexts: Enabling a Transformative Body Politic*. Palgrave Macmillan, 2011.

Garland-Thomson, Rosemarie. "Integrating Disability, Transforming Feminist Theory." *NWSA Journal*, vol. 14, no. 3, *Feminist Disability Studies*, Autumn 2002, pp. 1-32.

Gee, James. "Discourses." *Social Linguistics and Literacies: Ideology in Discourses, Critical Perspectives on Literacy and Education*. New York, 1990.

Gordon, Charles. "Impossible People, Queer Futures: Dean Spade and Critical Trans Politics." Review of Dean Spade. Normal Life: Administrative Violence, Critical Trans Politics, and the Law. *Postmodern Culture: Journal of Interdisciplinary Thought on Contemporary Cultures*. 10 Jun. 2015. Accessed 25 Jan. 2018.

Howells, William Dean. "Letters of an Altrurian Traveller: Plutocratic Contrasts and Contradictions." *The Cosmopolitan*, March 1894, pp. 558-569.

Jefferson, Thomas. *Notes on the State of Virginia. The Heath Anthology of American Literature*, 5th ed., vol. A: Colonial Period to 1800, edited by Paul Lauter et al., Houghton Mifflin Co, 2006, pp. 994-99.

Jost, John T., et al. "Social inequality and the reduction of ideological dissonance on behalf of the system: evidence of enhanced system justification among the disadvantaged." *European Journal of Social Psychology*, vol. 33, 2003, pp. 13–36.

Kafer, Alison. *Feminist, Queer, Crip*. Indiana UP, 2013.

Komlos, John. "The Root Cause of Protest: Radical Income Inequality." *Evonomics: The Next Evolution of Economics*, 25 Sept. 2016, evonomics.com/protest-income-inequality-african-americans-john-komlos/. Accessed 15 Jan. 2018.

McRuer, Robert. *Crip Theory: Cultural Signs of Queerness and Disability*. NYUP, 2006.

Mingus, Mia. "Changing the Framework." *Leaving Evidence*, 12 Feb. 2011, leavingevidence.wordpress.com/2011/02/12/changing-the-framework-disability-justice/. Accessed 29 Mar. 2018.

Nussbaum, Susan. *Good Kings Bad Kings*. Algonquin, 2013.

"Reward Work, Not Wealth." *Oxfam International*, n.d., www.oxfam.org/en/research/reward-work-not-wealth/. Accessed 29 Mar. 2018.

Sensoy, Özlem, and Robin DiAngelo. *Is Everyone Really Equal? An introduction to Key Concepts in Social Justice Education*. Teachers College Press, 2017.

Spade, Dean. *Normal Life*. South End Press, 2011.

Stewart, Duncan. "Hollywood and Diversity: How the Media Informs Social Identities." *National Organization for Women*, 8 Oct. 2014, now.org/blog/hollywood-and-diversity-how-media-construct-social-identities/. Accessed 22 Feb. 2018.

"Theatrical Market Statistics 2016." *Motion Picture Association of America*, n.d., www.mpaa.org/wp-content/uploads/2017/03/MPAA-Theatrical-Market-Statistics-2016_Final-1.pdf/. Accessed 10 Feb. 2018.

United States Department of Labor. "Economic News Release." *Bureau of Labor Statistics*, 27 Jun. 2017, www.bls.gov/news.release/atus.t01.htm/. Accessed 22 Feb. 2018.

Wolff, Edward N. "Household Wealth Trends in the United States, 1962–2013: What Happened Over the Great Recession?" *Pursuing the American Dream*, 2013, www.pewtrusts.org/~/media/legacy/uploadedfiles/pcs_assets/2012/pursuingamericandreampdf.pdf/. Accessed 29 Mar. 2018.

CRITICAL
CONTEXTS

Caste: The Engine That Runs (Ruins) India

Arundhati Roy's novels *The God of Small Things* and *The Ministry of Utmost Happiness*_____

Lucky Issar

"Fiction dances out of me. Non-fiction is wrenched out by the aching, broken world I wake up to every morning,"[1] writes the Indian author Arundhati Roy. This broken world appears poignantly in her novels, revealing the darker aspects of Indian society. Poverty, oppression, inequality, and gender violence are not unique to India; these injustices exist elsewhere too. However, it is the sheer scale and schizophrenic nature of socioeconomic inequities of the Indian social landscape that are baffling—millions of impoverished people living and dying on the streets while a few hold the entire wealth of the country. Roy fiercely questions these injustices and takes an unpopular but bold stand against the structures of power. She uses everything in her "power to flagrantly solicit support for that position."[2]

Almost the entire body of her work gives veracity to this claim. Even though her works deal with a range of issues, the tenor of her politics and vision has always remained consistent. However, this essay focuses only on the depiction of class and gender in her two novels—*The God of Small Things* and *The Ministry of Utmost Happiness*. It further links class- and gender-based violence to the Indian caste system. Caste undoubtedly affects the lower castes and the 'Untouchables,' but it equally impacts the upper castes. This essay explores how caste perpetuates class and gender violence in contemporary India and how it damages the whole Indian society.

Caste and Class Violence

In this section, I will look at the novel *The God of Small Things* to show what caste does to the practitioners of caste—irrespective of their position in the caste hierarchy—and how caste is rigidly maintained through varied forms of violence. Since Indian

Independence, caste has been abolished by the Indian constitution, and yet a cursory glance at contemporary Indian society reveals that instead of becoming obsolete, caste modernizes itself.

In her novel *The God of Small Things* (*GST*), Roy takes us into the intimate and private world of dizygotic twins, Rahel and Estha, and their divorced mother, Ammu, who is an upper-caste woman with a lower caste, Untouchable lover, Velutha. As the book unfolds, we see Velutha as a kind, skilled, "flat muscled and honey coloured" man. But we also know that he is a "Paravan," the lowest in caste-hierarchy. To be a "Paravan" means to suffer gross abuses of the upper castes. Once their secret affair is known, Velutha is imprisoned on false charges by Ammu's family, and he is tortured to death in police custody. In a caste-based society, such transgressions are punished. In his case, he gets killed for loving an upper-caste woman and breaking the "Love (caste) Laws. That lay down who should be loved. And how. And how much" (Roy, *GST* 31).

Interestingly, Velutha, though a "Paravan" with all its social handicaps, is the only male character in the novel who is morally impeccable. The upper-caste male figures, such as the twin's maternal uncle Chacko, their maternal grandfather Pappachi, Ammu's ex-husband, and the communist politician comrade Pillai in the neighborhood are portrayed as warped and violent. Chacko sees himself as a defender of human-rights, but he exploits the poor.

Despite his class and caste-based privileges, Chacko is a failure both on a personal and professional front. His English wife leaves him. Ammu, Chacko's sister, makes fun of his unprofitable pickle-making business and his model airplanes that always come down. The underprivileged Velutha, on the other hand, is like a magician with his hands. Even as a child "he could make intricate toys— tiny windmills, rattles, minute jewel boxes out of dried palm reeds; he could carve perfect boats out of tapioca stems and figurines on cashew nuts" (Roy, *GST* 74). Ammu's mother Mammachi concedes that "if only he hadn't been a Paravan, he might have become an engineer" (75). This remark, with its strange logic, reveals her deep-seated prejudice against the lower castes, even toward an eleven-year-old child. Velutha, in spite of this hostile and prejudiced environment, learns to excel in carpentry.

Ammu's parents often let Velutha in the house whenever his help is needed, but otherwise, he is forbidden to enter the house. Velutha works in the factory owned by Chacko. He practically runs the factory. Even though Velutha is far more efficient and skilled than other workers, he is paid less because of his low caste. The other workers and even the local politician resent his presence in the factory. The communist politician warns Chacko that "whatever job he (Velutha) does, carpenter or electrician or whateveritis [*sic*], for them he is just a Paravan . . . You should be cautious. Better for him you send him off" (Roy, *GST* 279). Ammu's family looks down on lower castes, but they are willing to exploit Velutha's labor. These attitudes show how the outcastes are (ab)used, and their work and contribution often discredited.

We further see that the communist politician Pillai's ideas about justice are actually ways to accumulate power. Velutha supports the Communist Party because he believes in its slogans that promise to annihilate caste from Indian society. In his distress, Velutha seeks the politician's help. It is a deeply troubling scene as Velutha cannot even utter his problem. The words, such as "love," "upper-caste Ammu," and "police" are unspeakable due to the centuries-old distance between the Untouchable man and the upper-caste politician (who pretends to work for equality). The politician, instead of helping Velutha, reprimands him. "This is a little village . . . people talk . . . It's not as though I don't know what's been going on" (Roy, *GST* 287). Velutha struggles to say something, but that "made no difference to the man he spoke to. His own voice coiled around him like a snake" (287). The politician who publicly claims to be against caste does not let Velutha inside his house. After a brief exchange, he tells Velutha that the party is not "constituted to support workers' indiscipline in their private life" (287). Velutha watches the communist politician fade from the door while the politician's disembodied voice continues. *"It is not in the party's interests to take up such matters. Individuals' interest is subordinate to the organization's interest. Violating Party discipline means violating Party Unity*" (287). The words "violation" and "indiscipline" essentially mean that he has transgressed caste-lines and has challenged the caste norms by loving an upper-caste woman. Therefore, the society punishes him: family, law, and politics join hands in bending democratic institutions, whenever caste order is threatened or challenged. Caste is so important to the upper castes because it is through caste that class is created and maintained.

Velutha is not vengeful toward the upper castes despite their violations of him. For instance, he loves Ammu's children Rahel and Estha. Rahel, later in life, reflects on how Velutha instinctively participated in their play "taking care not to decimate it with adult carelessness. Or affection" (Roy, *GST* 190). On the other hand, the children are often neglected by their mother, uncle Chacko, aunt, and even grandmother. After Ammu's untimely death, Rahel is raised by her uncle and grandmother. Later in life, Rahel observes with an adult hindsight that "they provided the care (food, clothes, money) but withdrew the concern" (15). At the core of this unconcern toward Rahel is her impure/hybrid caste. Ammu's family look down at 'Untouchables'; however, it is ironic that they unconsciously cast the same caste-ist gaze at Rahel.

The society that brands people like Velutha as "Paravans" lives on their labor. For centuries, they have been exploited by the upper castes. Even in the recent past, the restrictions enforced on lower castes are quite chilling. The "Paravans" have to follow a whole list of rules imposed on them by the upper castes. They are not allowed to touch what upper caste people touch, to walk on public roads, or to cover their upper bodies, and "they were expected to crawl backwards with a broom, sweeping away their footprints so that Brahmins [the uppermost caste] . . . would not defile themselves by accidentally stepping into a Paravan's footprint" (Roy, *GST* 74). The novel explicitly describes the degradations that "Untouchables" are subjected to by the upper castes and more subtly shows us how the caste system distorts the upper castes—an aspect of caste that goes unexamined.

Apparently, it is only through the practice of caste that a large part of society is kept firmly on a leash. Since the caste system is sanctioned in ancient religious texts, such as *the Manusmriti*,[3] it persists in the Indian society. In fact, caste in India is practiced across religions; although religions such as Christianity, Islam, and Buddhism emphasize equality and do not recognize caste in any form, caste is practiced. Even when upper-caste Hindus convert to other religions, they continue to maintain their caste. For instance, Ammu's family, even after converting to Christianity a long time ago, endorse and practice their upper-caste status. On the other hand, when the Untouchables convert to Christianity in order to escape the scourge of untouchability, they are called "Rice Christians" in local parlance. Furthermore, "[t]hey were made to have separate churches, with separate services, and separate priests. As a special favor they were given their own separate Pariah Bishop" (Roy, *GST* 74). Consequently, the caste-based inequalities continue in society. Caste enables the upper castes to control everyone else, and, therefore, it is never relinquished.

This obsession with caste in Indian society is partly a consequence of religious beliefs and partly the greed of the upper castes for power. Even though India is a democracy and its constitution accords equal rights to all its citizens, caste is so deeply embedded in everyday life that it is almost impossible to eradicate it. Caste is played out in ceremonies related to marriage, birth, death, and religious festivals. It is through these sacred sites that caste derives its strength, and perpetuates processes of exclusion, particularly of the lower castes—treatment that cannot be challenged in a court of law.

The caste system is such that people only think about the welfare of their own caste and its interests. In Indian thought, it is believed that one's situation in life, including caste, is the outcome of one's actions, *Karma*, committed in a former life. This conception has a firm grip on the Indian mind. This also explains why an ordinary tourist is baffled to see immense poverty in India; a regular Indian, on the contrary, seems quite indifferent toward the appalling poverty he encounters on a daily basis.

For quite some time now, the Indian state has told grand stories about its success in global markets. However, these stories are only half-true. We only hear about the rising middle class and the tiny Indian elite. The downside of this story is not so celebratory; it is, in fact, embarrassing. Even when a few are getting richer, a vast majority of people are pushed into darkness and poverty—from cities to the edges of the city, from the edges to farther away, as if the state expects its poor to disappear into oblivion. The poor are considered largely a nuisance in the city, so the city administration forces people living in unauthorized colonies, slums, or even on the streets, out of the city.[4]

This trend is emerging in semi-urban and even in remote areas across India. The tribal populations that have been living in forests and remote regions for centuries are not particularly enriched by the global processes; they, in fact, become impoverished by the market-driven interventions. Rich industrialists, mine owners, big companies exploit these regions for profit making. Profit and politics take precedence over the welfare of tribal people. The government seeks only to appease capitalists and middle/upper-middle classes, and in its frenzy to maintain its GDP, industrial needs, and vote bank, politics goes out of its way to thwart any opposition. This involves the abuse of human rights. In order to make India *great*, India silences, imprisons, oppresses, and kills the dissenters—its own marginalized and disfranchised people.[5]

In the novel, when Rahel, Ammu's daughter, returns to her village as an adult, she sees the impact of capitalism on her village, its environment, and the poor. She describes the idyllic river of her childhood that has now shrunk; it "greeted her with a ghastly skull's smile, with holes where teeth had been" (Roy, *GST* 124). The river's flow is regulated in exchange for votes from the influential paddy-farmer lobby. "More rice, for the price of a river" (124) is the governing mantra. Just for the sake of profit, everything seems to be up for sale in India: mountains, rivers, forests, air. Rahel further notices that the population has swelled, whereas the river is reduced to a swollen drain. Once this river evoked fear through its power, but now it is tamed by the profit-making industry. Consequently, the river now looked as if "its teeth were drawn, its spirit spent. It was just a slow, sludging green ribbon lawn that ferried fetid garbage to the sea. Bright plastic bags blew across its viscous, weedy surface like subtropical flying-flowers" (124). In addition, we see that now on the steep mud banks of the river, shanty villages have cropped up. As the population increases, the safer areas are taken by the middle classes, while the lower castes are pushed to live in vulnerable areas. Historically, the lower castes have always lived on the periphery of a village or town—at a considerable distance from the upper castes.

In modern-day India, this pattern continues. As the Indian society focuses more on money-making pursuits, it bypasses every ethical consideration. This is reflected in how villages are structured and how modern-day towns and cities are evolving. Very strategically, the marginalized are pushed out of core residential areas. Both in towns and cities, the poor live in areas prone to floods and least connected to streets, schools, means of transport, and hospitals. This effectively keeps the poor in conditions of impoverishment, which thereby make them more vulnerable to exploitation by the upper castes.

The novel locates class discrimination in the portrayal of Velutha, the Untouchable. The power of caste finally crushes Velutha. It further shows how each key component (such as law, family, and religion) of Indian society tacitly plays a part in removing Velutha, as his defiance of caste-norms becomes unmanageable and dangerous. Whereas a fictional narrative demands artistic restraints in dealing with themes such as injustice and brutality, nonfiction does not. Commenting on India of the last three decades, Roy says that the most secessionist struggle that has ever been waged in India is the secession of middle- and upper-middle classes to a country of their own. Referring to the greed of the upper-caste Indian elite, she trenchantly says that the upper castes have always used fruits, branches, and leaves of a tree, but what is so ruthless and unprecedented today is that this elite now want to scrape and usurp even the roots. Furthermore, she implicates the transnational/ global elite as well and pointedly asks, "Can you leave the water in the rivers, the trees in the forest? Can you leave the bauxite in the mountain?"[6]

Caste and Gender Violence

Caste demands sexual order, which essentially means patriarchy. The caste-infested society imposes heteronormativity on people—it forces women to marry within the folds of caste and denies sexual rights to LGBT people. Any deviation from caste rules is seen as a direct threat to the Indian caste system, and therefore, the powerful upper castes punish transgressors who defy caste borders. Caste is maintained by regulating and controlling desire, especially of women and those who do not fit into the heteronormative framework.

In *The God of Small Things*, both Velutha and Ammu are punished by the society obsessed with notions of caste purity. The novel evinces that the society has different rules for men and women and for upper castes and Untouchables. After leaving her alcoholic husband, Ammu returns to her parental home along with her two children, where she is treated like an unwanted guest. Her kids are considered fatherless waifs and always made to realize that they "lived on a sufferance in the Ayemenem House" (Roy, *GST* 45). Ammu's paternal aunt often suggests that a married daughter has no position in her parent's home. Ammu's love for Velutha proves disastrous for both. Their story is despised when it becomes public. "The story of a man and woman, standing together in the moonlight. Skin to skin" (255). An untouchable man and an upper-caste woman "had made unthinkable, thinkable and the impossible really happen" (256). Ammu's family whispers among themselves. "He must go . . . Tonight. Before it goes any further. Before we are completely ruined" (257). This outrage shows the potency of caste borders in Indian society. It is not only Ammu's family that is outraged, but Velutha's own father implores forgiveness on Velutha's behalf and offers "to kill his son. To tear him limb from limb" (256). He apologizes for Velutha's transgressive act of loving Ammu to Ammu's mother, who spits on him in fury and calls him "Drunken dog! Drunken Paravan liar!" (256).

Ammu's brother Chacko suffers no such recriminations from his mother. He, in the guise of helping young women, sexually abuses them. His mother explains this by saying that "[h]e can't help having a Man's Needs" (Roy, *GST* 168). For the same need,

Ammu is traumatized to death. Within the safe domains of family, Ammu experiences prejudice just because she is a divorcée with two children.

Outside the family, society is even more intolerant toward her and the children. As Ammu realizes that Velutha has been falsely accused by her family, she goes to the police station to free him. The upper-caste policeman calls her *Veshya* (prostitute) and her children bastards and further warns her to go away. He taps her breasts with his baton in order to instill fear in her. "[I]t was not a police man's spontaneous brutishness on his part . . . it was a premeditated gesture, calculated to humiliate and terrorize her. An attempt to instill [caste] order into a world gone wrong" (Roy, *GST* 146). He does not mean to do her any real harm. "Inspector Mathew seemed to know whom he could pick on and whom he couldn't. Policemen have that instinct" (8). In fact, in this case, he is working at the behest of Ammu's family.

Not only the major female characters, but even the minor ones reveal how the whole society is structured, and how caste demands subjugation of women. From early childhood, girls are largely expected to be submissive. Rahel, though a bright child, is reprimanded and expelled from her school because she would hide behind doors and deliberately collide with older girls to find out if their breasts hurt. Apparently, in her institution (and in schools across India), ". . . breasts were not acknowledged. They were not supposed to exist, and if they didn't could they hurt?" (Roy, *GST* 16). Girls are forbidden to ask questions (concerning body and desire) because questions pose a threat to the status quo.

Even when women follow caste norms, they are still subjected to violence. Ammu suffers the indignities inflicted upon her by her alcoholic husband. She eventually leaves him because he wants her to sleep with his boss. Ammu's mother, Mammachi, in her younger day, shows talent for piano, but her bureaucrat husband does not support her. He does not like the idea of his wife being independent. Sometimes out of rage and jealousy, he beats his wife and young daughter. After beating them, if his anger still remains, he continues with violence. In fury, "he tore down curtains, kicked furniture and smashed a table lamp" (Roy, *GST* 181). Once, he flogs his daughter, but she does not cry. In order to really hurt her, he destroys her favorite gumboots. He uses pink shears. "The scissors made snicking scissor sound . . . it took ten minutes for her beloved gumboots to be completely shredded . . . her father looked at her with cold, flat eyes . . . surrounded by a sea of twisting, rubber snakes" (181). Even after his retirement, when Mammachi establishes herself as a successful pickle-maker, he turns extremely ruthless and venomous toward her. Apart from Ammu and her family, we meet the communist politician's wife, Kalyani. She acts like an efficient and well-behaved servant who keeps the house tidy, feeds her husband and his guests, and only speaks when spoken to—that, too, only with a subdued, hesitant nod.

Through the portrayal of these female characters, the novel links caste to gender violence. Caste operates by subjugating women at each stage of life. The dominance on women is consistently exercised. The *Manusmriti* professes that women should never be made independent, a virtuous woman must remain subservient to her husband and the male members of her family, and the list goes on. It grants unbridled power to men over women. Guided by these atrocious principles, men subdue women. Violence toward women turns lethal if they flout the caste norms. Even a privileged woman like Ammu cannot protect herself—her own family turns against her.

In Roy's recent novel, *The Ministry of Utmost Happiness* (*MUH*), we see even a crueler trope of caste. In the first half of the book, we witness the birth of a "hermaphrodite" or intersex child. In Indian parlance such a child is called "Hijra." The book narrates how the mother responds to her own child, once she recognizes that the child is intersex. She feels tormented, helpless, and unhinged. In her world, everything has a gender, even the non-living things. A gender-less child cannot participate in life's ritual, and if such a child has no place in his biological family, one cannot imagine what place this child will have in the larger society. As she oscillates in her fears, doubts, questions, and ignorance about the queer body of her child, she unconsciously suffers the fear of losing caste and entering some kind of horror-chamber with no escape routes. She recoils from "what she has created while her bowels convulsed a thick stream of shit ran down her legs" (Roy, *MUH* 4). Her visceral indescribable dread toward the queer anatomy of her own child reveals itself in "a soundless, embryonic howl" (5).

The mother raises the child as a boy named "Aftab." Aftab turns out to be exceptionally talented at singing but is teased and snickered at by the other children. *"He's a she. He's not a He or a She. He's a He and a She. She-He, He-She Hee! Hee! Hee!"* (Roy, *MUH* 8). Consequently, Aftab feels like a family embarrassment and stops going to school. Aftab leaves home, joins a group of "Hijras" and takes the name "Anjum." In her struggles, we see that without a caste, one is invariably excluded and shunned—one cannot participate in life in any meaningful way. Anjum goes through a series of turbulent events and eventually ends up living in the graveyard.

Through Anjum's journey, one witnesses the apathy of society toward queer-bodies, or the sexual minorities who do not fit into the conventional roles of man and woman. Caste only recognizes those ideas, bodies, and practices that strengthen it, while everything else is considered egregious to Indian ethos. If a child is born with indeterminate sex, it is given to "Hijras" voluntarily by the parents. One can imagine the inherent cruelty, ignorance, and fear underneath the act of giving away the child. How deep the ideas of pure-impure, legitimate-illegitimate run in Indian people. Consequently, the bodies that do not fit into the caste matrix are seen as a threat to the caste system , and therefore, they are discarded. The parents know well that the child, thus given away, will live a life of extreme vulnerability; they accept it as his (and their) fate. In addition, a "Hijra" is of no use as it cannot forward the caste or participate in any of life's rituals. In short, the parents cannot imagine any way of including such a child. This also demonstrates how caste shapes the category of "Hijra" and its unique subculture in the Indian setting. It only exists because caste exists.

The novel (*MUH*) suggests that all those who are marginalized face violence. This vast population, both in urban and semi-urban regions, are primarily the lower castes and the Untouchables. They have no access to any kind of security net. We see how society's excluded are pushed out of the city. They come to live with Anjum in the graveyard.

In India, very often gender violence does not even seem like violence. Unlike rape, dowry deaths, or mental torture that can be condemned and dealt with in courts, there are forms of violence that go unnoticed. For instance, there are cities in India where widows, victims of sexual abuse, older women, and sick women go to live because they are disowned by their families.[6] These women go to cities like Vrindavan—the city of widows—to live almost like beggars.[7] No one examines this because it seems like these women chose to come here for religious purposes. They are mostly thrown-out by their families as their presence is largely a burden to them, or these women just run away from mad fathers, corrupt policemen, alcoholic husbands, and brothers who seek to cut their hair and punish them for being women as is shown in *The God of Small Things*.

Looking back at Ammu, we see that even as a privileged woman, she is violently hindered from making independent choices. After her secret relationship with Velutha is known, she sees policemen in her dream approaching her with "snicking scissors, wanting to hack off her hair" (Roy, *GST* 161). This is usually done as a cultural practice in regard to widows, but also as a punishment to those women who transgress the sexual norms of the society. Ammu with all her privileges feel these fears in her bones; one wonders what happens to women who are lower caste and marginalized in every possible way. In fact, in *The God of Small Things*, we do not meet any Untouchable woman. It is perhaps such a dark place that the writer leaves it out and focuses only on upper-caste women. The upper-caste women are safe as long as they follow the caste norms. Any deviation from caste norms means losing the caste, and without caste, they do not belong anywhere.

The novel shows the callous attitude of men towards women in general, and lower castes in particular, even though both these categories are intrinsic to the genealogy of the caste system. One can imagine the daily struggles of those who are unfit for a conventional marriage, or those who opt-out of such a system that is only designed for heterosexuals. Anjum is marked as undesirable at her birth. "Hijras" in India learn how to survive the hostile surroundings. They use vulgar language and exaggerated gestures just to intimidate a potential abuser. They use these gimmicks as armor. Anjum is no exception. The exact opposite of Anjum is Estha (in *GST*), Rahel's twin, who has been sexually abused as a child and is traumatized to the extent that he stops speaking. Even though he is not a "Hijra," he does not fit easily into a neat gender category. Estha, unlike Anjum, deals with the hostile and uncaring world by not engaging with it. Not with the gunshot-like claps of "Hijras," but with silence. "Over time he had acquired the ability to blend into the background of wherever he was . . . it usually took strangers a while to notice him . . . even longer to notice that he never spoke. Some never noticed at all" (Roy, *GST* 10-11). As a young adult, he prefers to stay at home and does household work. He goes around in the world like "[a] quiet bubble floating on a sea of noise" (11). "Like a fisherman in a city. With sea secrets in him" (13). Estha, we see, "occupie[s] very little space in the world" (11). As the queerness spreads in him, he shrinks into himself.

Reading these two novels, one questions how and why the upper castes stick to the caste system, and how the practice of the caste system entails class- and gender-based violence in India. One can still ask why the country that claims to be the largest democracy is so obsessed with caste. In *The God of Small Things*, we see how the epistemology of class- and gender-based violence is played out in the ancient Indian text the *Mahabharata*. It is the story of Kaurva brothers and Pandva brothers. The stepbrothers go to war to settle the ownership dispute concerning the kingdom of "Kuru." We hear the high points of the epic in the novel. We meet Karna, a skilled warrior of unknown lineage, who fights against Pandvas on the battlefield: "Karna the abandoned child . . . the most revered warrior of them all" (Roy, *GST* 231). Unlike Pandvas and Kaurvas, Karna is fatherless, casteless and therefore unworthy in the hierarchy of caste—notwithstanding his being an accomplished, admirable, and invincible warrior. One of the Pandvas makes fun of Karna and reviles him "for being a lowly charioteer's son" (233). Under the guidance of the *just* Krishna, one of the Pandava brothers kills Karna on the battlefield by stealth. Karna dies "unfairly, unarmed . . . stoned out of his skull"(232). The story reverberates with what happens to Velutha. The keepers of law and justice (the police and the politician) unite to eradicate Velutha for eroding caste lines. Similarly Krishna and upper caste Pandavas collaborate to kill the lowly born Karna by cunning.

In the novel, we are told that Karna is actually the half-brother of Pandvas. Pandvas' mother, Kunti, gave birth to him before her marriage. However, she abandons him because he is born out of wedlock and therefore he is illegitimate—without caste. Apparently, Kunti goes through the same kind of inner torment that the mother of a "Hijra" child experiences (in *MUH*). Kunti abandons the child because there is no father in sight, and Indian society is ruthless to children who are born out of wedlock. Likewise the mother of the "Hijra" child suffers too because of the inappropriate body of her child, which cannot sustain and carry forward the caste. The child's very body makes it unfit to participate in life. Therefore, the society discards those who do not fit into the caste system.

Furthermore, the Pandavas, in a game of dice, stake their wife, Draupadi. Having won Draupadi, the Kaurvas publicly humiliate her. Ammu, too, suffers the same kind of humiliation. Her own husband, just to keep his job and carry on with drinking, suggests that she should sleep with his Boss. She leaves him and returns to her parental home, where she is not really welcomed. In the epic, Draupadi is insulted and objectified by warring men—the Pandvas (her husbands), who stake her, and the Kaurvas, who win her. Several centuries later, someone like Ammu is ill-treated by her husband as well as by her father and brother.

Using these significant episodes, Roy connects her narratives to the seminal Sanskrit text the *Mahabharata*. She locates the genesis of class- and gender-based violence in ancient texts that emphatically justify caste-discrimination and gender-violence. Obviously, such conceptions harm Indians. The novels show that any society in which a large section of population is enslaved and exploited on the basis of class and gender can never be a healthy and free society. In both novels, Roy shows how caste not only destroys the "Untouchables," but its venom also seeps into the privileged upper castes. Since the very fundamentals of caste are premised on cruelty and injustice, it breaks both the upper castes and the 'Untouchables' in different ways. It is this appalling, unexamined, and painful reality of the Indian society that Roy wakes up to every morning—the aching, broken world that howls like a hot wind—that demands nothing less than justice.

Notes

1. Arundhati Roy, *The Ordinary Person's Guide*, p. 3.
2. From Arundhati Roy's essay "Free Speech: Your Take."
3. An ancient code of conduct manual for Hindus. Throughout this essay, I use the words "Hindu" and "Indian" to describe people of India.
4. See Kalyani Menon-Sen and Gautam Bhan, *Swept off the Map: Surviving Eviction and Resettlement in Delhi.*
5. From Arundhati Roy's essay "Walking with the Comrades."
6. Watch Deepa Mehta's films *Water* and *The Forgotten Woman.*
7. From Arundhati Roy's essay "Mr Chidambaram's War."

Works Cited

Ambedkar, B. R. *Annihilation of Caste*. 1936. Verso, 2014.

Mehta, Deepa, director. *The Forgotten Woman.* David Hamilton, 2008.

_____. *Water.* David Hamilton, 2005.

Roy, Arundhati. "Free Speech: Your Take." *Outlookindia.com*, 14 Jan. 2002.

_____. *The God of Small Things.* Flamingo, 1998.

_____. *The Ministry of Utmost Happiness.* Hamish Hamilton, 2017.

_____. "Mr Chidambaram's War." *Outlookindia.com*, 9 Nov. 2009.

_____. *The Ordinary Person's Guide to Empire.* Flamingo, 2004.

_____. "Walking with the Comrades." *Outlookindia.com*, 29 Mar. 2010.

Sen, Kalyani Menon, and Gautam Bhan. *Swept off the Map: Surviving Eviction and Resettlement in Delhi.* Yoda Press, 2008.

Punishment, Spirituality, and Materialism in the Anti-Utopia

Fyodor Dostoyevsky's novels *Poor Folk, Notes from the Dead House, Winter Notes on Summer Impressions, Notes from the Underground,* and *Crime and Punishment*

Roger Chapman

In Tsarist Russia the novelist Fyodor Dostoyevsky (1821–1881) lived in the context of an ongoing debate on inequality. His literary outpourings, complex and voluminous in a mixed style of realism and romanticism, "depicted the grim face of early industrialism and dealt with social problems, notably the plight of the newly liberated serfs" (Mathews, Platt, and Noble 512). Although he was also a writer of short stories, the truth is his mode of thinking was not conducive to an abbreviated format; as H. E. Bates explains, a short story "cannot tolerate a weight of words or a weight of moral teaching" (37). When comparing himself with the important Russian writers (i.e., Pushkin, Lermontov, Gogol, Turgenev, and Tolstoy), Dostoyevsky pointed out that he was different from the rest in that he was not of the landed gentry. He believed that due to the vantage point of his social background, he was able to depict a truer picture of Russia, in particular the upheaval and chaos of average Russians as industrialization undermined many aspects of traditional life (Frank, *Dostoevsky: The Seeds* 6).

Dostoyevsky's father was a surgeon who had ascended to the legal status of the nobility after being awarded the order of St. Anna third class for his service at a charity hospital in Moscow. Though the role of physician was respectable, the doctor's profession neither conferred high social status nor generated great wealth. The Dostoyevsky apartment was cramped, but they kept up the pretense of nobility by having six servants. They even possessed a country estate of some three thousand acres and a hundred serfs, but this family was not of the landed gentry. Dostoyevsky's father may have been embittered due to his low station—he convinced his seven children that they had descended from ancient Lithuanian aristocrats, but due to lack of documentation, the family was denied the privileges of its elite background. Still, the children were provided a good education with private tutors, and both Dostoyevsky and his older brother, Mikhail, were able to attend boarding school in St. Petersburg (Frank, *Dostoevsky: The Seeds* 8-10).

After becoming a widower, the father retired to the cottage on the country estate. Less than two years later, he died, possibly murdered at the hands of his serfs who were tired of his harshness (Frank, *Dostoevsky: The Seeds* 85-86). It was at this estate that the young Dostoyevsky spent summers, frolicking outdoors, interacting with peasants, and observing the milieu of village life. At the time of his father's death, Dostoyevsky was a student at the Army Engineering College in St. Petersburg—the last letter exchange he had with his father was over money. As a cadet, he tried maintaining a lifestyle similar to his peers of higher social rank, thus straining his father's finances. Some, such as Sigmund Freud, suppose that Dostoyevsky's guilt over his spendthrift ways and his father's death led to a physiological reaction that brought about epileptic attacks (Frank, *Dostoevsky: The Seeds* 88)—for the rest of Dostoyevsky's life, he would be dogged by seizures that would randomly come and go.

Whatever guilt Dostoyevsky may have had, it was not enough for him to pursue the military career that his father had mapped out for him. After graduating from engineering school, soon as he could, he resigned from his military commission and began pursuing a literary career. The social consciousness he was so keenly aware of from his lowly nobility status as well as perspective gained from observing up close the haves and the have-nots afforded him writing material. If there was any bitterness, he turned it into sympathy for the poor and downtrodden and all those who suffer. Dostoyevsky's first writing success, at age twenty-four, was the epistolary novel *Poor Folk* (1846). Vissarion Belinsky, a literary critic at the time, hailed *Poor Folk* as a great work of social awareness and pronounced the debut novelist as Nikolai Gogol's successor (Fitzgerald 161). Gogol was the author of *Dead Souls* and "The Overcoat" and was famous for sensitively depicting people living in abject poverty, such as low-level civil service workers. *Poor Folk* includes such characters and, like Gogol, the narrative upholds the dignity of people so poor that when they walk, they tread carefully so that their boots will not wear out too quickly (139). In another work by Dostoyevsky, a satirical story about social class, "A Christmas Tree Party and a Wedding" (1848), a middle-aged man, a banker, scopes out a little girl to later marry because she is of the landed gentry and will inherit a fortune; at the end of the story, a few years after the Christmas party where the banker met the little girl, there is the wedding, but there is no love except the love of rubles.

In 1847, Dostoyevsky joined a socialist reading group known as the Petrashevsky Circle. The evidence suggests that certain members of the group were on the cusp of engaging in direct action by publishing socialist propaganda critical of the Tsarist system (Kjetssa 64-65). Exactly how committed Dostoyevsky was to this radical action is inconclusive, but he was never put to the test because Tsarist police in 1849 conducted a sweep and arrested all of the participants. It was a dangerous time to be part of a radical group in Russia, as the government was in a reactive mode due to the previous year's riots and revolutions that had wracked the Continent (Kjetssa 61). The upheavals of 1848 are why Karl Marx and Friedrich Engels wrote *The Communist Manifesto*, as they hoped to blow on those coals and cause even greater unrest. On December 22, after being found guilty of subversion, Dostoyevsky and his co-conspirators were taken to a public square to be executed—but just as the firing squad was about to carry out the punishment, a messenger dramatically galloped up on horseback and announced the Tsar's reprieve. The sentence was reduced to penal servitude in Siberia. From 1850 to 1854, Dostoyevsky was a convict at the Omsk prison. This was followed by a stint of compulsory military service. Finally, in 1859, he was allowed to return to St. Petersburg. Dostoyevsky would have an interest in politics, economics, and current affairs for the remainder of his life; however, while his sympathy for the poor and contempt for the landed gentry remained strong, he exchanged a revolutionary viewpoint for a spiritual one.

His first major novel following the end of his exile was *Notes from the Dead House* (1861), and it produced quite a sensation, for it was the first literary effort to depict the penal system of Siberia. This prison memoir was realistic, but it sympathetically portrayed the convicts as human beings worthy of some respect. As Joseph explains: "Dostoevsky made no effort to conceal their sometimes horrendous crimes; but he saw them as sentient beings whose behavior deserved to be understood if not pardoned" (*Between Religion* 10). The Omsk experience, with Dostoyevsky in contact on a daily basis with peasants, was a turning point for him. His interaction with these men of the lowest social class, representatives of the majority, made him realize that they were the possessors of authentic Russian culture. He eventually concluded that their worldview was superior to the Westernized borrowings of the intelligentsia. In fact, the higher classes seemed like foreigners who had forgotten their country or else had allowed their materialism to deaden their spiritual faculties. Also, Dostoyevsky became convinced of the spiritual value in suffering, something he knew firsthand, suffering as he did from being deprived of all reading material except for the Bible. Now, instead of giving consideration to Western ideas, such as secular socialism, Dostoyevsky was convinced that Russia's traditional culture was the answer. He evolved into a Slavophile, a Russian nationalist and an Orthodox believer. *Poor Folk* and *Notes from the Dead House* are more or less similar in sentiment about the lower classes, but they may as well have been written by two different authors.

Back in St. Petersburg, Dostoyevsky tried making up for his lost decade. He joined with his older brother Mikhail in launching a literary magazine, *Vremya* (Time). After that periodical ran afoul with the authorities, they started a second one, *Epokha* (Epoch). When the brother suddenly died, however, Dostoyevsky assumed his debts and took over financial responsibility for his dependents. Prior to his world turning upside down, which included the death of his first wife, Dostoyevsky was able to take a couple of months off and travel to Europe. Major stops were Germany, France, and England. Afterwards, he published a travelogue, *Winter Notes on Summer Impressions* (1863), a work that anchors the ideological mindset of Dostoyevsky and provides the framing for his classic works, such as *Notes from the Underground* (1864) and *Crime and Punishment* (1866) and even the minor work *The Gambler* (1866).

Winter Notes on Summer Impressions is not touristy, but rather it is a severe critique, a prejudicial one, of Western Europe. Indeed, the work comes across as polemical and harshly judgmental. The 1863 trip helped crystallize Dostoyevsky's worldview that would be infused in all subsequent writings (Chapman). Germany was an important stop on the excursion because of the opportunity to gamble at the casinos. Some have suggested that Dostoyevsky's penchant for losing at the roulette wheel was in part due to his desire of *becoming* and *not being* rich (Lord 70), but either way, he seems to have had a gambling addiction. He rationalized his gambling as an attempt to win a big payout in order to help many people, which prompted his wife to sarcastically dub him the "benefactor of mankind" (Lord 80).

Later, when pressed with a looming deadline in which he had to deliver a novel or else surrender the copyright of all his past and future works to the publisher, he found a stenographer and quickly produced *The Gambler*, a psychological examination of the gambler's malady. The novel portrays the quest of materialism as a type of hell, which was Dostoyevsky's attitude. As explained by Temira Pachmuss, "Throughout his life, Dostoevsky despised the bondage of money. His longing was to be free from concern over such worldly matters in order that he might live by the spirit" (47). The main character Aleksey has a relationship problem with his lover Polina and believes he will be regarded by her as a somebody if he wins big: "Through money, through gambling, he imagines he will become a different man" (Jackson 196). In the story, the importance of the casino being in the West is that it serves as a lesson of what happens to a Russian when he leaves his native land and its unique culture. The person in the story who comes across as truly liberated is the grandmother who, after losing some money at the roulette wheel, returns to Russia and devotes her resources to building a church.

In *Winter Notes on Summer Impressions*, Dostoyevsky laments how Western Europe has long been the standard for aspiring Russian elites. Dostoyevsky ridicules the Russian desire to imitate Westerners and suggests that it leads to a philosophy of life that is oppressive toward others, a type of rationalization "such as using Holy Scriptures to prove the necessity of the slave trade, like the Americans in the southern states" (*Winter* 63). In the desire to become more like Europeans, the Russian elites speak critically of their own country, referring to their own culture as "barbarism" (72). Dostoyevsky admits that he once considered Europeans better off than Russians, but now he has seen firsthand the "melancholy" and "continual anxiety" on European faces (75).

In the chapter "Baal" in *Winter Notes on Summer Impressions*, Dostoyevsky offers his perspective of London after a week's stay. Here the great industrial city is described as polluted and crowded, featuring the Crystal Palace that was the venue of the industrial exhibition (the first world's fair) and housed the material wonders and latest inventions and, alongside it, Whitechapel "with its half-naked, savage, and hungry population" (Dostoyevsky, *Winter* 90). The industrial exhibition Dostoyevsky contemptuously regards as "something out of Babylon," requiring everyone "to accept the material world as your ideal. . ." (91). In other words, the industrial age was turning the civilized into idolaters. Moreover, the process of industrialization was dehumanizing people, the workers, and reducing them to poverty as they paradoxically made the world richer. The "colossal setting" zapped the working poor of their dignity, leading to alcoholic debauchery with gin, contributing to insensibility and "zombie-like" living, with some either rejecting traditional Christianity outright or "seek[ing] salvation morosely and bitterly in Mormonism or something similar" (92).

As observed by Ernest Simmons, "Trips abroad disillusioned him [Dostoyevsky] about the political and social structure there and strengthened his faith in the future high density of Russia if it could be kept free of the materialistic poison of the West" (115).

Both Paris and London convinced him that the materialism of the West came at too high of a price. Regarding the French, he sneered at their motto of liberty, fraternity, and equality. As Dostoyevsky presents it in *Winter Notes on Summer Impressions*, liberty in France is freedom and freedom is for anyone who "has a million"; equality before the law should be "a personal insult" to all French because it is obviously not true; and fraternity "still forms the chief stumbling block of the West" (108-109). Among other things, "thought of profit" stands in the way of brotherhood; the Western emphasis on selfish individualism will not allow for fraternity (113-114). Most worrisome for Dostoyevsky was the Western penchant for developing systems for control in order to develop an artificial unity. For him, the Crystal Palace symbolized this controlling mechanism, this utilitarian quest to impose on the globe what the ideologues felt would bring about the greatest happiness for the most people. For Dostoyevsky, the Crystal Palace, with its emphasis on products, productivity, consumption, uniformity, free trade, and globalization, all heralded in quasi-religious terms, represented a dangerous mechanization of humanity, utilizing a rationalistic utilitarian and algorithmic approach to force an artificial brotherhood out of fear that everyone would otherwise turn cannibalistic. In his own words, what was being played out was "the mortal struggle between the individualistic basis of the whole Western world and the necessity of finding some way to live together" (89). This was an affront to his spiritual instincts.

The Crystal Palace would come up in his subsequent works, namely *Notes from the Underground* and *Crime and Punishment*. The context for those books has to do with what happened shortly after Dostoyevsky returned from his first trip abroad. Nikolai Chernyshevsky, a socialist radical of St. Petersburg, was arrested, and while awaiting his case to be heard, he wrote and had published *What Is To Be Done?*, a utopian novel. In that work, he offered his vision of a future socialist society. In Chernyshevksy's story, the character Vera Pavolovna has a series of dreams and in the fourth one appears the future Russia after the socialist revolution. The new society is housed in the Crystal Palace:

There stands a building, a large, enormous structure such as can be seen only in a few of the grandest capitals. No, now there's no other building like it! It stands amidst fields and meadows, orchards and groves. The fields grow grain, but they aren't like the ones we have now; rather, they're rich and abundant. . . . There's nothing at all like it now. No, there is one building that hints at it—the palace at Sydenham: cast iron and crystal, crystal and cast iron—nothing else. No, that's not all; it's merely the shell of the building, its external façade. Inside there's a real house, a colossal one, surrounded by this crystal and iron edifice as if by a sheath. . . . (Chernyshevsky 369-370)

As W. J. Leatherbarrow explains, the Crystal Palace was for Chernyshevsky "the new spirit of scientific optimism and heroic materialism" as well as "a symbol of the secular paradise on earth that man would achieve through socialism" (8). And that is exactly what made Dostoyevsky livid about Chernyshevsky's novel. Ironically, both novelists saw the Crystal Palace as a potent symbol of that which puts materialism above everything else, whether achieved by capitalism or socialism. (Queen Victoria and Prince Albert hosted the first world's fair in order to promote free trade and to ward off radicalism by educating their subjects on the promise of the new industrial order; they would thus have been aghast hearing that their Crystal Palace was being co-opted as a symbol of Russian socialism.) The two men were in disagreement not about capitalism versus socialism, but about materialism. Interestingly, Chernyshevsky's novel was read and raved over by Vladimir Lenin, who wrote a pamphlet in 1901 that utilized the same title—*What Is to Be Done?*—and presented Marxist-Leninism as the answer to the question.

Dostoyevsky was convinced that modernity and its emphasis on material abundance and consumption was pulling humanity in a direction of what would today be termed a dystopia. This is what he alludes to in the novella *Notes from the Underground*, a work that is credited with being the first to make use of the "antihero" literary device. (Mathews, Platt, and Noble 512). In this case, the unnamed narrator, the antihero, rants against the superfluous man (the privileged Russian who typically embraces Western ideas). The narrator is a champion of freedom and freewill and is angry, suspicious, and even fearful of the possibility of a utopian society. At one point, the underground man proclaims that he would stick his tongue out at the Crystal Palace and prefer living in a hencoop instead (Dostoyevsky, *Notes* 24), as he regarded the idea of the Crystal Palace as a threat to his freedom. According to Robert Lord, the underground man believes that science and so-called scientific laws, including utilitarianism, are nonhuman and fail to take into account the individual desire for freedom above everything else (40-41). In fact, as Lord continues, freedom is such a strong desire, if not instinct, that humans will choose self-destructive and wicked deeds in order to prove they are their own masters (42).

The antihero of *Notes from the Underground* also mocks rationalism. He boasts that he has no interest in being rational, and he sneers about his superior honesty. The underground man is conscious of his duality (the contradictory nature, as characterized by lofty ideals on one hand and baseness on the other) and feels smugly superior because he believes all people are double-minded even though most are unaware of their true condition. (Dualism, as Pachmuss points out, was a major theme of Dostoyevsky's writings, including *The Double*, a novel examining the concept.) The programs offered by the utopian-minded, whether proponents of capitalism or socialism, were regarded by Dostoyevsky as in disharmony with human nature and out of synch with spiritual truths. For him, people will never capitulate to the demands of an ordered society, even if material abundance is guaranteed.

The more the world becomes rational, the antihero in *Notes from the Underground* fumes, the worse it becomes. Civilization itself does not elevate people as much as people think. For instance, civilization offers a "variety of sensations—and absolutely nothing more." Civilized people have engaged in horrific wars even though they regard bloodshed as "abominable." But there are those who "are fully convinced" that this will change "when common sense and science have completely reeducated human nature and turned it in a normal direction." According to the antihero, the utilitarians believe humankind "will cease from *intentional* error" because of the development of rationalism (Dostoyevsky, *Underground* 16). "Consequently," he sarcastically continues,

> we have only to discover these laws of nature, and man will no longer have to answer for his actions and life will be exceedingly easy for him. All human actions will then, of course, be tabulated according to these laws, mathematically, like tables of logarithms up to 108,000, and entered in an index; or, better still, there would be published certain edifying works of the nature of encyclopedic lexicons, in which everything will be more clearly calculated and explained that there will be no more incidents or adventures in the world. (Dostoyevsky, *Underground* 17)

While it would be too simplistic to say that the underground man is channeling Dostoyevsky, it is true that they both rejected the optimism regarding the notion of human progress being accompanied by greater economic wellbeing.

In *Notes from the Underground*, the author clearly has Chernyshevsky in mind when the antihero acknowledges the utopian dream of socialists: "Then—this is all what you say—new economic relations will be established, all ready-made and worked out with mathematical exactitude, so that every possible question will vanish in the twinkling of an eye, simply because every answer to it will be provided. Then the 'Palace of Crystal' will be built" (Dostoyevsky, *Underground* 17). But the antihero warns that planned economy might lead to a situation in which life becomes "frighteningly dull" even though it is "extraordinarily rational." He goes on to warn that people will never be satisfied and they will not be grateful that, in fact, "in the midst of general prosperity a gentleman with an ignoble, or rather with a reactionary and ironical, countenance" will suggest "'we better kick over the whole show and scatter rationalism to the winds, simply to send these logarithms to the devil, and to enable us to live once more at our own foolish sweet will'" (17).

Dostoyevsky was very skeptical of those who had ready-made schemes for ending inequality. In the attempt to make an ideal world, he believed, there will be short-term atrocities committed for the sake of the long-term—in his opinion, unattainable—good. This is one of the ideas he explores in his detective thriller *Crime and Punishment*. In this story, Rodion Romanovich Raskolnikov, a college student deeply in debt and living in St. Petersburg, regards himself as having the character and courage of Napoleon. He seems to have the mentality of Nietzsche's superman, rising above good and evil (Panichas 30). He wants to test himself, but he also wants to do something that contributes to making a better world. So he comes up with the plan to murder an old female pawnbroker in order to steal her money and valuables so that he can give the bounty to the poor. The utilitarian logic was that since she was old, and had long taken advantage of the economically downtrodden, it would be better to do away with her life and redistribute her wealth. So Raskolnikov tiptoes down the thirteen steps of the back stairwell (in order to avoid meeting his landlord, whom he owes rent) and slays the pawnbroker. The murderer, after burying the stolen property and buckling under the pressure, confesses his crime and goes to Siberia. Nothing good came out of the scheme.

One clue that *Crime and Punishment* is a morality tale aimed at Chernyshevsky is that shortly after committing the murder, Raskolnikov visits a tavern called the Crystal Palace, which is sarcastically described as a "very well-ordered and spacious" place (Dostoyevsky, *Crime* 177). In the tavern, the murderer reads about his crime in the newspaper, and in the same edition, there are articles reporting about the numerous arson fires in St. Petersburg that were being set by young socialists in a senseless bid to jumpstart revolution. The fires actually did happen, and sometime prior to Chernyshevsky's arrest, Dostoyevsky had approached him (the two men knew each other) and implored him to use his influence to put a stop to these fires (Frank, *Dostoevsky: The Stir* 151-155). Obviously, the subtle point (subtle because for many readers *Crime and Punishment* is simply a suspenseful murder thriller with masterful descriptions of psychological aspects) was that in the quest to achieve some ideal state, there will invariably be misdeeds. Interestingly, when Iraqi dictator Saddam Hussein was captured by American forces in December 2003, he was found to be reading a copy of *Crime and*

Punishment. Whether the dictator was simply distracting himself in his fugitive status or was thinking about how the novel might apply to his oppressive Baathist regime or the overly optimistic American project to spread democracy across the Middle East, Dostoyevsky would have been struck by the surrealistic poignancy.

A major implication of both *Notes from the Underground* and *Crime and Punishment* is Dostoyevsky conceding that inequality is inescapable. Human beings, in their sinful fallen state, could never cooperate enough for there to be equipoise. For him, two humans can be equal only in being human. In the novel *The Devils* (1872), sometimes translated as *The Possessed*, he takes on socialist radicals. In a letter to an acquaintance Dostoyevsky explained that *The Devils* was "like *Crime and Punishment* even nearer to reality" (Jones 237). The issue of inequality, the reason why revolutionists, at least in theory, wish to change the social order, is not addressed because it was irrelevant to Dostoyevsky. The evils that emerge in the process of carrying out revolution or some Western ideological program is what primarily interests this novelist. When he wrote the novel, he was in debt and so was living outside of Russia in order to be out of the reach of his creditors. Despite his personal problems with not enough money, he was certain that a socialistic revolution was not the answer. He originally considered calling the novel *The Atheist* because that was one of his major problems with the socialists: their atheism and their belief that materialism was the answer to the human condition. Similarly, in *The Brothers Karamazov* (1880) Dostoyevsky opined: "For socialism is not merely the labour question, it is before all things the atheistic question, the question of the form taken by atheism today, the question of the tower of Babel built without God, not to mount to heaven from earth but to set up Heaven on earth" (21).

Until the early twentieth century, Dostoyevsky was largely an obscure author outside of Russia. If he was read, it was either in French or German, though English translations of *House of the Dead*, *Crime and Punishment*, and *The Insulted and the Injured* appeared between 1890 and 1895. Constance Garnett, the first major English translator of Dostoyevsky's work, considered him to be a careless writer, much inferior to his contemporaries Ivan Turgenev and Leo Tolstoy. But it was her 1912 translation of *The Brothers Karamazov* that created an enthusiasm for Dostoyevsky. Though she did not really care for his works, commercial necessity drove her. By 1920, she had translated twelve volumes of Dostoyevsky, and ever since, this Russian author has been highly regarded in the English-speaking world (Moser 435). As Peter Kaye notes, many of the English authors of that time—including D. H. Lawrence, Virginia Woolf, Joseph Conrad, and Arnold Bennett—read him, but most did not appreciate what he had to offer. This was perhaps due to a collective failure to grapple with Dostoyevsky's complex polyphonic approach.

In Russia, Dostoyevsky's fame grew following his death. But after the Bolsheviks took over, the communist consensus was that the author of *The Possessed*, a damning critique of socialist revolutionaries, was a reactionary writer. Though he had a statue of Dostoyevsky erected, Lenin regarded the author's works as "trash" (Simmons 102). During the Stalin period, the Soviet Union largely ignored Dostoyevsky. After Khrushchev came to power following the death of Stalin, the Soviet government introduced The Thaw (a period of cultural relaxation with less censorship), and all of Dostoyevsky's works were republished and sold throughout the nation (Slonim, 144). The famous Soviet dissident Andrei Sinyavsky suggested that Dostoyevsky was one of the first to discern the quasi-religious aspect of the Russian revolutionaries of the nineteenth century (9). With "The Legend of the Grand Inquisitor" (as embedded in *The Brothers Karamazov*) and certain revolutionary characters in *The Possessed*, Dostoyevsky became the progenitor of the "antiutopian" novel. According to Sinyavsky,

> When Dostoyevsky wrote these antiutopias, few believed him. We believe him because we have experienced the twentieth century. This attests, as does the antiutopian wave, to the fact that the Soviet people live in a real-life utopia and know the cost. The antiutopian novel isn't simply a rejection or contradiction of the utopia, it depicts utopia found, the real-life absolute. (32)

Later, when the Soviet dissident Alexander Solzhenitsyn offered his gulag novel *One Day in the Life of Ivan Denisovich* (1962), many Russians could not help but compare it with *House of the Dead*. (Solzhenitsyn, like his literary forebear, was a Slavophile, regarded communism as a Western imposition, and embraced the teachings of the Orthodox Church.)

With respect to Fyodor Dostoyevsky's legacy on the debate of inequality, his writings side with the poor, but they do not sound a battle cry for social justice. As Maxim Gorky critically noted in his "Notes on the Petty Bourgeoisie" (1905), Dostoyevsky had a passive attitude about social problems (Simmons, 96). The passivity, a consequence of his insights gained from his Siberian experience, was imbued with a damnation of materialism. In other words, Dostoyevsky was a spiritualist. As he saw it, schemes to create abundance of material goods or redistribute wealth were empty promises that in the attempt of being carried out would only cause greater harm by undercutting humanity's more important underlying needs. That the Crystal Palace, the capitalist venue for the first world's fair, could be readily used as a symbol of socialist utopia demonstrated in Dostoyevsky's mind that both "isms" were two sides of the same coin, a coin not worth keeping. This was a position he developed over time, and it crystallized during and after he was an inmate in Siberia when he began to consider that the Western influences of the Enlightenment and industrialization are far from being holy writ.

Works Cited

Bates, H. E. *The Modern Short Story*. The Writer, 1976.

Chapman, Roger. "Fyodor Dostoyevsky, Eastern Orthodoxy, and the Crystal Palace." *Historic Engagements with Occidental Cultures, Religions, Powers*, edited by Anne Richard and Iraj Omidvar, Palgrave Macmillan, 2014, pp. 35-55.

Chernyshevsky, Nikolai. *What Is To Be Done?* Translated by Michael R. Katz, Cornell UP, 1989.

Dostoevsky, Fyodor M. *Winter Notes on Summer Impressions*. Translated by Richard Lee Renfield, McGraw-Hill, 1965.

Dostoyevsky, Fyodor. *The Devils*. Translated by David Magarshack, Penguin Books, 1971.

_____. *The Gambler: Stories of the 1860s*. Raduga Publishers, 1990.

_____. *The Insulted and the Humiliated*. Raduga Publishers, 1989.

_____. *Notes from the Dead House*. Translated by Guy Cook and Elena Cook, Raduga Publishers, 1989.

_____. *Notes from the Underground*. Translated by Constance Garnett. Dover, 1992.

_____. *Poor Folk*. Boni and Liveright, 1917.

Fitzgerald, Shelia, editor. "Feodor Mikhailovich Dostoevski." *Short Story Criticism*, vol. 2, Gale, 1989.

Frank, Joseph. *Between Religion and Rationality: Essays in Russian Literature and Culture*. Princeton UP, 2010.

_____. *Dostoevsky: The Seeds of Revolt, 1821–1849*. Princeton UP, 1976.

_____. *Dostoevsky: The Stir of Liberation, 1860–1865*. Princeton UP, 1986.

Jackson, Robert Louis. "Polina and Lady Luck in *The Gambler*." *Fyodor Dostoevsky*, edited by Harold Bloom, Chelsea House, 1988, pp. 187-209.

Jones, John. "The Possessed." *Fyodor Dostoevsky*, edited by Harold Bloom, Chelsea House, 1988, pp. 237-267.

Kaye, Peter. *Dostoevsky and English Modernism, 1900–1930*. Cambridge UP, 1999.

Kjettsa, Geir. *Fyodor Dostoyevsky: A Writer's Life*. Fawcett Columbine, 1987.

Leatherbarrow, W. J. *Dostoevskii and Britain*. Berg, 1995.

Lord, Robert. *Dostoyevsky: Essays and Perspectives*. U of California P, 1970.

Mathews, Roy T., F. Dewitt Platt, and Thomas F. X. Noble. *Experience Humanities*. McGraw-Hill, 2014.

Moser, Charles A. "The Achievement of Constance Garnett." *American Scholar*, vol. 57, no. 3, Summer 1988, pp. 4311-438.

Pachmuss, Temira. *F. M. Dostoevsky: Dualism and Synthesis of the Soul*. Southern Illinois U P, 1963.

Panichas, George A. *Dostoevsky's Spiritual Art: The Burden of Vision.* Transaction Publishers, 2005.

Simmons, Ernest J. *Introduction to Russian Realism.* Indiana UP, 1965.

Sinyavsky, Andrei. *Soviet Civilization: A Cultural History.* Arcade Publishing, 1988.

Slonim, Mark. *An Outline of Russian Literature.* Oxford UP, 1958.

Leveling the Playing Field: Cultural Relativism and Inequality

Kurt Vonnegut's novel *The Sirens of Titan* and short story "Harrison Bergeron"_____

Adam T. Bogar

Vonnegut and Anthropology: An Introduction

In his 1989 essay "The Concept of Fiction" ("El concepto de ficción"), Argentinean writer Juan José Saer mentions the expression "speculative anthropology" ("antropologia especulativa") as a "suggested definition of fiction" (Hemer 180). Although he never goes on to elaborate on this definition, according to Oscar Hemer, Saer "quite obviously uses the word [speculative] in an affirmative sense—speculative as *uninhibited, unpredictable, transgressive*" (182). The fiction of American writer and public intellectual Kurt Vonnegut (probably best known as the author of the seminal novel *Slaughterhouse-Five*) fits that bill perfectly for a variety of reasons. This chapter will provide a reading of Vonnegut's novel *The Sirens of Titan* and his short story "Harrison Bergeron" as well as a selection of his nonfiction works. Through this reading, I will explore the ways in which Vonnegut's study of anthropology informs his thought and writing, to the extent that his fiction becomes speculative anthropology itself. I will also elaborate on the interrelatedness of anthropological and political thinking in his works, apparent in his treatment of, and comments on, social and economic inequality.

Vonnegut had a somewhat unconventional educational history. Coming from a family of hardware salespeople and, later on, architects, there was a family pressure on him to study science: "Although [Vonnegut] would have preferred to study literature or the humanities, or to become an architect like his father and grandfather before him, both Kurt, Sr., and his older brother, Bernard, pushed him toward the sciences. . . " (Farrell 5). He first started studying biochemistry at Cornell University in 1940, but left in 1942, partly due to his enlistment in the US Army, but partly due to his displeasure with studying science. After his enlistment, "Vonnegut was sent back to college as part of the Army Specialized Training Program (ASTP), where he studied mechanical engineering, first at Carnegie Technical Institute and later at the University of Tennessee" (5). In 1944, he was shipped over to Europe as part of the 106th Infantry Division to fight in World War II, where he was captured and held as a prisoner of war in Dresden, Germany. He survived the Allied firebombing of the city in 1945 and returned to the US in May 1945. It was only after all this, in December 1945, that Vonnegut enrolled as a graduate student at the University of Chicago, initially "as an undeclared major" (Shields 86).

Trying to decide what to study, he started with physical anthropology, which he found "tedious" (*Wampeters* 177), and archeology, but neither of those appealed to him. As Vonnegut writes, "I went to my faculty adviser, and I confessed that science did not charm me, that I longed for poetry instead" (178). The adviser suggested he tried social or cultural anthropology, which he described as "poetry which *pretends* to be scientific" (178). Although he left the University of Chicago without a degree, his studies in anthropology have had a profound influence on his works, particularly on those written during the 1960s and 70s.[1]

One of the most pervasive influences of Vonnegut's study of anthropology is that he learned of the idea of "folk societies," a term most famously employed by then-University of Chicago professor and renowned anthropologist Robert Redfield, whom Vonnegut called "the most satisfying teacher in [his] life" (*Wampeters* 178). Redfield describes and elaborates on this ideal type of society in a 1947 article, which he characterizes as being "small, isolated, nonliterate, and homogeneous, with a strong sense of group solidarity" (Redfield, "Folk" 293). According to Shiela Pardee, "Redfield's ideas continued to resonate in [Vonnegut's] fiction throughout his career. He credited Redfield for his thematic emphasis on the human need to belong to a small, supportive social group" (187).

In his 1971 address to the National Institute of Arts and Letters, Vonnegut describes his "biochemical-anthropological theory" through which he can explain *"everything"* (*Wampeters*

182, emphasis in original): "And I say to you that we are full of chemicals which require us to belong to folk societies, or failing that, to feel lousy all the time. We are chemically engineered to live in folk societies, just as fish are chemically engineered to live in clean water—and there aren't any folk societies for us anymore" (180). In short, Vonnegut "believed that the need for belonging to a group small enough for everyone to be known and to have roles to play was innate and biological" (Pardee 187). Pardee goes on to describe various appearances of such folk societies in Vonnegut's works as "sense-making systems" (I borrowed the expression from Peter Freese [145]), as his proposed ways of overcoming "a longing for community" (Standish 79). This chapter will explore a different aspect of Vonnegut's folk societies, namely, the role such communities play in trying to address different forms of social and economic inequality.

Equality as Dystopia?

Although Vonnegut touches upon the subject of social inequality in many of his works, most notably in his essays, speeches and other nonfiction writing, I will discuss two main texts where the issue of inequality features very prominently or even takes center stage. The first one of these two is Vonnegut's 1959 novel *The Sirens of Titan*, which describes the Church of God the Utterly Indifferent, one of Vonnegut's invented religions. Members of the Church are required to wear weights and other handicaps to level the playing field "in the race of life:"

> [The Reverend C. Horner Redwine had a] blue canvas bag of lead shot [. . .] strapped around his wrist. There were similar bags of shot around his ankles and his other wrist, and two heavy slabs of iron hung on shoulder straps—one slab on his chest and one on his back. These weights were his handicaps in the race of life. He carried forty-eight pounds—carried them gladly. A stronger person would have carried more, a weaker person would have carried less. Every strong member of Redwine's faith accepted handicaps gladly, wore them proudly everywhere. The weakest and meekest were bound to admit, at last, that the race of life was fair. (Vonnegut, *Sirens* 224)

As Reverend Redwine explains to Malachi Constant (one of the novel's protagonists), the Church requires this type of forced equality so that "no one could then reproach you for taking advantage of the random ways of luck" (Vonnegut, *Sirens* 230). "Unbelievers," that is, those who object to such an idea of equality, are threatened to face "the righteous displeasure of crowds" that are present "in every part of the world. The total membership of Churches of God the Utterly Indifferent was a good, round three billion" (231). People are monitored and, in a sense, controlled by the "disciplinary arm of the Church [which] was in crowds everywhere" (231).

Although the narrator describes followers of the Church as "happily self-handicapped people," who are apparently happy because "nobody took advantage of anybody any more" (227), the idea of such equality that is controlled and forced onto people still implies a controlling agent, an enforcer. In *The Sirens of Titan*, this role of the enforcer would suit Winston Niles Rumfoord, who founded the Church of God the Utterly Indifferent and gave it its two main teachings: "Puny man can do nothing at all to help or please God Almighty, and Luck is not the hand of God" (183).[2] His system of controlled equality is coupled with the elimination of the ideas of destiny and exceptionalism, to create a world where everyone lines up for the race of life with equal chances (or more precisely, equal lack of chances) to succeed amidst unpredictable "accidents."

Elaborating on almost exactly the same idea, Vonnegut's 1961 short story "Harrison Bergeron" is probably his most up-front treatment of the issues of egalitarianism and equality, or more accurately, the misunderstandings surrounding these ideas. The story briefly describes a dystopian society in the year 2081, where

> . . . everybody was finally equal [. . .] every which way. Nobody was smarter than anybody else. Nobody was better looking than anybody else. Nobody was stronger or quicker than anybody else. (Vonnegut, "Harrison" 7)

Due to the 211th, 212th and 213th Amendments to the Constitution, and on the orders of the United States Handicapper General, strong people carry weights; beautiful people wear hideous masks; and talented professional dancers in a TV performance dance off rhythm and in a somewhat clumsy way (so that nobody would feel bad about not being as good a dancer as they are); and smarter, more intelligent people have radio transmitters in their ears that frequently emit different distracting noises "to keep [such people] from taking unfair advantage of their brains" (Vonnegut, "Harrison" 7). In short, everyone is wearing some sort of a handicap in order to make sure that all people are truly equal in every possible way. The handicaps are assigned and monitored by the office of Diana Moon Glampers, the Handicapper General. In the story, we see an otherwise highly intelligent husband George Bergeron and his perfectly average wife Hazel watching a dance performance on TV. They discuss—in rather simplistic terms—the goods of their equality-based society and contrast it to "the dark ages [that had] everybody competing against everybody else" (9).

Suddenly a news bulletin interrupts the TV program and an announcement is read to inform viewers that "Harrison Bergeron, age fourteen [. . .] has just escaped from jail, where he was held on suspicion of plotting to overthrow the government. He is a genius and an athlete, is under-handicapped, and should be regarded as extremely dangerous" (Vonnegut, "Harrison" 10). He was recently taken from George and Hazel's home by officers of the Handicapper General. Suddenly, amidst great noise and earthquake-like shaking of the ground, Harrison busts his way onto the scene through a door. George immediately realizes it must be his son, but "the realization was blasted from his mind instantly by the sound of an automobile collision in his head" (11). Harrison proclaims himself Emperor and cries that everyone must obey him. He initially wears a huge amount of cripplingly heavy handicaps:

> Instead of a little ear radio for a mental handicap, he wore a tremendous pair of earphones, and spectacles with thick wavy lenses. The spectacles were intended to make him not only half blind, but to give him whanging headaches besides. Scrap metal was hung all over him. Ordinarily, there was a certain symmetry, a military neatness to the handicaps issued to strong people, but Harrison looked like a walking junkyard. In the race of life, Harrison carried three hundred

pounds. And to offset his good looks, the H-G men required that he wear at all times a red rubber ball for a nose, keep his eyebrows shaved off, and cover his even white teeth with black caps at snaggle-tooth random. (Vonnegut, "Harrison" 11)

Harrison removes all of his handicaps, orders the musicians on scene to play to the best of their abilities (and removes their handicaps as well), and asks if there's a woman brave enough to join him as Empress. One of the ballerinas rises, Harrison removes her handicaps and her mask, and she turns out to be stunningly beautiful. They start dancing intensely to the music, they literally elevate and go higher and higher in exaltation until they "kiss the ceiling [. . .] and then, neutralizing gravity with love and pure will, they remained suspended in air inches below the ceiling, and they kissed each other for a long, long time (Vonnegut, "Harrison" 13). At this moment, Diana Moon Glampers, the Handicapper General herself, enters the scene with a gun, and shoots both Harrison and the ballerina dead. She then gives everyone ten seconds to put their handicaps back on. George and Hazel's TV tube burns out, and Hazel wants to say something about it to George, but he has gone out to the kitchen for a beer. When he returns, he asks whether Hazel's been crying, as there are tears on her cheek. She says that she did about "something real sad on television," but she doesn't really remember, as it's "all kind of mixed up in [her] mind" (14). George suggests that she "forget sad things" (14), and they go back to their lives, apparently as if nothing has happened.

It is a natural first reaction to sympathize with Harrison when he is shot dead by the Handicapper General, the apparent oppressor of individuality, amidst his attempt at escaping the (quite literal) bondages of such a society. But, as Darryl Hattenhauer points out, "[t]hose who hold Harrison up as a model of freedom overlook the fact that he is a would-be dictator" (391). He proclaims himself the "Emperor," and he also says that "everybody must do what I say at once" (Vonnegut, "Harrison" 12). On the surface, Vonnegut seems to have written a short story about the impossibility, absurdity, and, indeed, ridiculousness of total equality, but on closer scrutiny, it is revealed that "Harrison Bergeron" (as well as *The Sirens of Titan*) is a very calculated and witty jab at what Leonard Mustazza calls "the cold arrogance of class-conscious America" (54).

In a short yet important article, Darryl Hattenhauer argues that the above jab is aimed to a large extent at "America's form of egalitarianism: anti-intellectual leveling" (390). Egalitarian social plans usually target economic inequality, especially in terms of income and wealth, and they "tend to rest on a background idea that all human persons are equal in fundamental worth or moral status" (Arneson). The idea of income redistribution is notably missing from "Harrison Bergeron," mainly because "equal income redistribution would contradict [America's dominant ideology, that is,] the fact that some are smarter than others (corollary: the rich are smart and the poor are dumb), and also contradict the fact that some are better looking or more athletic than others (corollary: attractive and athletic people deserve wealth)" (Hattenhauer 390). All that is left is a carefully wrapped-up satire about the "American common sense version of equality," which is "nonsense" (391).

Here we can turn back to Winston Niles Rumfoord in *The Sirens of Titan* as well and see that even though he proposes an egalitarian society of sorts, he proposes it for everyone else but not for himself. And he does all that from the convenient and privileged position of a wealthy and powerful American aristocrat, who can afford becoming "the first person to own a private space ship, paying fifty-eight million dollars out of his own pocket for it" (Vonnegut, *Sirens* 23). Rumfoord is "a member of the one true American class. The class was a true one because its limits had been clearly defined for at least two centuries [. . .] The strength of his class depended to some extent on sound money management—but depended to a much larger extent on marriages based cynically on the sorts of children likely to be produced. Healthy, charming, wise children were the desiderata" (21-22). As seen earlier, true egalitarianism is supposed to be based on the idea that every human being is of equal worth and dignity (see Arneson), but Rumfoord "has been content to manage human affairs by virtue of nothing more than his own sense of self-worth, a kind of social Darwinism at its worst" (Mustazza 54).

Inequality and Vonnegut's Anthropological Social Plans

The Sirens of Titan and "Harrison Bergeron" provide just two examples of Vonnegut's satirical takes on the misinterpretation of egalitarian societies and social plans. Groups and elements, devised to provide isolated individuals with such a sense of inclusive community, abound in Vonnegut's novels, from the *karasses* of the invented Bokononist religion in *Cat's Cradle*, through the artificial extended families in *God Bless You, Mr. Rosewater* and *Slapstick*, all the way to the chrono-synclastic infundibula of *The Sirens of Titan* (". . . where the smartest daddies from different places can all be right at the same time, even though they all disagree" [Pardee 193]). These communities of course have a quality of irony in themselves, but they are certainly not mere jokes. Much rather they are "lovely dream[s]" (Vonnegut, *Wampeters* 178) through which Vonnegut can communicate his deep-rooted concern for those at the bottom of the social pyramid, the poor and the lonely.[3]

Much of what Vonnegut has to say about social issues in general, and inequality in particular, is of course political in nature. He frequently speaks about the poor who are "urged to hate themselves" and who "mock themselves and glorify their betters," and he blames the rich and the powerful for doing "less for their poor, publicly and privately, than any other ruling class" and for creating "a mass of undignified poor [. . . who] do not love one another because they do not love themselves" (Vonnegut, *Slaughterhouse* 161-62). In spite of the obvious political charge of his message, however, Vonnegut's concern for those left behind and his firm stance against social inequality is to a very significant extent informed by his study of anthropology. As pointed out earlier, a truly egalitarian system should recognize people's equal fundamental worth, which resonates deeply with the idea of cultural relativism, which was a prevalent trend in American anthropological thought around the time when Vonnegut was attending the Department of Anthropology at the University of Chicago: "At that time they were teaching that there was absolutely no difference between anybody. [. . .] Another thing they taught was that no one was ridiculous or bad or disgusting" (Vonnegut, *Slaughterhouse* 9-10). Although this is of course an oversimplified summary of cultural relativism, the essence of the idea is indeed something similar. One of the most important early proponents of this idea was American anthropologist Franz Boas, who wrote that "emotional reactions which we feel as natural are in reality culturally determined," and in order to understand behaviors and cultures that are different from our own, we "must lay aside many points of view that seem to us self-evident, [. . . so that we can] view our own civilization objectively" (qtd. in Bunzel, Introduction 5).

This idea is also an important feature in the works of Robert Redfield, whose lectures, as mentioned earlier, had a lasting effect on Vonnegut's thought and writing. Redfield (and others as well, see e.g., Bunzel, *Economic* 381 or Burns 129) conceives of folk societies as egalitarian communities. This does not necessarily mean that everyone is equal "every which way." There are members in such a folk society who are stronger or more beautiful than others. There are people who are better at carrying out certain tasks than others. They can even take advantage of others. The important thing is that in such folk societies, there exists a web of relationships among the members, which ensures that the community is working and looking out for the individual as well, not just the other way round. In folk societies, this is usually taught "through example," so that children can learn "about their relationship to the group and the moral behavior honored by the community" (Burns 129). In this sense, the organization of folk societies involve an "elementary equality" not only among the individual members, but also between the individual and society, so that they "both served each other" and "drew strength from each other" (129). This complex system of relationships involves and includes every member of the community, equally, regardless of who they are and what they can do.

Outside of stories about his own family and ancestors and their ways of life, Vonnegut had personally witnessed the workings of a community, which, in his eyes, resembles this ideal very closely. In 1970, he was in the then-Republic of Biafra, in present-day Nigeria. Biafrans declared their independence from Nigeria in 1967. However, after two and a half years of civil war, they surrendered unconditionally, and the territory was reintegrated into Nigeria. While there, Vonnegut described that "a more typical Biafran family might consist of a few hundred souls," and that "families took care of their own—perfectly naturally" (*Wampeters* 150). A Biafran military commander, General Chukwuemeka Odumegwu-Ojukwu, for example, told him that his family was "three thousand members strong," and "he knew every member of it by face, by name, and by reputation" (150). Such a community of relatives comes quite close to embodying Redfield's idea of a folk society, where relations are not simply personal but "familial" (Redfield, "Folk" 301).

Redfield was, of course, aware that the folk society he describes in his 1947 article is an ideal concept, which never aligns perfectly with the myriad ways real-world communities are organized, that in real life, "no known society precisely corresponds with it" (Redfield, "Folk" 294; see also *Community* 144). Vonnegut was also aware of this. Just a year after his visit to Biafra, he wrote (with some bitterness) that "the generation gap is an argument between those who believe folk societies are still possible and those who know they aren't" (*Wampeters* 181). The anthropological social plan of the folk society may be only a "lovely dream," but writing provided the opportunity for Vonnegut to make this ideal a reality, if only in his fiction. Anthropological thought thoroughly permeates his novels and his short fiction as well; moreover, it is not only informed by anthropological ideas and concepts but in turn his fiction can be seen as a form of speculative anthropology itself. According to Oscar Hemer, anthropology "shares a very crucial feature with literature; it can encompass everything" (180). Fiction has a "dual character, which inevitably blends the empirical with the imaginary" (180), which is exactly the way in which Vonnegut creates his fictional worlds and peoples and applies the ideas and concepts of his speculative anthropology to them.

Notes

1. Vonnegut submitted thesis proposals for his master's degree, all of which were rejected, but eventually, "in 1971, the University of Chicago accepted the novel *Cat's Cradle* [. . .] as a thesis and awarded him a master's degree in anthropology" (Whitlark 77).

2.   In the novel, Rumfoord pilots his private spaceship into an "uncharted chrono-synclastic infundibulum two days out of Mars" and as a result, he "existed as wave phenomena" (Vonnegut, *Sirens* 7). In this state, he got to know everything past and future and used his knowledge to orchestrate and implement a range of global events, such as the invasion of Earth by a Martian colony, or the founding of the Church of God the Utterly Indifferent. Later on in the novel, it turns out that in fact all of human history, including Rumfoord's schemes, was controlled by an extraterrestrial race of robots from the planet Tralfamadore. This of course complicates Rumfoord's status as "enforcer" of the Church's regulations, but for the purposes of this chapter, it is a reasonable thing to say. For more thorough analyses of the questions of free will and agency in *The Sirens of Titan*, see Bogar and Calvo Pascual.

3.   Apart from his expressed preference of a type of government that looks out for the "Losers" (Vonnegut, *Wampeters* 187; see also *A Man Without a Country* 95-96 and Hattenhauer 387-88), such concern is clearly shown by Vonnegut's admiration of famous American Socialist and labor organizer Eugene Victor Debs: "Next to the Sermon on the Mount, the words Vonnegut quotes most often in his work were spoken by his fellow Hoosier, Eugene V. Debs, while running for president on the Socialist Party ticket: 'While there is a lower class I am in it. While there is a criminal element I am of it. While there is a soul in prison I am not free'" (Wakefield).

Works Cited

Arneson, Richard. "Egalitarianism." *The Stanford Encyclopedia of Philosophy*, edited by Edward N. Zalta, Summer 2013, plato.stanford. edu/archives/sum2013/entries/egalitarianism/.

Bunzel, Ruth. "The Economic Organization of Primitive Peoples." *General Anthropology*, edited by Franz Boas, D.C. Heath and Co., 1938, pp. 327-408.

_____. Introduction. *Anthropology and Modern Life*, by Franz Boas, W.W. Norton, 1962, pp. 4-10.

Burns, E. Bradford. *Patriarch and Folk: The Emergence of Nicaragua, 1798–1858*. Harvard UP, 1991.

Farrell, Susan. *Critical Companion to Kurt Vonnegut: A Literary Reference to His Life and Work*. Infobase, 2008.

Freese, Peter. "Vonnegut's Invented Religions as Sense-Making Systems." *The Vonnegut Chronicles: Interviews and Essays*, edited by Peter J. Reed and Marc Leeds, Greenwood, 1996, pp. 145-64.

Hemer, Oscar. "The Writer as Anthropologist." *The Anthropologist as Writer: Genres and Contexts in the Twenty-First Century*, edited by Helena Wulff, Berghahn, 2016, pp. 172-87.

Mustazza, Leonard. *Forever Pursuing Genesis: The Myth of Eden in the Novels of Kurt Vonnegut*. Bucknell UP, 1990.

Pardee, Shiela Ellen. "Anthropology across the Universe: Folk Societies in the Early Novels of Kurt Vonnegut." *Critical Insights: Kurt Vonnegut*, edited by Robert T. Tally Jr., Salem Press, 2013, pp. 185-205.

Redfield, Robert. "The Folk Society." *American Journal of Sociology*, vol. 52, no. 4, 1947, pp. 293-308. *JSTOR*, http://www.jstor.org/stable/2771457/.

_____. *The Little Community / Peasant Society and Culture*. U of Chicago P, 1967.

Standish, David. "*Playboy* Interview." 1973. *Conversations with Kurt Vonnegut*, edited by William Rodney Allen, UP of Mississippi, 1988, pp. 76-110.

Vonnegut, Kurt. "Harrison Bergeron." 1961. *Welcome to the Monkey House*, Dial Press, 2006, pp. 7-14.

_____. *A Man Without a Country*. Random House, 2007.

_____. *The Sirens of Titan*. 1959. Dial Press, 2009.

_____. *Slaughterhouse-Five; or the Children's Crusade*. 1969. Dial Press, 2009.

_____. *Wampeters, Foma & Granfalloons (Opinions)*. 1974. Dial Press, 2006.

Wakefield, Dan. "Kurt Vonnegut: Christ-Loving Atheist." *Image: Art, Faith, Mystery*, no. 82, 2014, pp. 67-75, www.imagejournal.org/article/kurt-vonnegut/.

Whitlark, James S. "Vonnegut's Anthropology Thesis." *Literature and Anthropology*, edited by Philip A. Dennis and Wendell Aycock, Texas Tech UP, 1989, pp. 77-86.

Structural Inequality, Labor Exploitation, and the Foundation of America

Solomon Northup's slave narrative *Twelve Years a Slave* and Frederick Douglass' slave narrative *My Bondage and My Freedom*_____

Jericho Williams

As testimonies illuminating the horrors of slavery, American slave narratives shocked and outraged nineteenth-century readers and exposed the troubling underpinnings of the American economy. Immensely popular in literary societies and among a general audience, they were bestsellers that appealed to wide swaths of American and British readers (Blight 16). They outsold many of the works from contemporary writers whom scholars now view as indispensable to the American Renaissance period, including Henry David Thoreau and Herman Melville. For example, Frederick Douglass's rhetorically sharp and direct *Narrative of the Life of Frederick Douglass, An American Slave* (1845) sold more than thirty thousand copies in its first five years, while readers only bought roughly sixty copies of Herman Melville's comparatively avant-garde masterpiece *Moby-Dick* (1851) during its first decade (Newman 26). With escalating sales came more attention from reviewers and critics who came to recognize slave narratives as a new and distinctively American genre (Gould 26). At the peak of their social and cultural relevance in the 1850s, the authors of these narratives advocated for the freedom and personhood of the slaves who comprised around a fifth of the nation's twenty million people, helping to fuel the movement that brought about the abolition of slavery after the Civil War (Kolchin 242).

For roughly a century or more after the abolition of slavery, many slave narratives disappeared into heaps of other antebellum documents as their cultural urgency gradually lessened. Historians and literary scholars have uncovered some of them during the past few decades and asserted their importance as canonical, nineteenth-century works. Yet questions about how to teach them and what they offer twenty-first century students still persist. Solving these conundrums is crucial because like other activist-minded texts that expose America's shortcomings, slave narratives are at risk of historical confinement, regionalist designation, and trivialization without careful attention. In an effort to encourage an additional means of engagement with this "large, rich, and wondrously complex and conflicted body of literature," this essay proposes a broader conceptual web in which to frame and teach slave narratives (Gardner 8). Through comparative analyses of Solomon Northup's story and two versions of Frederick Douglass's narrative, it asserts that slave narratives occupy a central place in the creation of an American subgenre of the literature of inequality.

Solomon Northup's *Twelve Years a Slave* (1853) and Frederick Douglass's *My Bondage and My Freedom* (1855) provide two thoughtful, paradigmatic examples of slavery and the fight for social justice. By contextualizing personal experiences within national and economic frameworks, they accomplish what John Ernest describes as one of the greater purpose of slave narratives: bringing to life the plights of people caught in a "system for controlling labor populations" (14). Theorized more broadly, these narratives speak to today's labor struggles by shedding light on abstract structural dynamics and damaging, systemic behaviors that still exist in updated attire.

In *Twelve Years a Slave,* Northup recounts the loss of his identity and freedom after he is drugged and sold into slavery. Changing from a respected citizen into a slave overnight, Northup reorients readers to the process of animalization and emotional distancing that slaves undergo, and which also ensnares slaveholders who seek justification for their behavior. To counter this process and its underlying assumptions, Northup elevates and distinguishes his story from other narratives by portraying the benefits slaves might provide if given an opportunity to freely pursue the professed ideals of white Americans. As Northup recounts his experience, readers descend deep into the heart of slavery and emerge with him as he relies on the intellect he nurtured as a free man to pursue an escape to freedom. In Frederick Douglass's second memoir, *My Bondage and My Freedom*, Douglass offers additional reflective insight about the machinations of the slave system and a greater extension from his prior work, *Narrative of the Life of Frederick Douglass* (1845). Instead of rehashing his story or providing its sequel, Douglass teaches unsuspecting audiences how to see the structures of abuse and understand the damage they cause. He details how slavery inverts the expectations of a civil society, warps relationships among slave owners and the enslaved, and scars subsequent generations. While championing the idea of a more educated society, Douglass professes that inequality not only undercuts the ideals of a great nation, but that it also sprouts most readily where society's most uneducated and vulnerable exist far removed from watchful eyes.

Solomon Northup's *Twelve Years a Slave* (1853)

Solomon Northup's *Twelve Years a Slave* recounts the story of a man's twelve-year journey into slavery. Working with an amanuensis named David Wilson, Northup begins by aligning his background and equally free status with the freedom of his readers. He writes,

> Having all my life breathed the free air of the North, and conscious that I possessed the same feelings and affections that find a place in the white man's breast; conscious, moreover, of an intelligence equal to that of some men, at least, with fairer skin, I was too ignorant, perhaps too independent, to conceive how any one could be content to live in the abject condition of a slave. (Northup 10-11)

Here, Northup distinguishes his account from other slave narratives by stressing his clear grasp of freedom prior to becoming a slave. He situates his point of view as equal or near equal to those of his readers, and he forges likenesses that help to humanize his story. For example, Northup works a variety of jobs to support his wife and three children, including farming, transporting materials by rafting, and playing his violin. He lives a reasonably quiet lifestyle until he receives an opportunity to travel to New York and then Washington, DC, to play music. While in the nation's capital, he accompanies a couple of new friends to a bar and consumes a drink laced with a drug that makes him disoriented and sick. Imagining that his three companions are taking him to see a doctor, he finds instead that they have kidnapped him, confiscated his free papers and money, and imprisoned him.

Northup pointedly notes that his kidnapping and enslavement take place in the most important city in the nation, where he would spend a full two weeks before relocation with other slaves (Fiske et al. 53). Held in the infamous Williams' Slave Pen, Northup remarks, "Strange as it may seem, within plain sight of this same house, looking down from its commanding height upon it, was the Capitol" (21). Aghast and befuddled by this detail, Northup repeats, "A slave pen within the very shadow of the Capitol" (22). Long before recounting his experiences as a slave, Northup levels perhaps his harshest criticism by highlighting the great contradiction of a nation—founded on the idea of personal freedom—housing slaves for sale within sight of its most culturally emblematic building. In a few sentences, he indicts generations of the nation's founding fathers and present-day politicians for their direct participation or nonchalant compliance with an unjust and inhumane system. Northup's perspective unravels dignified visions of Washington, DC, in the 1840s by criticizing its leaders from a slave pen. Moreover, it calls attention to how people's beliefs in their country's ideals can prevent them from seeing the dangers and the inequities it fosters in name of prosperity.

Unlike other slave narratives, Northup's first few chapters cast slavery as more of a potential trap door for free African Americans than a cruel institution the enslaved strive to escape. The loss of his freedom and identity in one night underscores the murky borders between freedom and slavery for African Americans. An educated and literate man, Northup slowly realizes that his concept of selfhood vanishes once he becomes a slave. His identity is no longer visible to the outer world or accepted by those around him. When he sees children clinging to their mother, a woman named Eliza, as they face potential separation from each other in the slave pen, Northup notes, "They nestled closely to her, as if *there* only was there any safety or protection" (28). At this point still a relative newcomer to slavery's crimes, he learns that Eliza's former master had promised her freedom prior to delivering her to the slave market in Washington. Once she was sold, he notes that the "hope of years was blasted in a moment" (29). Northup alludes to her death two sentences later, linking the removal of Eliza's freedom and a life without her children as a sentence too difficult to bear. Encountering Eliza soon after his kidnapping helps Northup to understand the indiscriminate nature of a system that exchanges people with dollars regardless of their background, family ties, or desires.

From this point, Northup documents the process of dehumanization within his new and depraved labor market. In the midst of his first beating, he vows that all of the "brutal blows could not force from my lips the foul lie that I was a slave" (Northup 23). Although he resists accepting his new name (Platt), Northup struggles in isolation with the fact that there is no one from his prior life around to reinforce what he knows to be true. During his more bewildered moments, "he does not know people's names, he does not necessarily know where he is, and most profoundly, he does not who he is" (Weinstein 126). In a key scene, he uses a small pocketknife to cut his initials into a tin cup as a personal reminder of his identity, and subsequently begins to provide a similar service for other slaves around him (Northup 36). As Northup begins his move south from Washington, he observes the great fear that the system internalizes within his fellow slaves. Subsumed "in fear and ignorance," he observes, they often cower in fear and struggle to keep secrets from their oppressors (41). From an outsider's point of view, Northup marvels at the ghastly efficient manner with which slavery fosters dependency and fear. He gradually pieces together how the dehumanizing system absorbs the lives of droves of men and women and silences them.

Because he has previously experienced life in a free society and occupies an outsider position as someone who participated in a labor force bereft of slavery, Northup also intuits another of the system's great wrongs: it prevents white Americans from viewing African Americans as equals in order to justify their attitudes and behaviors. If, as Kenneth Warren notes, "the advent of the [slave narrative] genre was insurgent through and through," it happened as part of a larger mission to undermine the great lies that justified the control and mistreatment of "the nation's vast agricultural laboring population" (185). The vantage point many slave narratives proffer—a courageous individual who overcomes great odds through cunning and intelligence—functions as a means to counter the great strength of beliefs rooted in biological superiority spread to justify the confine and control people for the purpose of free labor. Northup's inexplicable descent into slavery positions him as an observer of the oppressive processes wrought by some of America's most educated and privileged men, who sought to maintain their sense of superiority and furthered the interests of their own social class. Perhaps most memorably and obliviously, President Thomas Jefferson defended slavery on the grounds of the inferiority of slaves. Jefferson believed that slavery must eventually come to an end, but he would take no part in prompting change. In *Notes on the State of Virginia*, Jefferson shares many of his troubling views while trying to justify Virginia's significant slave population, which was pivotal in accruing profits. Showing little sense of human understanding and an aloof view of agricultural labor, Jefferson writes, ". . . their disposition [is] to sleep when abstracted from their diversions, and unemployed in labor. An animal whose body is at rest, and who does not reflect, must be disposed to sleep of course" (146). Jefferson appallingly either fails to realize or else refuses to admit the link between the work of its hardest laborers and their need for rest. It becomes another detail in passing that casually validates paternal management and the continuation of slavery, and Jefferson's likening of slaves to animals positions white men as benevolent caretakers and slaves as little more than that of a domesticated animal in need of care.

Northup seizes upon the propagandized notion of slaves as animals to expose not only its means of perpetuation, but also how its practical failure inspires extraordinary abuse. First, he notices that for the purposes of the market, "unsoundness in a slave, as well as a horse, detracts materially from his value" (Northup 33). Describing how the slave pen operator James H. Burch interacts with slaves,

Northup writes that he "was out among his animals early," and questioning his own reality in reference to the situation, he adds, "Could it be possible . . . that I had been driven through the streets like a dumb beast . . . herded with a drove of slaves?" (46-47). In each scenario, he forces readers to confront the powerlessness of people as capable of complex thought and communication as their owners or their associates. Violent force and coercion lies in the shadow of every transaction Northup observes, as bidders judge slaves by their appearances to estimate the degree that they might resist work or rebel. In connecting the marketing and selling of slaves with their treatment as animals, Northup highlights the great fabrications set in place and reinforced to uphold the American economy and justify oppressive behavior. He insinuates that as long as slaveholders and their entourage of middlemen falsely animalize African Americans "as mere live property, no better, except in value, than [a] mule or dog," slaves who rightly resist must bear the extreme violence of interactions designed to uphold an unjust labor system that enriches a few to the great detriment of all (120).

Northup's belief in the integrity of work and fair treatment for workers came from his own background as a free laborer with varying job experiences as a farmer and a musician. Not long after his immersion into the slave system, he intuited that in the course of time, the "consequences of oppressive labor systems" permeate "the landscape itself" and that the institution of slavery threatened the continued health of the entire nation (Smith 324). In contrast to the prevailing insistence on the control and efficiency in the management of slaves, he routinely observes that the slave owners "who treated their slaves most leniently, were rewarded by the greatest amount of labor" (Northup 62). Northup illustrates this notion by explaining how he helped his first master, William Ford, increase the profitability of his lumber business by proposing a transport system via stream instead of land (57). Later, Northup concocts the means to obtain better food for himself by constructing a fish trap. In each scenario, Northup calls attention to the innovative potential of humans who had been enslaved. Although his greatest worry at the close of his narrative is the possibility that he has too heavily emphasized positive moments amidst indescribable struggles, he also sees and conveys the lost opportunities for functional alternatives within a system that seeks to control and oppress. Like some other slave narrators, Northup points to the inability of words to captures slavery's horrors, but he also suggests that the failure to trust an entire race of people and to foster better working conditions ultimately spiraled America towards accelerating levels of inequality that prefaced a great split in national interests and a devastating Civil War.

Frederick Douglass's *My Bondage and My Freedom* (1855)

Writers of slave narratives faced the dual challenge of capturing their resistance and escape from slavery without revealing too many details and also rhetorically molding their stories into activist documents that would expose and undermine the system of slavery (Cassuto 95). Altogether, narratives were meant to move readers personally and politically. Frederick Douglass's *Narrative of the Life of Frederick Douglass* (1845) remains a foundational and popular example as a courageous escape story and principled plea against the institution. In *My Bondage and My Freedom*, his full-length successor to his first slave narrative, Douglass adds a more reflective layer while also explicating the psychological effects of slavery within an ostensibly civil society upholding the institution. Selling 18,000 copies in three years, *My Bondage and My Freedom* was immensely successful (Andrews 4). Whereas Douglass composed his first narrative as an escaped slave who had been born into the system, the second narrative was crafted from years of experience living as a freedman and veteran activist. As a result, *My Bondage and My Freedom* presents an independent voice divorced from slavery and the antislavery movement from which Douglass emerged; it dissects slavery in a panoramic manner that shows how slavery's labor-related abuses afflict and denigrate all involved.

Two glaring shifts in perspective announce the evolution of Frederick Douglass's thought at the opening of *My Bondage and My Freedom*. First, whereas the *Narrative of the Life of Frederick Douglass, An American Slave* begins with a preface and letter by two leading abolitionists, William Lloyd Garrison, the founder of the American Anti-Slavery Society, and Wendell Phillips, the organization's president, *My Bondage and Freedom* features a preface comprised largely of one of Douglass's letters to his editor and then an introduction by James McCune Smith, a prominent African American doctor. With this change, Douglass sought to highlight his autonomy and distance himself from white abolitionists. Within the context of the white abolitionist movement during the mid to late 1840s, he felt constrained and often used for political purposes, so Douglass founded *The North Star*, an anti-slavery newspaper published from 1847 through 1851, partly as a means to disassociate himself with William Lloyd Garrison and other abolitionists (Bruce 266). He also became more and more careful to assert that his voice be recognized as his own. Within the letter the editor cites in the preface of *My Bondage and My Freedom*, Douglass notes, "Not only is slavery on trial, but unfortunately, the enslaved people are also on trial. It is alleged, that they are, naturally, inferior; they are *so low* in the scale of humanity, and so utterly stupid, that they are unconscious of their wrongs, and do not apprehend their rights" (7). This version of the narrative, then, seeks to counter this notion from the perspective of a wiser and more conscientious writer whose thoughts stand on their own without framing or approval of white abolitionists.

Second, and as a result of the disentanglement from his prior supporters, Douglass focuses more on environment and culture rather than his story, a move that enables him to better spotlight the structural inequalities of slavery. In the first sentence of *Narrative of the Life of Frederick Douglass, An American Slave*, Douglass writes, "I was born in Tuckahoe, near Hillsborough, and about twelve miles from Easton in Talbot County, Maryland" (47). In its successor, he opens with a three-paragraph description of Tuckahoe, a "thinly populated" town characterized by "the barrenness of its soil, and the ignorance, indolence, and poverty of its people" (29). Only at the end of third paragraph does he identify his relationship to Tuckahoe. Douglass writes, "It was in this dull, flat, and unthrifty district, or neighborhood, surrounded by a white population of the lowest order . . . that I—without any fault of mine—was born, and spent the first years of my childhood" (30). He implores readers to pardon his lengthy description of Tuckahoe because he believes that one must know where an autobiographical writer hails from in order apprehend his or her value or importance as a speaker. Then, in the following two sentences, Douglass drops the weight of slavery upon readers and places them within its a tumultuous atmosphere. He is as accurate about Tuckahoe's geography and social strata, for example, as he is unsure of the knowledge of the time of his birth and his parents' background.

Slowly unraveling slavery's consequences within a broader framework, Douglass seeks to account for the various ways that it situates slaves to endure exploitation and abuse within the greater purpose of labor, while also reorienting readers to the fundamental ways that the institution inverts the ideals of a dominant society. Whereas his first narrative contained eleven chapters, *My Bondage and My Freedom* contains twenty-five, and Douglass organizes them within sub-headings that preface each chapter. His journey becomes a tour of horrors. The "grand aim" of the entire system, Douglass writes, is "to reduce man to a level with the brute" by establishing barrier after barrier to steer African Americans away from the possibility of attaining membership among the status quo or even the semblance of what constitutes acceptable social positions (32). Slavery first enforces a reconceptualization of the idea of family. Douglass describes a carefree boyhood purposefully devoid of behavioral pressures and routines white children experience that concludes around the ages of seven or eight. From this point forward, he notes that a heightened sense of coercion and control define the remainder of a slave's working life, as the journey from even the most carefree childhood leads to the impossibility of ever reaching what the dominant American society conceives of as adulthood. Instead of the gradual growth toward the formation of a nuclear family and generational bonds, slavery fosters separation as a norm in the creation of highly efficient workforces. As children grow, Douglass writes, "the order of civilization is reversed," since "slavery has no use for either fathers or families" beyond their potential to serve and work (41). To illustrate this point, Douglass confesses that when he learns about his mother's death, he feels "no strong emotions of sorrow for her . . . with very little regret" (47). Here, he shows how the system strives to sever any deep emotional bonds, and how it isolates children who grow to experience life as discrete units whose value corresponds with their ability to work. The death of his mother serves as one of many passing events in his life as opposed to a painful loss. The productive plantation, "a little nation of its own" devoid of oversight of the nation or the state, also fosters harmful divisions (50). Within it, the natural world metamorphoses into a venue of terror, linking the conquest of southern landscapes with overwork, no pay, mistreatment, and perversion (Gerhardt 515). Human beauty becomes a curse for young women subject to destructive violence and sexual abuse from white slave holders and overseers, and hard work and productivity beget greater labor demands instead of rewards or compensation. Literacy and civic participation are lost, as slave owners and their representatives prevent and effectively criminalize them at all costs, while also encouraging diversions such as drinking, gambling, and sports during the Christmas holidays as a scant reward for a year's worth of labor. Douglass shows that by striving to completely disempower and distract their workers, slave owners reinforced a system bent upon maximizing profit at the expense of improving human life.

As the inequities multiply, with expanding plantations and increasing slave populations that enable lavish lifestyles for proportionally small percentages of slave owners and their families, Douglass asserts that the conditions corrode the physical and mental health of everyone involved. Freedom, which Douglass imagined at this point as a "self-possessive individualism," remains absent except for the choice few with the capital to establish and maintain their plantations; these slaveholders must denounce the abolition of slavery (Bercovitch 648). Yet, Douglass persistently suggests that the slave owners are trapped as well. He writes, "The slaveholder, kind or cruel, is a slaveholder still—the every hour violator of the just and inalienable rights of man; and he is, therefore, every hour silently whetting the knife of vengeance for his own throat"

(Douglass 197). With anger and resentment festering nearby and all of his family members and dependents subject to the enforced inequities and debasement in the name of profit, the slaveholder also suffers psychologically and morally. The most lavish plantation still imprisons its inhabitants, tethered to the land and to an unsustainable lifestyle that necessitates oppression. Cementing this point, Douglass writes, "To the pampered love of ease, there is no resting place. . . . Neither to the wicked, nor to the idler, is there any solid peace" (84). Without a fairer system of labor, wages, and freedom, and with an abundance of plantations operating far from the eyes and judgments of others, an entire society of slaves, middle managers, bosses, and their faraway consumers bear the weight of unjust society nearing its brim of dissolution via rebellion or war.

Though championed as historically significant and as powerful individual stories, Solomon Northup's *Twelve Years a Slave* and Frederick Douglass's *My Bondage and My Freedom* remain pivotal texts in the fight against inequality. Speaking from within and beyond slavery, they peel back the gilded surfaces of nineteenth-century American wealth to reveal its disquieting foundations. They interrogate a capitalist economic system that fostered the dehumanization of African Americans and propagated ongoing struggles with inequality. Synthesizing years of consideration about the institution of slavery, Northup and Douglass both articulate the process of animalization and degradation that would later reappear and inform perceptions of lower-class immigrants at the turn of the twentieth century and beyond. They also foresaw the dangers of the gap between available work and sufficient pay that would come to define The Great Depression, and they understood the beginnings and functions of government-sanctioned surveillance as means to monitor African Americans and subsequent waves of immigrants and minorities as part of an effort to maintain the status quo. As a result, *Twelve Years a Slave* and *My Bondage and Freedom* vocalize the great toil and losses of the dispossessed at the expense of the empowerment of a privileged nineteenth-century few. In the process, Northup and Douglass exalt the first-person account as a means to undermine hidden labor injustices that continue to prop up and fuel the American economy, in the forms of overseas sweatshop labor and the burgeoning gig economy.

Works Cited

Andrews, William L. "Introduction." *Critical Essays on Frederick Douglass*. Edited by William L. Andrews, G.K. Hall & Co., 1991, pp. 1-17.

Bercovitch, Sacvan. "The Problem of Ideology in American Literary History." *Critical Inquiry*, no. 12, summer 1986, pp. 631-653.

Blight, David W. "Introduction: 'A Psalm of Freedom.'" *Narrative of the Life of Frederick Douglass, An American Slave, Written by Himself (1845)*. Edited by David W. Blight, Bedford, 1993, pp. 1-23.

Bruce, Dickson D., Jr. *The Origins of African American Literature, 1680–1865*. U of Virginia P, 2001.

Cassuto, Leonard. *The Inhuman Race: The Racial Grotesque in American Literature and Culture*. Columbia UP, 1997.

Douglass, Frederick. *Narrative of the Life of Frederick Douglass, An American Slave*. 1845. Penguin, 1986.

_____. *My Bondage and My Freedom*. 1855. Penguin, 2003.

Ernest, John. Introduction. *The Oxford Handbook to the African American Slave Narrative*. Edited by John Ernest, Oxford UP, 2014, pp. 1-17.

Gardner, Eric. *Unexpected Places: Relocating Nineteenth-Century African American Literature*. U of Mississippi P, 2009.

Gerhardt, Christine. "The Greening of African-American Landscapes." *Mississippi Quarterly*, no. 55, fall 2002, pp. 515-533.

Gould, Philip. "The Rise of the Slave Narrative." *The Cambridge Companion to the African American Slave Narrative*, edited by Audrey Fisch, Cambridge UP, 2007, pp. 11-27.

Jefferson, Thomas. *Notes on the State of Virginia*. 1785. Penguin, 1999.

Kolchin, Peter. *American Slavery, 1619–1877*. Hill and Wang, 2003.

Newman, Judie. "Slave Narratives and Neo-Slave Narratives." *The Cambridge Companion to Literature of the American South*. Cambridge UP, 2013, pp. 26-38.

Northup, Solomon. *Twelve Years a Slave*. 1853. Penguin, 2012.

Smith, Kimberly. "Environmental Criticism and the Slave Narratives." *The Oxford Handbook to the African American Slave Narrative*, edited by John Ernest, Oxford UP, 2014, pp. 315-327.

Warren, Kenneth W. "A Reflection on the Slave Narrative and American Literature." *The Oxford Handbook to the African American Slave Narrative*, edited by John Ernest, Oxford UP, 2014, pp. 183-195.

Weinstein, Cindy. "The Slave Narrative and Sentimental Literature." *The Cambridge Companion to the African American Slave Narrative*, edited by Audrey Fisch, Cambridge, 2007, pp. 115-134.

CRITICAL
READINGS

Racial Classifications and Crossing the Color Line
Nella Larsen's novel *Passing*

Almas Khan

> One three centuries removed
> From the scenes his father loved,
> Spicy grove, cinnamon tree,
> What is Africa to me?
> > (Countee Cullen, "Heritage," *Color* [1925], lines 7-10)

This epigraph opening Nella Larsen's *Passing* (1929) suggests one of the novel's central preoccupations: the tortuous relationships between racial identity and place for African Americans living in Jim Crow America.[1] Over thirty years earlier, in the notorious *Plessy v. Ferguson* (1896) case, the Supreme Court had upheld the constitutionality of "separate but equal" laws in the context of a state statute mandating racially segregated railroad cars (548). As Justice John Marshall Harlan argued in his famous dissent there, the decision seemed to signal a reversion to the antebellum period, when slave codes restricted enslaved peoples' mobility (555). Other spatial constraints on African Americans abounded during the so-called Jazz Age of the 1920s, when Larsen's novel is set, belying the Constitution's promise of "equal protection of the laws" after the Civil War. For instance, through restrictive covenants, people of color were frequently barred from owning houses in predominantly white areas, with African American physician Ossian Sweet in 1925 facing a homicide trial for attempting to defend his home from a white supremacist mob (Boyle 186). It was in this spatially and racially fraught milieu that Nella Larsen, the daughter of a Danish mother and West Indian father (Kaplan xiii), published *Passing*.

The novel's title evokes a racial and spatial phenomenon wrought by inequality, having deep historical antecedents and a long lineage of literary representations. W. E. B. Du Bois in *The Souls of Black Folk* (1903) elicited a geographic metaphor in deeming "the problem of the twentieth century" as "the problem of the color-line—the relation of the darker to the lighter races of men in Asia and Africa, in America and the islands of the sea" (17). "Passing" dating to the antebellum era and into the 1920s was an attempt to transgress these inegalitarian racial lines and particularly connoted African Americans "passing for white," although the term can more broadly "refer to the crossing of any line that divides social groups" (Hobbs 31; Sollors 247). *Passing* indicates several motivations for African Americans taking this immense risk during the early twentieth century, when hysteria about racial subterfuges permeated the popular press (Kaplan xv). Clare Kendry, a mixed-race woman who passes for white in the novel, describes her desire "'to get away, to be a person and not a charity or a problem, or even a daughter of the indiscreet Ham. Then, too, I wanted things'" (Larsen 19). Passing could be seen as African Americans' means to have their citizenship and humanity recognized before the civil rights revolution spanning from the 1940s through 1960s, which legally overturned *Plessy* (Ackerman 5-6).

Larsen's novel followed in a literary tradition of "passing novels" by both white and African American authors, whose texts collectively demonstrated the arbitrariness of inequitable postbellum racial classifications. William Dean Howells's *An Imperative Duty* (1891), Frances E. W. Harper's *Iola Leroy, or Shadows Uplifted* (1892), Mark Twain's *Pudd'nhead Wilson* (1894), and James Weldon Johnson's *The Autobiography of an Ex-Colored Man* (1912) are among prominent works in the genre. *Passing* adapts and critiques conventions from these novels as a Harlem Renaissance text published amidst a flourishing of African American cultural achievements starting at the end of World War I in 1918 until the cusp of World War II in 1937 (Hutchinson 2, 7). While the novel depicts rising middle-class and upper-class African Americans in relatively privileged spaces during this period, the precarity of the characters' positions overshadows the text. And perhaps no character is more vulnerable than Clare Kendry, who is married to a wealthy, jet-setting white supremacist unaware of her heritage, but

---

who yearns for African American spaces she had seemingly chosen to spurn before.

Spatial inclusion and exclusion in *Passing* reifies communal and national recognition (or lack thereof), with Clare—who is unable to be "'place[d]'" and whose "identity" is in flux (Larsen 12)—exemplifying the perils of inter- and intra-racial policing of domestic spaces. Clare's death in the novel evinces the impossibility of escaping spatial-racial bounds prescribed by custom at the time and reinforced by law; her ordeal nonetheless also suggests the potential for an equitable transformation of domestic spaces. Clare's sophisticated understanding of identity as in part a fluid personal construction rather than an immutable genetic, social, and legal inheritance represents a vision of self-forging aligned with American Dream ideals. Yet *Passing*'s answer to Cullen's question "What is Africa to me?" remains ambivalent, with the novel criticizing racially essentialist rhetoric that impedes integration while acknowledging the emotional appeal of racial solidarity and exclusive spaces to preserve an inequitable, but ostensibly comfortable, status quo.

Passing and the Complex Origins of Racial Inequality

Passing depicts racial inequities being fortified between as well as within groups; inequality is shown to be a multifaceted problem, with a racial border patrol existing not only between whites and African Americans, but within the African American community. The novel thus exposes how a historically marginalized group may, wittingly or unwittingly, uphold the conditions keeping the group subordinated. Indeed, Clare's husband John Bellew and her mixed-race childhood acquaintance Irene Redfield are portrayed as doubles. Bellew not only "'dislike[s]'" African Americans but "'hate[s] them,'" claiming to "'draw the line at that. No niggers in my family. Never have been and never will be'" (Larsen 29).[2] Irene, meanwhile, "adhere[s] to her own class and kind; not merely in the great thing of marriage, but in the whole pattern of her life as well" (24-25). Irene questions the "genuineness" of Clare's apparent return to the racial fold after marrying Bellew, concluding that Clare actually "cared nothing for the race," and should therefore be refused "recognition" (34, 36). Although Irene conceives herself not to be "snob" who "care[s] greatly for the petty restrictions and distinctions with which what called itself Negro society chose to hedge itself about" (17), she consistently espouses and enacts such discriminations. Irene reflects on how inviting Clare to Idlewild, an African American resort, would subject Irene to opprobrium, and deliberately neglects inviting Clare to a party (17, 61).

Irene's racial judgmentalism is censured in *Passing*, but it is also shown to arise from an innate source: the almost universal human longing for "safety" and "security," two words that pervade the text and are "all-important" values for Irene (Larsen 47). Larsen's novel, however, underscores the personal and social downsides of an overzealous commitment to these ideals, illuminating who and what may be sacrificed in return. Irene and Clare seem to embody two polarities on a figurative safety and security spectrum, with Irene envisaging herself as devoted to upholding familial and racial security, which Clare's presence appears to threaten. Irene views the "hazardous business of 'passing'" as "a breaking away from all that was familiar and friendly to take one's chance in another environment" (17) and believes that Clare perches "on the edge of danger" yet, selfishly, refuses to withdraw regardless of "any alarms or feeling of outrage on the part of others" (5) and in spite of the threat to the "'security'" of Clare's own daughter (48).

Irene strives to insulate her family, including her husband and two sons, from racial dangers but is haunted by the potential of her plans coming to naught: "Was she never to be free of it, that fear which crouched, always, deep within her, stealing the sense of security, the feeling of permanence, from the life which she had so admirably arranged for them all, and desired so ardently to remain as it was?" (Larsen 40). Irene's commitment to the status quo endures despite her younger son being called a "'dirty nigger'" at school (73), and despite her living in the mid-1920s, at a time when 50,000 members of the Ku Klux Klan paraded through Washington, DC (Rothman). Irene chides her husband for disrupting the seeming placidity of their sons' domestic life by discussing a lynching, as she would prefer the boys be "'happy and free'" without knowledge about "'the race problem'" (73). In a moment of candor, while conversing with Clare, however, Irene admits "'that no one is ever completely happy, or free, or safe'" (48), although elaborate measures may be undertaken to conceal this reality in the face of flagrant injustices.

Passing implies that the possibility for real, widespread, long-term security may be compromised for an illusory security that may only transiently safeguard individual interests, but that cannot be dismissed as an entirely irrational choice. Irene's dilemma when contemplating whether to "out" Clare as African American reflects these catch-22 options: "She was caught between two allegiances, different, yet the same. Herself. Her race. Race! The thing that bound and suffocated her. Whatever steps she took, or if she took none at all, something would be crushed. Clare, herself, or the race. Or, it might be all three" (Larsen 69). Moreover, regardless of her condemnation of Clare's passing, Irene selectively passes as well for expedient reasons, separating those motivations in her mind from more problematic "social" rationales: "'I don't believe I've ever gone native [i.e., passed as white] in my life except for the sake of convenience, restaurants, theatre tickets, and things like that. Never socially, I mean, except once'" (70).

The novel's verdict on Irene's and Clare's actions as mixed-race women living in a racist and sexist age[3] remains ambiguous, but is best captured in Clare's postscript from a letter to Irene. Clare there ponders: "It may be, 'Rene dear, it may just be, that, after all, your way may be the wiser and infinitely happier one. I'm not sure just now. At least not so sure as I have been" (Larsen 34). Rather than perceiving of passing as an unethical act constituting a form of race betrayal, readers of Larsen's novel are prompted to scrutinize the underlying conditions giving rise to the phenomenon, including how the construction of domestic spaces may exacerbate inequalities. For, as Werner Sollors argues, "only a situation of sharp inequality among groups would create the need for the emergence of a socially significant number of cases of 'passing'" (248).

Domestic Spaces, Foreign Spaces, and the Spaces in Between

The title of Allyson Hobbs's monograph on passing, *A Chosen Exile: A History of Racial Passing in American Life*, suggests the spatial liminality of racial passers as within the nation, yet foreign to it as well as to the African American community. *Passing* conceptualizes domestic spaces on three interrelated levels—familial, racial, and national—and Clare undercuts Irene's worldview about the firm borders around these spaces. Irene feels, but is unwilling to admit, that "all other ways [aside from hers], she regarded as menaces, more or less indirect, to that security of place and substance" welding her family (Larsen 43). She abhors changes "affect[ing] the smooth routine of her household" (41), with these households in the novel including Irene's New York City home, the African American community in Harlem, and the United States. Clare's warmth toward Irene's family, coupled with Clare's frequent trips to Harlem, deeply perturb Irene, who often derogatorily associates Clare with foreign places, people, and items that threaten the integrity of Irene's multiple hearths.

Clare ensconces herself in Irene's life as a prelude to becoming more active in the African American community. Before a Negro Welfare League dance, Clare visits the Redfield boys in their playroom, standing in the threshold space of a doorway while pleading for the youths', and more generally the African American community's, acceptance. The boys' faces are unwelcoming, being described as "blank" and resentful, which leads Clare to apologize for disturbing them: "'Please don't be cross. Of course, I know I've gone and spoiled everything. But maybe, if I promise not to get too much in the way, you'll let me in, just the same'" (Larsen 52). Like Irene, the boys are not initially enthusiastic at encountering Clare, but one of them permits her to enter the playroom: "'Sure, come in if you want to. . . . We can't stop you, you know'" (52). The boys soon "conceiv[e] for her an admiration that verged on adoration" (57). Abjuring Irene's classism, Clare also "descend[s] to the kitchen" to converse with African American domestic workers; Irene "secretly resent[s]" these intrusions into intimate spaces (57).

Irene even observes how Clare occupies Irene's favorite chair (46), as if to supplant Irene in the home.

Irene eventually comes to be convinced that she has been replaced in her husband's affections by Clare, despite scant circumstantial evidence; Irene perhaps reasons that an affair is the next logical step in the line of Clare's domestic infringements. The circumspect Irene notably shatters a teacup into "white fragments" while hosting a party at her home soon after learning about the apparent illicit liaison (Larsen 66). Irene seems elated at being "'rid of it [the cup] forever,'" a possibly ominous reference to Clare. Earlier in the novel, Irene had characterized Clare as being an ideal belle in "'the old South if she hadn't made the mistake of being born a Negro,'" and the cup is claimed to have belonged to Confederates (61, 66). Later, after Clare's husband learns of her heritage and maligns her as "'a damned dirty nigger'" (79), his rage at Clare's ostensible domestic duplicity is shown to partially resemble Irene's. Bellew's fury appears to splinter Clare, though according to Irene, Clare remains oblivious to "the whole structure of her life . . . lying in fragments before her" following the confrontation (79).

Passing is sensitive to how Irene's life is also fractured because of racism and sexism, although she endeavors to maintain a sanctuary at home. Toward the novel's end, Irene applies what scholars would later term "intersectionality theory" to her plight as a mixed-race woman. Intersectionality denotes "the critical insight that race, class, gender, sexuality, ethnicity, nation, ability, and age operate not as unitary, mutually exclusive entities, but as reciprocally constructing phenomena that in turn shape complex social inequalities" (Collins 2). Paradoxically, it is while Irene would appear to an observer to be most serene in the hearth that she experiences her acutest moment of agony about injustices: "Sitting alone in the quiet living-room in the pleasant firelight, Irene Redfield wished, for the first time in her life, that she had not been born a Negro. . . . It was, she cried silently, enough to suffer as a woman, an individual, on one's own account, without having to suffer for the race as well" (Larsen 69). Irene is nevertheless committed to intimate domestic stability and patriotism, contemplating "ways to keep Brian by her side, and in

New York. For she would not go to Brazil. She belonged in this land of rising towers. She was an American. She grew from this soil, and she would not be uprooted" (76). Irene correlates her relatively advantaged class status by dint of marriage with the national iconography of skyscrapers, while recognizing the tenuousness of both apparently solid edifices.

Clare, contrastingly, is linked with the foreign in Irene's consciousness, thereby being "othered" during a period when racist laws against "undesirable" immigrants proliferated. The Immigration Act of 1924 established strict quotas for Southern and Eastern European immigration while excluding Asian immigrants, who were ineligible for citizenship; the statute was liberalized in 1952 (Daniels 16, 51-52). Alien Land Laws meanwhile functioned comparably to restrictive covenants, preventing Asian immigrants from owning property in the early to mid-twentieth century until the Supreme Court invalidated the statutes in *Oyama v. California* (1948) (Villazor 984), the same year that it effectively nullified restrictive covenants in *Shelley v. Kraemer*. Clare's troubling foreignness is perceived by Irene to extend to the very paper on which Clare writes. Unlike the rest of Irene's "ordinary and clearly directed" mail, Clare's "long envelope of thin Italian paper with its almost illegible scrawl seem[s] out of place and alien" to Irene (Larsen 5); Clare is subsequently described by Irene as having "exotic" eyes (21). Later in the novel, Irene seems to jettison Clare from her life as a friend and fellow African American by referring to Clare as a "stranger" separated from Irene by an insurmountable "barrier": "[T]hey were strangers. Strangers in their ways and means of living. Strangers in their desires and ambitions. Strangers even in their racial consciousness. Between them, the barrier was just as high, just as broad, and just as firm as if in Clare did not run that strain of black blood" (44). Irene deems Clare an outsider despite the women being raised in the same neighborhood.

Drawing this connection between Clare and foreign influences, Irene progressively affiliates her husband's restlessness to immigrate to Brazil—in Irene's view, to be "loose[ned] from his proper setting" (Larsen 45)—with Clare. Clare, for whom "[e]ighteenth-century

France would have been a marvellous setting," according to Irene (61), thus becomes an amplified threat to Irene's personal, racial, and national security. Brazil is for Irene "some place strange and different," and Brian's craving to escape "'this hellish place'" (74) of Jim Crow America is said to require "strenuous efforts" from Irene "to repress" (35). Clare's husband is also dismissive of Brazil, though for different reasons than Irene, ironically remarking to her while she is passing: "'Coming place, South America, if they ever get the niggers out of it. It's run over—'" (31). Bellew conceives of the African diaspora as sullying South America, much as Irene believes her family would be contaminated if they were to immigrate to Brazil, a place as "strange" as Clare.

Bellew and Irene, in varying ways, are both obsessed with slotting people into categories as a means of containment, with Irene relegating Clare to the past (pre-revolutionary France and the antebellum US) to more readily dismiss her. Clare is even reduced by Irene to foreign bric-a-brac. After Irene becomes aware of Clare's ostensible affair with Brian, she chats with party guests about Brian's purchasing a cheap, "'hideous'" item from Haiti (Larsen 63-64); earlier, Irene had alluded to Clare's "'decorative qualities,'" as opposed to her having "'[r]eal brains'" (61-62). Clare's spatial-racial hybridity in refusing to definitively choose between foreign and domestic spaces (28) or to embrace a single racial identity confounds Irene (33), whose fealty to the African American communities in Chicago and New York potentially precipitates Clare's death.

Urban Landscapes and the Geographic Inscription of Inequality

Passing is set in Chicago and New York City, two major cities among the places to which six million African Americans migrated during the Great Migration of 1915–70. Although African Americans at the time left the South for more hospitable racial climes in the North (Wilkerson 8-9; Boyle 3-4), they also confronted racism there (Sokol xxiii-xix), as Larsen's novel delineates through Clare's and the Redfields' experiences. Clare and Irene both grew up in Chicago, which was in the early twentieth century starkly segregated, and the city remains racially divided into today (Moser). The "south side" was (and continues to be) associated with African Americans, who were concentrated largely in a "black belt," while more affluent north-side areas were populated principally by whites (Grossman 123, 126). Clare and Irene meet again as thirty-something adults when transgressing into one of these uptown spaces: the swank Drayton hotel. Clare's prosperous white supremacist husband's praising the hotel as a "'[n]ice place'" where he had previously stayed (31) codes the Drayton as a privileged white space.

Seeking "immediate safety" from a humid Chicago summer—a metaphor for the heat of racism—Irene pines for a "'roof somewhere'" and accepts a cab driver's recommendation to try the Drayton, as "'[t]hey do say how it's always a breeze up there'" (Larsen 8). Beginning from her entry through the hotel's "wide doors" (8), the experience does not disappoint. The elevator trip up to the Drayton's roof is analogized by Irene to "being wafted upward on a magic carpet to another world, pleasant, quiet, and strangely remote from the sizzling one that she had left below" (8). Situated at a table by a window, Irene scorns "people creeping about in streets" and gazes upon "lower buildings" as Lake Michigan sparkles in the distance (8). Her reverie is interrupted by Clare, however, whom she observes scrutinizing her. Terror follows: "Did that woman, could that woman, somehow know that here before her eyes on the roof of the Drayton sat a Negro?" (10). Irene claims not to be "ashamed of being a Negro, or even of having it declared," but of "being ejected from any place, even in the polite and tactful way in which the Drayton would probably do it" (11). Having been granted admission to an elite domestic space, which can be read as a synecdoche for her full inclusion in the nation, Irene fears eviction at Clare's hands.

This dire eventuality for Irene does not ensue, as Clare is situated similarly, but Clare's earlier *de facto* exclusion from the local African American community because of perceived spatial trespasses is highlighted. Though Clare was raised in an impoverished home on the south side, her father's death when she was fifteen resulted in her living with white aunts on the west side, and at her aunts' behest, her visits to the south side ceased (Larsen 5, 12-13). The aunts had forbidden her from even mentioning African Americans or the south side to neighbors (19), as if conceiving of the area as a tainted space. Clare's being seen with whites in fashionable places such as Lincoln Park on the north side, meanwhile, resulted in rumors circulating among the African American community of her being a "fallen woman": "Working indeed! People didn't take their servants to the Shelby for dinner. Certainly not all dressed up like that" (13-15). During their conversation at the Drayton, Clare informs Irene of being forced to choose between spaces and racial communities upon dating Bellew and marrying him at eighteen: "'I stopped slipping off to the south side and slipped off to meet him instead. I couldn't manage both'" (20).

Meeting Irene revives Clare's desire for African American companionship and spaces, which Clare characterizes as a flight from "this pale life of mine" (Larsen 7). Two years after their Chicago encounter, Clare seeks to use Irene as an entrée point to the thriving African American community in Harlem. Irene, however, strives to repel Clare's attempt to re-enter African American spaces, cautioning about "the folly of Harlem" for Clare: "'I can't help thinking that you ought not to come up here, ought not to run the risk of knowing Negroes'" (46). Clare's response reflects her pain at seemingly being rejected by the local black community through Irene: "'You mean you don't want me 'Rene?' Irene hadn't supposed that anyone could look so hurt" (46). Citing the pull of racial loyalty, Irene acquiesces to Clare visiting her home and attending events in "black Harlem" (69). However, once Irene begins to suspect Brian's infidelity and learns of Clare's possibly divorcing Bellew, coming to live in Harlem, and being "'able to do as I please,'" Irene strategizes ways to "rid her[self] forever" of Clare (69, 75).

Clare's murky death at the novel's end in Harlem casts her as a "tragic mulatta" figure whose conflicting racial loyalties, which bring to the fore issues of national inclusion and exclusion, fate her demise (see Raimon 12; Durán 122-23). Spatially, the conclusion mirrors the Drayton episode, with African American hosts Felise and Dave Freeland living at "'the very top'" of a six-story apartment building (Larsen 77), paralleling the Drayton's roof. Clare and the

Redfields are invited to the Freelands' home for dinner, but the party is transmogrified when Clare's husband intrudes into the African American space, the inverse of the Drayton scene, and accuses his wife of racial deception.[4] Tumult ensues as Felise warns Bellew: "'Careful, you're the only white man here'" (79). Irene meanwhile becomes "possessed" by the fear of Bellew's divorcing Clare (79) and setting in motion a cascade of domestic disturbances in Irene's life. What exactly follows these overt and covert hostilities to Clare is unclear, but the novel terminates with her falling out of a window that Irene had purportedly opened after feeling warm on a cold December day; Clare's flaming loveliness is extinguished in a snowy street (78-80). Whereas Clare had ascended to a privileged domestic space near the novel's opening, she appears to have been punished, Icarus-like, for flying too close to the sun by *Passing*'s close.

The anticlimax features inconsistent accounts of who volitionally or accidentally caused Clare's demise. Bellew and Clare herself are mentioned as possible actors, but evidence also strongly indicts Irene. The guests generally conclude that Clare "had fainted or something like that," and officials believe that the death was likely accidental; however, Bellew's disappearance after the fall is suspicious (Larsen 81-82). Moreover, Irene had, in her anxiety, touched Clare's arm immediately before the fall and claims that she was as close to Clare as Bellew was then (81-82), which may signify that both of them contributed to Clare's physical death, if not her emotional one as well. Given their fury toward Clare, it may be surprising that Bellew and Irene suffer with her loss; Bellew is said to groan "like a beast in agony," while Irene is initially relieved but later collapses and is plunged into darkness (79-82).

Passing thus decisively substantiates Justice Harlan's contention in *Plessy* that "separate but equal" laws limiting spatial liberty would redound profoundly, "render[ing] permanent peace impossible" and "keep[ing] alive a conflict of races the continuance of which must do harm to all concerned" (561). Although the novel's ending suggests this conflict's persistence, with death constituting the sole escape, hope resides in readers toiling to eradicate the spatial-racial lines hindering democratic promises from materializing into domestic realities.

Notes

1. Jim Crow was a highly exaggerated black character serving as shorthand for a collective racial epithet before the Civil War (1861–65), but the phrase was subsequently associated with laws constricting African American rights ("Jim Crow Laws").

2. Abolitionist David Walker's *Appeal* (1830) argued that African Americans in the antebellum period were perceived to be "not of the human family" (33), a metaphor for race that was, in turn, linked to the nation. One southern senator at the turn of the twentieth century had pronounced that African Americans could not then "'be admitted to the family circle of the white race'" ("The South and Negro Suffrage" 292).

3. For example, only with the Nineteenth Amendment's ratification in 1920 were women granted the constitutional right to vote in federal elections (Flexner and Fitzpatrick x). Discrimination against women in employment and education, among other spheres, remained rampant well into the twentieth century, with Title VII of the Civil Rights Act of 1964 and Title IX of the Education Act of 1972 finally legally barring such practices ("The Civil Rights Act").

4. The sensational Rhinelander trial, which inspired *Passing* and is cited in the novel (71), involved this claim. The case arose in 1925 when Leonard Rhinelander, scion of a wealthy white family, accused his mixed-race wife, Alice Jones, of not disclosing her racial heritage before their marriage; he sought an annulment on grounds of fraud but lost the case (Smith-Pryor 4, 229).

Works Cited

Ackerman, Bruce. *We the People: The Civil Rights Revolution*, vol. 3. Harvard UP, 2014.

Boyle, Kevin. *Arc of Justice: A Saga of Race, Civil Rights, and Murder in the Jazz Age*. Henry Holt, 2004.

"The Civil Rights Act of 1964 and the Equal Employment Opportunity Commission." *National Archives*, 7 Aug. 2017, www.archives.gov/education/lessons/civil-rights-act/.

Collins, Patricia Hill. "Intersectionality's Definitional Dilemmas." *Annual Review of Sociology*, vol. 41, Aug. 2015, pp. 1-20, www.annualreviews.org/doi/10.1146/annurev-soc-073014-112142/.

Cullen, Countee. "Heritage." *Collected Poems*, edited by Major Jackson, Library of America, 2013, pp. 28-32.

Daniels, Roger. *Guarding the Golden Door: American Immigration Policy and Immigrants Since 1882*. Hill and Wang, 2004.

Du Bois, W. E. B. *The Souls of Black Folk*. 1903. Edited by Henry Louis Gates Jr. and Terri Hume Oliver, Norton, 1999.

Durán, Maria del Mar Gallego. *Passing Novels in the Harlem Renaissance: Identity Politics and Textual Strategies*. Transaction, 2003.

Flexner, Eleanor, and Ellen Fitzpatrick. *Century of Struggle: The Woman's Rights Movement in the United States*, enlarged ed., Harvard UP, 1996.

Grossman, James R. *Land of Hope: Chicago, Black Southerners, and the Great Migration*. U of Chicago P, 1991.

Harper, Frances E. W. *Iola Leroy, or Shadows Uplifted*. 1892. *Three Classic African-American Novels*, edited by Henry Louis Gates Jr., Vintage, 1990, pp. 225-463.

Hobbs, Allyson. *A Chosen Exile: A History of Racial Passing in American Life*. Harvard UP, 2014.

Howells, William Dean. *An Imperative Duty*. *Harper's New Monthly*, Jul.-Nov. 1891. *An Imperative Duty*, edited by Paul R. Petrie, Broadview, 2010, pp. 33-122.

Hutchinson, George. Introduction. *The Cambridge Companion to the Harlem Renaissance*, edited by George Hutchinson, Cambridge UP, 2007, pp. 1-10.

"Jim Crow Laws." *Encyclopedia of African American History, 1896 to the Present: From the Age of Segregation to the Twenty-First Century*, vol. 3, edited by Paul Finkelman, Oxford UP, 2009.

Johnson, James Weldon. *The Autobiography of an Ex-Colored Man*. 1912. Edited by Jacqueline Goldsby, Norton, 2015.

Kaplan, Carla. "Introduction: Nella Larsen's Erotics of Race." *Passing*, by Nella Larsen. 1929. Edited by Carla Kaplan, Norton, 2007, pp. ix-xxvii.

Larsen, Nella. *Passing*. 1929. Edited by Carla Kaplan, Norton, 2007.

Moser, Whet. "Chicago Isn't Just Segregated: It Basically Invented Modern Segregation," *Chicago Magazine*, 31 Mar. 2017, www.chicagomag.com/city-life/March-2017/Why-Is-Chicago-So-Segregated/.

Oyama v. California, 332 U.S. 633 (1948).

Plessy v. Ferguson, 163 U.S. 537 (1896). .

Raimon, Eve Allegra. *The 'Tragic Mulatta' Revisited: Race and Nationalism in Nineteenth-Century Antislavery Fiction*. Rutgers UP, 2004.

Rothman, Joshua. "When Bigotry Paraded Through the Streets." *The Atlantic*, 4 Dec. 2016, www.theatlantic.com/politics/archive/2016/12/second-klan/509468/.

Shelley v. Kraemer, 334 U.S. 1 (1948).

Smith-Pryor, Elizabeth M. *Property Rites: The Rhinelander Trial, Passing, and the Protection of Whiteness*. U of N Carolina P, 2009.

Sokol, Jason. *All Eyes are Upon Us: Race and Politics from Boston to Brooklyn*. Basic, 2014.

Sollors, Werner. *Neither White Nor Black Yet Both: Thematic Explorations of Interracial Literature*. Oxford UP, 1997.

"The South and Negro Suffrage." *New York Tribune* 25 Nov. 1898, p. 6. Reprinted in *The Marrow of Tradition*, by Charles W. Chesnutt. 1901. Edited by Werner Sollors, Norton, 2012, pp. 291-92.

Twain, Mark. *Pudd'nhead Wilson*. 1894. Penguin, 2004.

Villazor, Rose Cuison. "Rediscovering *Oyama v. California*: At the Intersections of Property, Race, and Citizenship." *Washington University Law Review*, vol. 87, no. 5, 2010, pp. 979-1042, openscholarship.wustl.edu/cgi/viewcontent.cgi?referer=https://www.google.com/&httpsredir=1&article=1101&context=law_lawreview.

Walker, David. *David Walker's Appeal*. 1830. Black Classic, 1993.

Wilkerson, Isabel. *The Warmth of Other Suns: The Epic Story of America's Great Migration*. Vintage, 2010.

Ideological Control and Human Nature in the Dystopian Society
George Orwell's novel *1984*_____

Boyarkina Iren

Science fiction is one of the few literary genres very closely concerned with the analysis and improvement of society. Any significant work of science fiction can be viewed as a kind of a scientific research laboratory in which the important trends in the development of society are studied, analyzed, and extrapolated to an imaginary world for further analysis. This imaginary world is like a metaphor, a model. In the case of negative trends observed in the society in the zero world, the author singles them out, exaggerates, and extrapolates them to the imaginary world, thus creating a dystopia in most of the cases. In doing so, the author tries to draw the attention of society to the existing problems, presenting a warning about the negative consequences if no measures are taken in due time. Thus, every dystopia, though often set in the far future, is a biting satire of the contemporary society. The novel *1984* by George Orwell is one of the best examples of this kind. Through the chilling dystopia set up in 1984, the novel provides a thorough explanation of the causes of inequality in human society (the society of the novel as well as our own society) from its origins to the present day, one of those causes being the kind of ideological control of consciousness that the dystopian society in the novel accomplishes with Newspeak. Ultimately, however, Orwell portrays egalitarian socialism as impossible because of the ruling class's desire for power and its ability to control consciousness in this way.

The description of the State of Oceania and the Party in the novel is a collective portrait and a biting satire of different dictatorships that flourished in Orwell's time. The writer was deeply concerned about drastic social changes (wars, revolutions, emerging dictatorships, etc.) in the world around him, and his novel was a warning about the possible negative consequences of this turmoil and of the emergence of monstrous dystopian powers (like Ingsoc in Oceania):

> It was only after a decade of national wars, civil wars, revolutions, and counter-revolutions in all parts of the world that Ingsoc and its rivals emerged as fully worked out political theories. But they had been foreshadowed by the various systems, generally called totalitarian, which had appeared earlier in the century, and the main outlines of the world which would emerge from the prevailing chaos had long been obvious. (Orwell, *1984* 258)

Speaking about wars, revolutions and counter-revolutions, Orwell seems to agree with Wells, who also claimed that the transition to a new world order would involve the collapse of the old one due to violence: "The collapse is not a simple one: it is the outbreak of reactionary violence, which is degenerating to gangsterism" (Stalin 1947). In H. G. Wells's speculative novel *The Shape of Things to Come*, this violence is manifested through the outbreak of a war, followed by a plague, barbarism, etc. Then the intellectual elite come to power. Orwell's narration might be seen as a zoom-in into this stage in the Wellsian novel.

In *1984*, the ruling Party came to power after the revolution and has adopted a very strict policy of total control and suppression of the ruled. First of all, compared to the Party members, the proletariat (*proles* in the novel) have been kept in devastating social and economic conditions and in complete ignorance, thus ensuring not only socioeconomic inequality between proles and Party members, but unequal rights for education as well. The Party has taken special care that the proles remained ignorant, otherwise they could understand the mechanisms of their suppression and overthrow the ruling Party. Hence, the slogan of the Party in the novel: "Ignorance is strength." Indeed, the ignorance of the proletariat has meant the strength and long reign of the Party. This is a reference to the dictatorships (for example in Italy, China, etc.) that kept their populations in ignorance to ensure their own power for as long as possible. Moreover, in some countries, the ruling parties are still using this principle to remain in power, which means that the novel is by no means obsolete.

In *1984*, society is very rigidly stratified, consisting of three groups: High, Middle, and Low. The High try to keep the power, the Middle try to win the power, and they both use the Low in their struggle for power. Once they obtain the power, they throw the Low back into the abyss of poverty and despair. This process has been going on since the origins of the human society, and the High together with the Middle try their best to keep it going forever. On the other hand,

> the aim of the Low, when they have an aim—for it is an abiding characteristic of the Low that they are too much crushed by drudgery to be more than intermittently conscious of anything outside their daily lives—is to abolish all distinctions and create a society in which all men shall be equal. Thus throughout history a struggle which is the same in its main outlines recurs over and over again. (Orwell, *1984* 253)

The Low are those with a true egalitarian impulse, but because Orwell suggests that such impulses are entirely relative to the amount of power the group possesses, we must believe that even those among the Low, were they to climb to the level of the High, would change their minds about equality. This might also be true because, despite the equality hypocritically proclaimed after the revolution, equality does not exist anywhere in the society, not even among the Party members. They all enjoyed different economic benefits and privileges, like the right to switch off a spying telescreen, the right to have servants, etc., thus confirming once again a famous Orwellian slogan about fake equality introduced in *Animal Farm*: "All animals are equal but some animals are more equal than others" (64).

> Between the two branches of the Party there is a certain amount of interchange, but only so much as will ensure that weaklings are excluded from the Inner Party and that ambitious members of the Outer Party are made harmless by allowing them to rise. Proletarians, in practice, are not allowed to graduate into the Party. The most gifted

among them, who might possibly become nuclei of discontent, are simply marked down by the Thought Police and eliminated. (Orwell, *1984* 264)

The Thought Police, used for the elimination of dangerous proles, also controls the Party members by means of an elaborate and cruel spy system, which consists of telescreens obligatorily installed in every room, microphones, spies, specially designed language, etc. Party members live with the idea of being constantly spied upon and controlled, which is reinforced by omnipresent posters stating BIG BROTHER IS WATCHING YOU. Moreover, people are encouraged to spy on their colleagues, friends, and family members and to report every suspicious issue to the authorities. Even kids are taught to spy on and report their own parents or siblings. Reported persons are often arrested at night and brought to the Ministry of Love, where they usually confess all their crimes after lengthy and cruel torture. Then their brains are "formatted," so that they start loving the Party and Big Brother; after that, they are usually eliminated. Because no one can ever have security, they can't imagine a world of equality and are trained from their earliest moments to think in terms of power and hierarchy.

Even a new language, Newspeak, has been specially designed to control inner thoughts and the slightest mood changes in Party members. A special Research Department in a dedicated ministry has been constantly working on further improvement of Newspeak, eliminating more and more words and parts of speech and abolishing undesirable word meanings. The final target of this meticulous process is the reduction of the human range of consciousness and the elimination of the very possibility of a *Crimethought*, that is, a thought contrary to the will of the Party.

[. . .] the whole aim of Newspeak is to narrow the range of thought. In the end we shall make thoughtcrime literally impossible, because there will be no words in which to express it. Every concept that can ever be needed, will be expressed by exactly one word, with its meaning rigidly defined and all its subsidiary meanings rubbed out and forgotten. [. . .] Every year fewer and fewer words, and the range of consciousness always a little smaller. . . . Even now, of course, there's no reason or excuse for committing thoughtcrime. It's merely a question of self-discipline, reality-control. (Orwell, *1984* 67)

Indeed, any good Party member should automatically stop thinking in the wrong direction; in Newspeak, it was called *Crimestop*. But in the end, there wouldn't be any need even for this, since there would be no words to commit thoughtcrime, hence the total thought control by the Party and the maintenance of status quo inequality will become automatic by means of language. Indeed, "The Revolution will be complete when the language is perfect. Newspeak is Ingsoc and Ingsoc is Newspeak" (Orwell, *1984* 67).

The abundance of combined words and abbreviations in Newspeak is striking, and

> this was not done solely with the object of saving time. Even in the early decades of the twentieth century, telescoped words and phrases had been one of the characteristic features of political language; and it had been noticed that the tendency to use abbreviations of this kind was most marked in totalitarian countries and totalitarian organizations. (Orwell, *1984* 186)

Here is another hint that the Party in *1984* is a satire on various totalitarian countries and organizations. In this satire, Orwell emphasizes and criticizes the ways in which totalitarian countries and organizations usurp the power and artificially maintain inequality among people.

The idea of Newspeak can be traced back to Wells's *The Shape of Things to Come*, in which Wells expressed his ideas about socialism and the evolution of the society. In this novel with a double-frame narration, Dr. Philip Raven predicts the future of mankind; he has gleaned these predictions from a dream he had, in which he was reading a history book written in 2106. His fragmented notes of what he can recall of this history book are arranged into a coherent book by his friend, who is actually narrating the story. The paradigm of the novel is the evolution of the humankind from the twentieth century, i.e., the Age of Frustration, to the establishment of the Modern World States around 2106. This evolution is divided into parts: the Age of Frustration, the birth of the Modern State, the Modern State Militant, the Modern State in control of Life. In this history of the future, Wells foreshadows some of the events and tendencies of the twentieth century, sometimes rather accurately. For example, Wells' concept of the World State and globalization foreshadowed the modern process of globalization in the world and influenced the ideas of many science fiction writers. Wells also foresees a gradual disappearance of religions in the twentieth century and gives a substantial analysis of the social, political, and economic motivations for the coming war (WWII), resulting from the Treaty of Versailles.

Wells suggests a modification of the real-life language of Basic English as the lingua franca for his future utopia. Basic English is an adjusted and simplified version of English, aimed at facilitating international communication as well as quick learning of this language. It was an invention of Cambridge scholar K. G. Ogden (1889–1990). Ogden "emerged with an English of 850 words and a few rules of construction which would enable any foreigner to express practically any ordinary idea simply and clearly" (Wells 1933: 337). In Wells's novel, "it was made the official medium of communication throughout the world by the Air and Sea Control, and by 2020 there was hardly anyone in the world who could not talk and understand it" (Wells 337). However, the main difference between Basic English in *The Shape of Things to Come* and Newspeak in *1984* lies in their main target. While the former was designed to facilitate communication between different parts of the world as well as to facilitate its learning, the latter was created to narrow the range of consciousness of the ruled as well as to control their thoughts (hence, life) completely.

> The purpose of Newspeak was not only to provide a medium of expression for the world-view and mental habits proper to the devotees of Ingsoc, but to make all other modes of thought impossible. It was intended that when Newspeak had been adopted once and for all and Oldspeak forgotten, a heretical thought—that is, a thought diverging from the principles of Ingsoc—should be literally unthinkable, at

least so far as thought is dependent on words. Its vocabulary was so constructed as to give exact and often very subtle expression to every meaning that a Party member could properly wish to express, while excluding all other meanings and also the possibility of arriving at them by indirect methods. (Orwell, *1984* 376)

Newspeak designers left only the necessary and sufficient number of words to express worldview and mental habits allowed to Party members, while all the undesirable and dangerous words were simply eliminated. Hence, if anybody wanted to express an idea contrary to the Party policy, s/he could not even do that because suitable words did not exist anymore. Since the Party wanted to keep the power and maintain inequality, all the words, which could enable any thought endangering Party's status quo, not to mention revolutionary ideas, were eliminated. In other words, the Party took away an instrument indispensable for any kind of dissident and revolutionary thoughts: the words to express these thoughts and impulses.

In *1984*, the Party comes to power after the Revolution and establishes its own power pyramid.

At the apex of the pyramid comes Big Brother. Big Brother is infallible and all-powerful. Every success, every achievement, every victory, every scientific discovery, all knowledge, all wisdom, all happiness, all virtue, are held to issue directly from his leadership and inspiration. Nobody has ever seen Big Brother. He is a face on the hoardings, a voice on the telescreen. [. . .] Big Brother is the guise in which the Party chooses to exhibit itself to the world. His function is to act as a focusing point for love, fear, and reverence. (Orwell, *1984* 261)

In terms of power, the Inner Party is just below Big Brother; the number of its members is something less than 2 percent of the population of Oceania. Below the Inner Party comes the Outer Party, which, if the Inner Party is described as the brain of the State, may be justly likened to the hands. The masses, 'the proles', constitute 85 percent of the population. In the terms of the earlier classification, the proles are the Low.

The Party governs the country (hence, maintains status quo inequality) by means of various ministries: Ministry of Peace, Ministry of Love, Ministry of Plenty, Ministry of Truth, or Minipeace, Minilove, Minitruth, Miniplenty, in Newspeak. The bitter irony and hypocrisy of the situation lies in the striking contrast between the ministry's name and its main function. For example, in the cellars of Ministry of Love, endless, inhumane torture is used to extort confessions from those considered guilty of thoughtcrime. The Ministry's of Peace function is to conduct the permanent war and improve the weapons. Ministry of Plenty constantly reports victories in the "production battle," while the whole country suffers constantly from the lack of something: shoelaces, razors, buttons, etc., and the food ratio is constantly reduced. Ministry of Truth constantly changes (read: falsifies) papers, books, films, videos, etc. according to the latest events: people eliminated, enemies and allies in the war changed, Party predictions not fulfilled, etc. Thus, the past is constantly changing according to the decisions of the Party; the mutability of the past is one of the principles of INGSOC (English Socialism in Newspeak). This is indicated in the Party slogan "Who controls the past, controls the future; who controls the present controls the past." Party members have to stick to the new state of affairs and carefully forget the old information, as if it did not even exist. Thus, people are rather disoriented and can hardly understand what is going on, which facilitates the Party's control over them. In fact, "All the beliefs, habits, tastes, emotions, mental attitudes that characterize our time are really designed to sustain the mystique of the Party and prevent the true nature of present-day society from being perceived" (Orwell, *1984* 265). And what is not perceived cannot be rebelled or fought against.

Another important means of maintaining inequality among people in the novel is the permanent state of war among three main world powers: Oceania, Eastasia, and Eurasia. Every once in a while, Oceania (where the action of the novel takes place) changes enemies. Immediately it will be declared that Oceania had been always at war with this enemy, and the other state of affairs never existed. The Ministry of Truth carefully deletes all the information contradicting the new status quo. This can be done periodically because the three world powers aren't fighting to conquer each other's territory, but to get control over cheap labor resources and to keep their own proles permanently in a state of misery and suffering, so that they cannot think of anything else except daily survival and hence remain supressed and under the control of the rulers.

> But though it is unreal it is not meaningless (war). It eats up the surplus of consumable goods, and it helps to preserve the special mental atmosphere that a hierarchical society needs. War, it will be seen, is now a purely internal affair. [. . .] In our own day they are not fighting against one another at all. The war is waged by each ruling group against its own subjects, and the object of the war is not to make or prevent conquests of territory, but to keep the structure of society intact. (Orwell, *1984* 251)

This explains one of the three main slogans of the Party: WAR IS PEACE. Paradoxically, according to the Party conviction, a constant war with an external enemy keeps the population of a country exhausted and under control; hence, it ensures peace for the rulers of the country.

Very closely connected to the theme of war is the theme of violence, which is used in the novel to maintain the inequality status quo. In *1984*, Orwell meticulously depicts psychiatric deviations, mainly violence, lack of empathy, etc. in beings obsessed by power and domination. The writer describes blood-chilling scenes of torture in the hidden, secret cells of Minilove. Orwell shows how torturers enjoy causing their victims pain and having them completely under control. This violence is not only physical but psychological as well, since not only are the bodies of victims tortured, but eventually, their brains are reformatted. Once the brain, associated with consciousness and personality, is clean of any information, a personality does not exist anymore in *sensy strictu*. Moreover, torture is unnecessary, since the victims are always killed at the end, so it must serve as an outlet for the sadistic inclinations of power-thirsty beings. Secrecy related to violence (hidden rooms and underground corridors of Minilove) is a very important metaphor in the novel. The acts of violence and its executors hide in underground corridors: the executioners want to enjoy the pain and complete surrender of victims, but they also want to preserve their good image as Party members to remain in power forever, so they do not want being seen in the act of torturing people. What is not seen cannot be fought against, according to these cynical Party members. Orwell shows how the Party manages to justify anything it does, while its only true goal is to keep power and money (which in the novel is symbolized by extra privileges for Party members).

Orwell's alternative history of the twentieth century explains how the State and Party described in *1984* might become possible:

> But by the fourth decade of the twentieth century all the main currents of political thought were authoritarian. The earthly paradise had been discredited at exactly the moment when it became realizable. Every new political theory, by whatever name it called itself, led back to hierarchy and regimentation. (*1984* 258)

Here Orwell uses the word "currents" to emphasize the almost organic change in twentieth century political thought, away from equality and toward hierarchy. Even when the material production of goods and services could finally have allowed equality, the thirst for power by the few maintained inequality for many.

> And in the general hardening of outlook that set in round about 1930, practices which had been long abandoned, in some cases for hundreds of years—imprisonment without trial, the use of war prisoners as slaves, public executions, torture to extract confessions, the use of hostages, and the deportation of whole populations—not only became common again, but were tolerated and even defended by people who considered themselves enlightened and progressive. (Orwell, *1984* 258)

Authoritarianism brings with it the kind of rigidity and lack of compassion that enables violence to be used overtly in order to maintain inequality.

Despite its clear condemnation of authoritarianism, *1984* is also rather critical of various forms of socialism because socialism is represented as betraying the ideals of liberty and equality. Moreover, once in power, socialists will be able to maintain that power forever. Orwell demonstrated one of the possible ways.

> Socialism, a theory which appeared in the early nineteenth century and was the last link in a chain of thought stretching back to the slave rebellions of antiquity, was still deeply infected by the Utopianism of past ages. But in each variant of Socialism that appeared from about 1900 onwards the aim of establishing liberty and equality was more and more openly abandoned. The new movements which appeared in the middle years of the century, Ingsoc in Oceania, Neo-Bolshevism in Eurasia, Death-Worship, as it is commonly called, in Eastasia, had the conscious aim of perpetuating UNfreedom and INequality. These new movements, of course, grew out of the old ones and tended to keep their names and pay lip-service to their ideology. But the purpose of all of them was to arrest progress and freeze history at a chosen moment. The familiar pendulum swing was to happen once more, and then stop. As usual, the High were to be turned out by the Middle, who would then become the High; but this time, by conscious strategy, the High would be able to maintain their position permanently. (*1984* 257)

Thus, Orwell seems to be in opposition to H. G. Wells's idea of creating an ideal utopian society where everyone is happy and satisfied, described in *The Shape of Things to Come*.

In *1984*, Orwell sees socialism as impossible because of the ruling classes' desire for power, in contrast with Wells's belief that perhaps socialism could be achieved. In the Wellsian novel, the conflict between the working class and financial oligarchy was solved by means of education and economic planning. In an interview with Joseph Stalin, Wells states, "If a country as a whole adopts the principle of planned economy, if the government gradually, step by step, begins consistently to apply this principle, the financial oligarchy will at last be abolished, and socialism, in the Anglo-Saxon meaning of the word, will be brought about" (Stalin 1947). Wells believes that it is possible to end the antagonisms between the old world order and the new one simply by some reforms and reorganizations in the society, for example by publishing a Declaration, and that people would accept the New World Government, though with some insignificant resistance. As Wells explains in the interview, "And it seems to me that when it comes to a conflict with reactionary and unintelligent violence, socialism can appeal to the law" (Stalin). Hence, in *The Shape of Things to Come*, we observe the international acceptance of Declaration, proclaimed by the New World Government; it manifests Wells's conviction that the counter-reaction of the old classes can be overruled by appealing to law and order. Even a year after publication of this novel, during his 1934 visit to the Soviet Union, Wells did not change his convictions and discussed with Stalin the merits of reformist socialism over Marxism-Leninism (Stalin 1947). Orwell does not seem to agree that it is possible to create such an ideal classless state without any revolution, by means of reforms only, as Wells described in *The Shape of Things to Come*. Orwell's novel appears to demonstrate his belief that there are three distinct groups (High, Middle, and Low) with irreconcilable goals and that they would not abandon their goals without a fight.

At the head of the reforms and reorganizations, Wells places the intellectual elite, which controls the progress of the World State: Sea and Air Ways Control, the First Council, the Second Council, etc. In *1984*, too, the intellectual elite controls everything: "What kind of people would control this world had been equally obvious. The new aristocracy was made up for the most part of bureaucrats, scientists, technicians, trade-union organizers, publicity experts, sociologists, teachers, journalists, and professional politicians." Orwell emphasizes some decisive (to his mind) qualities of these intellectuals: "they were less avaricious, less tempted by luxury, hungrier for pure power, and, above all, more conscious of what they were doing and more intent on crushing opposition. This last difference was cardinal" (259). Thus, in *1984*, he warns about the dangers of intellectual elite seizing the power to ensure the transition of the state to its final utopian phase: it will happen that the elite wants to keep the power forever, cultivating unfreedom and inequality forever.

According to Orwell, there are not so many possibilities for the ruling elite to lose power:

There are only four ways in which a ruling group can fall from power. Either it is conquered from without, or it governs so inefficiently that the masses are stirred to revolt, or it allows a strong and discontented Middle group to come into being, or it loses its own selfconfidence and willingness to govern. These causes do not operate singly, and as a rule all four of them are present in some degree. A ruling class which could guard against all of them would remain in power permanently. Ultimately the determining factor is the mental attitude of the ruling class itself. (*1984* 261)

Of these four ways, Orwell says, only the last one can really occur and be dangerous. Indeed,

From the point of view of our present rulers, therefore, the only genuine dangers are the splitting-off of a new group of able, under-employed, power-hungry people, and the growth of liberalism and scepticism in their own ranks. The problem, that is to say, is educational. It is a problem of continuously moulding the consciousness both of the directing group and of the larger executive group that lies immediately below it. The consciousness of the masses needs only to be influenced in a negative way. (*1984* 262)

The fact that this problem is educational and involves molding consciousness explains why the Party in the novel pays so much attention to education and to controlling the consciousness of its members through language, spying telescreens, Hate sessions, Thought Police, war, etc. The final target of the Party is always to keep the power and inequality status quo in the society.[1]

Orwell's novel emphasizes that throughout human history, the High and the Middle have been always fighting for power, using the Low for this end, "enlisting the Low on their side by pretending to them that they are fighting for liberty and justice. As soon as they have reached their objective, [they] thrust the Low back into their old position of servitude" (*1984* 264). The Low, or proletariat, was always used in these "power games" and never really enjoyed freedom or equality that the High or Middle were falsely promising to them:

> Of the three groups, only the Low are never even temporarily successful in achieving their aims. It would be an exaggeration to say that throughout history there has been no progress of a material kind. Even today, in a period of decline, the average human being is physically better off than he was a few centuries ago. But no advance in wealth, no softening of manners, no reform or revolution has ever brought human equality a millimetre nearer. From the point of view of the Low, no historic change has ever meant much more than a change in the name of their masters. (Orwell, *1984* 255)

Although Orwell describes this state as perpetual, he observes that in the early twentieth century, the industrial development of society created the conditions for the elimination of all kinds of inequality among people:

> as early as the beginning of the twentieth century, human equality had become technically possible. It was still true that men were not equal in their native talents and that functions had to be specialized in ways that favoured some individuals against others; but there was no longer any real need for class distinctions or for large differences of wealth. [. . .] Even if it was still necessary for human beings to do different kinds of work, it was no longer necessary for them to live at different social or economic levels (*1984* 257)

The fact that it still exists only means that it is profitable for some groups in the society, the High and the Middle, and they maintain this situation on purpose because they want to keep their power. Hence, they invent various justifications for the existence of inequality, religion included.

> By the late nineteenth century the recurrence of this pattern had become obvious to many observers. There then rose schools of thinkers who interpreted history as a cyclical process and claimed to show that inequality was the unalterable law of human life. This doctrine, of course, had always had its adherents, by aristocrats and

by the priests, lawyers, and the like who were parasitical upon them, and it had generally been softened by promises of compensation in an imaginary world beyond the grave. (Orwell, *1984* 253)

Here Orwell cleverly observes that for centuries, those people who wanted to keep the power have been using all possible methods to do it and all possible and impossible rationalizations for it: they have controlled the consciousness of the masses and kept dissatisfied and embittered masses content and obedient by using the church's promise of a kind of justice after death, and they have claimed they have the right to keep the power because of their aristocratic birth, wealth, church membership, etc. The legislative state system has been thus used to maintain this status quo power in very similar ways to those in our own society.

Like the fathers of science fiction, H. G. Wells and Olaf Stapledon, George Orwell was deeply concerned about the true essence of human nature. His rich life experience in Britain, India, and Spain contributed greatly to his contemplation of this issue. In *1984*, he summarized his observations on human lust for power and control, corruption on every state level, human cruelty and greediness of every kind, which are still very diffuse and as up-to-date as in his times. Indeed, "Orwell insisted until his death in 1950, that the book was a warning against corruption in general, regardless of the political system that engenders it" (Bloom 12). Moreover, Orwell warns that whenever such a Party as described in *1984* comes to power, there is no hope left for equality, justice, and democracy in any society.

Note

1. For the same reasons, in *Brave New World*, children are exposed to the constant radio "education" from a very young age.

Works Cited

Bloom, Harold, editor. *Bloom's Guides: George Orwell's* 1984. Chelsea House, 2004.

Huxley, Aldous. *Brave New World*. Chatto and Windus, 1932.

Orwell, George. *1984*. 1949. *Free Ebooks*, n.d., www. Planet eBook.com/.

Orwell, George. *Animal Farm*. 1945. *Free Ebooks*, n.d., www. Planet eBook.com/.

Stalin, Joseph. *Joseph Stalin-H.G. Wells: Marxism VS. Liberalism. An Interview.* New Century Publishers, 1947.

Wells, Herbert. *The Shape of Things to Come*. Edited by John Partington, Penguin Books, 2005.

The "Closet" and Marginalized Identities
James Baldwin's story "The Outing" and novel *Giovanni's Room*_____

Sonia Mae Brown

As a literal place, the closet is a space of containment or storage. Images or discussions of closets are often accompanied by notions of secrecy, suppression, and seclusion. As a metaphor and a theoretical tool, the closet refers to those whose sexuality must be hidden from public view; the term "closet" illuminates public and private aspects of sexual identity. The motif of the closet as space and place is evident in the works of James Baldwin. In his use of the closet as a rhetorical device, Baldwin documents the coping strategies marginalized peoples—in this case gay men—employ in the expression of their day-to-day realities. In his fiction, Baldwin uses the trope of the closet to "out" or bring to light the dehumanization of marginalized peoples. Baldwin's stories are "outings" in two senses: characters emerge out of the private space into the public realm, and characters engage in and undergo psychological journeys and quests in the attempt to find their individual subjectivities.

The closet as safe space
The closet is an important term in the academic field of queer theory, one that conveys the specificity of oppression based on norms of gender/sexuality. In his text *Closet Space*, queer theorist Michael P. Brown provides definitions of the closet and its history. Brown writes, "As a transitive verb, [to closet] means to isolate, hide, or confine something. As an adjective, it suggests secrecy, covertness" (5). Modern definitions of the closet highlight the functionality as well as the perception of the closet. The closet can also be used as a vehicle of expression. Brown notes, "It allows [individuals] to speak [their] anger and pain about lying, hiding, being silenced, and going unseen" (1). Seen in this way, the closet is a tool through which identity can be interrogated, questioned, and examined.

Queer identity, homosexuality, and the closet are the focus of Baldwin's 1954 essay titled "The Male Prison." In this essay, Baldwin affirms that the closet is a defining feature of gay identity, and he advises use of the closet as a literary, social, and interpretive tool. Discussing French author Andre Gide's story of his marriage, *Madeleine*, Baldwin writes, "And his homosexuality, I felt, was his own affair which he ought to have kept hidden from us, or, if he needed to be so explicit, he ought at least to have managed to be a little more scientific—whatever, in the domain of morals, that word may mean—less illogical, less romantic" (156). In this essay, Baldwin suggests that Gide should have kept his own sexuality in the literary closet and instead been a little more "scientific" or objective in his portrayal of homosexuality. Baldwin notes the fact that Gide had not come to terms with his own homosexuality and had not recognized it as an inherent aspect of his identity in this book. Gide's blatant homosexual themes caused Baldwin to feel uneasy even though Baldwin praises Gide's "devotion to a very high ideal" (155). For Baldwin, one's sexuality is a private affair and not a public matter.

The closet and the good/evil binary

Baldwin's portrayal of the closet and its relation to homosexual experience can be seen in his short story "The Outing" and his novel *Giovanni's Room*. In "The Outing," Baldwin uses the metaphor of the closet as a way to scientifically encode a discussion of sexual identity amid a narrative of teenage angst and religious experience. Published in 1951, "The Outing" ("Outing") is a short story that explores the closeted subjectivity of a young African American boy named Johnnie, who engages in a metaphorical and literal "outing." Simply put, the story is about a group of young boys who attend a church outing to Bear Mountain. During the trip, the boys wrestle with presenting Sylvia, a fellow churchgoer, a birthday gift. The boys also bear witness to a melodramatic church service in which Johnnie discovers a hidden—or suppressed—aspect of himself. In this text, Baldwin employs the metaphor of the closet in several ways. He deconstructs the good versus evil binary, revealing the presence of the closet as metaphor for homosexual existence. The closet can also be seen in the "triangulated desire" that exists between characters in the text. Moreover, Baldwin uses the closet to explore the private nature of identity and its public (re) presentation. In this text, Baldwin uses the closet to present the difficulties and tensions specific to black male queer experience.

By analyzing binaries, readers can uncover a narrative of closeted subjectivity within the religious context of "The Outing." Of all the binaries, the most fruitful for analysis is the good/evil dichotomy, which can be seen in the plot as well as in the language in the text. The good/evil binary suggests other binaries, for example, saint/sinner, us/them, normal/abnormal, etc. The outing, sponsored by the Mount of Olives Pentecostal Assembly, is referred to as the "whosoever will" outing, described this way because non-members –"Gentile, Jew or Greek or sinner" (29)—are allowed, even though the outing is for the members of the church. The church members are seen as saints, as holy and pure, while the sinners, non-members, are seen as tainted and in need of salvation. The presence of both groups (saints and sinners) on this outing creates a tension, division, or split onboard the boat, which becomes apparent when the church service begins on the lower level. Baldwin writes:

> From all corners of the boat there was the movement of the saints of God. They gathered together their various possessions and moved their chairs from top and bottom decks to the large main hall. [...] A few of the strangers who had come along on the outing appeared at the doors and stood watching with an uneasy amusement. The saints sang on, raising their strong voices in praises to Jehovah and seemed unaware of those unsaved who watched and who, some day, the power of the Lord might cause to tremble. (43-44)

When the service begins, the saints assemble themselves and begin singing and rejoicing. Baldwin notes the "uneasiness" of the sinners (unsaved strangers) who stand at the door to the hall. Here the division between the saved and unsaved is measured as a literal and physical separation. From the doorway, the unsaved stand and watch as the saints praise the Lord. Unable to enter into the hall, the unsaved are separated from the realm of the saved.

In addition to this saint versus sinner juxtaposition, the good versus evil binary is also perpetuated by the language in the text that refers to both David and Johnnie as demons. Baldwin notes the "perverse demon" that impels David (34) to sympathize with Johnnie when Johnnie's father, Gabriel, rebukes him. Gabriel also tells his wife about the "proud demon" that has taken over Johnnie (40). In addition, Sylvia's mother tells her to stay away from David because "that child's got a demon" (41), and jokingly, Sylvia chides David as a "black-eyed demon" (55). The repetition of *demon* in the midst of the religious context of the text sets up the notion that the young boys are different from, other than, and unlike the saints. This view of the boys as deviant can also be seen when the boys enter the revival. Baldwin writes, "No matter how careful their movements, these movements suggested, with a distinctness dreadful for the redeemed to see, the pagan lusting beneath the blood-washed robes" (48). To the saints of the church, the boys are seen as pagans, demons, or "other." This juxtaposition of the young, unsaved boys to the religious saints aids in establishing the saint/sinner, good/evil dichotomy that pervades the story. Baldwin sets up this good/evil dichotomy in which the boys represent the evil side of the spectrum because they are unsaved and other; however, within this narrative, there is a hidden story of closeted identity.

The good versus evil binary that runs throughout the text engenders the metaphor of the closet. As an unsaved person in the presence of saints, Johnnie is aware of a presence that affects his spirit. As the saints are shouting and catching the Holy Ghost, Johnnie becomes aware of a satanic presence that looms about (and within) him, for "it was Satan, surely, who stood so foully at his shoulder" (50). Here Baldwin is suggesting that Johnnie is influenced by an evil (or satanic) presence. While this declaration can be read metaphorically, it can also be interpreted literally in the respect that David is the being who is standing next to Johnnie. In acknowledging the presence of David, Johnnie is also recognizing that David represents something that is evil and illicit. This illicitness can also be seen when Baldwin writes about Johnnie's internal turmoil during the religious service. Baldwin notes, "Johnnie stood beside him [David], hot and faint and repeating yet again his struggle, summoning in panic all his forces, to save him from this frenzy. And yet daily he recognized that he was black with sin, that the secrets of his heart were a stench in God's nostrils" (48). Baldwin's use of alliteration is interesting here. The repetitive s- sound (stood, struggle, summoning, save, sin, secrets, stench) reads like the hiss of a serpent. In the bible, the serpent appeared to Eve and encouraged her to tempt Adam with the apple from the tree of knowledge. As a biblical animal, the serpent represents temptation or evil. Aside from this minor, almost coincidental detail, the words show that Johnnie is aware of evil (sin) within him. Baldwin's diction here is telling of the situation that Johnnie faces. Standing by David, Johnnie struggles with the intense religious scene before him and the reality within him. In this battle, he is aware of the "black sin" within him that exists in comparison to the white-washed robes of the saintly. This "black sin" is a secret. A secret that he knows is ungodly and wrong. The secret of his heart is his desire for David.

Further analysis of the scene reveals Johnnie's closeted homoerotic desire for David, which can be read as Satanic or evil in the consideration of the religious context. As the saints revel in and testify to their love for God, Johnnie becomes aware of the object of his love. Baldwin writes:

> Johnnie felt suddenly, not the presence of the Lord, but the presence of David [...]. From the corner of his eye he watched his friend, who held him with such power; and felt, for that moment, such a depth of love, such nameless and terrible joy and pain, that he might have fallen, in the face of that company, weeping at David's feet. (51)

While the saints are praising and relishing the presence of the Lord or Holy Ghost, Johnnie becomes aware of a powerful presence that captivates him. In this timeless moment, Johnnie is bound by the power of David. For Johnnie, David is the incarnate Christ figure. Unlike the saints who are focusing on God and His presence, Johnnie only sees the presence of David. Not only does he see David, but also

Johnnie becomes aware of his love for David. While this love can be interpreted as love in a brotherly sense, the presence of dualities in the text suggests that the love that Johnnie experiences is a romantic love.

Here, this love is situated in a romantic-religious context in the suggestion that Johnnie desires to fall and weep at David's feet. Biblically speaking, Johnnie's desire to weep at the feet of David is similar to the story of the woman who fell at the feet of Jesus and washed his feet with her tears. In the bible, this woman prostrated herself before Jesus to show her love for him (Luke 7. 37-39). Like the woman who submits herself to the feet of the Lord and weeps to show her love, Johnnie desires to prostrate himself in reverence at the feet of David. In his desire to prostrate himself to David, he is affirming his homoerotic love and admiration of David. Through the use of the closet as metaphor, Baldwin reveals a narrative of homoeroticism within the larger religious dialogue of the text and "scientifically" encodes a homoerotic connection between David and Johnnie.

Triangulated desire as closeted desire

The triangle of desire is a concept theorized by French philosopher Rene Girard that helps to analyze relationships among characters in a text. According to Girard's theory of triangulated desire, desire is fixed by a subject (person a) on an object (person b) and is resolved by the existence of another object (person c) (10). The relationships in Baldwin's "The Outing" mirror this triangulated desire; Johnnie fixates desire on David, and this illicit desire is mediated by the presence of Sylvia.

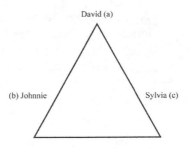

David (a)

(b) Johnnie   Sylvia (c)

Girard's theory suggests that desire is possible between all characters that occupy space on the triangle. It proposes that David's desire for Sylvia mimics Johnnie's desire for Sylvia, which suggests David's potential desire for Johnnie. The triangle of desire hints at the presence of closeted desire among individuals, thereby insinuating that the closet plays a role in the relationship between characters.

In the text, Baldwin engages this paradigm to explore the relationship between Johnnie and David. In his use of the triangle as a paradigm, Baldwin pits David's interest in Sylvia against Johnnie's interest in David. This can be seen in the text when the young boys are discussing what to get Sylvia for her birthday. Baldwin writes, "but David did not think it [the gift] was so bad; Johnnie thought it pretty enough and he was sure that Sylvia would like it anyway; ('When's *your* birthday?' he asked David)" (30 *Italics in orig.*). Here, Baldwin's use of punctuation is significant. While parentheses aid the reader in recognizing the dialogue that is occurring between the boys, the use of parenthesis here sets up an aside or helps disclose an idea or focus (David and his birthday) that is essential and antithetical to the original focus or topic (Sylvia). In addition to the parenthesis, Baldwin uses italics to further emphasize Johnnie's interest in David. This use of italics highlights or makes clear Johnnie's true concern. In italicizing *your*, Baldwin emphasizes Johnnie's curiosity about David and not Sylvia.

Johnny's curiosity about David can also be seen in another scene in which the triangulation of desire is also present. When the boat arrives at its intended destination, the boys try to find a way to give Sylvia her gift without the presence of the "saints." Baldwin writes:

> Johnnie swallowed his jealousy at seeing how Sylvia filled his comrade's mind [...]. Johnnie, frowning, fell into silence. He glanced sidewise at David's puckered face (his eyes were still on Sylvia) and abruptly turned and started walking off. "Where you going, boy?" David called. "I'll be back," he said. And he prayed that David would follow him. (52)

David is focused on figuring out how to get Sylvia alone in order to present her with the gift, but Johnnie is fixated on spending time with David. Unlike the others, Johnnie simply wants to give Sylvia the gift so that he can "explore the wonders of Bear Mountain" with David, but he realizes that David will not do so "until this mission [giving the gift to Sylvia] should have been fulfilled" (51). Johnnie's anger at David stems from the fact that he "was looking forward to the day with David" (31). Jealous and angry with David and his attentiveness to Sylvia, Johnnie walks away and realizes that "he had no interest in the birthday present, no interest whatsoever in Sylvia—that he had had no interest all along" (53). Johnnie's solitary reflection reveals his true concern for David and the fact that he has only been engrossed in this situation because of David.

Baldwin's use of the closet as a metaphor in "The Outing" is ingenious. The text is appropriately named the "The Outing;" while the text does recount the day trip or brief excursion taken by the church members and their guests, the text also recounts the public disclosing of Johnnie's private identity. Arguably, the outing process here is a personal one. Johnnie is "outed" to himself in becoming aware of his own homoerotic inclinations. In the same respect, Johnnie is also "outed" to readers of the text. The text then becomes a public statement of Johnnie's private identity. While Baldwin may not have been familiar with the contemporary usage of the term "outing" and its reference to the disclosure of homosexual identity, he was familiar with the concepts of narrative irony and homonymy, and this familiarity can be seen in his strategic "scientific treatment" of Johnnie's sexual identity in "The Outing." The text, itself, "outs" or exposes the homosexual nature that is closeted within the story.

In the struggle between the spiritual and the sensual, Johnnie realizes the terrifying, depthlessness of his identity (53). Baldwin writes, "But now where there had been peace there was only panic and where there had been safety, danger, like a flower, opened" (57). The closet, as place and space, allows Johnnie to exist within the religious context of his society. As place, Johnnie retreats to the closet to reconcile his loneliness and alienation from the others. As space, the closet allows Johnnie the possibility for safety. From the safety of the closet, Johnnie is able to interact with David and avoid judgment and condemnation. Baldwin shows the ways individuals become aware that the closet can be an essential tool in the negotiation between their public and private lives. "The Outing" thus provides readers with Baldwin's vision of the politics of otherness. As an "other" within his society, Johnnie uses the closet to make sense out of his reality.

The closet as Plato's cave

The politics of otherness and the complex nature of identity and subjectivity are also present in Baldwin's *Giovanni's Room* (1956). This introspective novel chronicles its main character David's psychological and moral growth from his sexual conquests as a youth in Brooklyn to his romantic pursuits as an adult in Paris. As indicated by the title, the room is significant to understanding the role of love and identity within the novel. The room is doubly representative of the location of illicit and illustrious acts and the space where David questions, responds to, and embraces his sexual identity.

The room in *Giovanni's Room* can be compared to the representation of the cave in Plato's *Allegory of the Cave*. The parable (or allegory) of the cave is an analogy used by the Greek philosopher Plato to describe the ways knowledge/understanding is created. In this parable, a group of people, who are chained in a cave facing a wall, watch shadows projected onto the wall by things passing in front of a fire behind them. As the figures are projected onto the wall, the prisoners begin to ascribe forms to the shadows. According to Plato, the shadows are the prisoners' representations or interpretation of reality. The prisoner, a stand-in for the philosopher, creates and/or determines his or her reality in response to events occurring around him/her. Like the philosopher in Plato's *Allegory of the Cave*, David is a prisoner who responds to the shadows on the wall of Giovanni's room (the cave) to rationalize his love for Giovanni. Analyzing the allegory of the cave within the text allows for a reading of the way Baldwin employs the closet as a metaphor for homosexual existence.

In this text, Baldwin represents Giovanni's room as a closet in which David's subjectivity is birthed. More so, the room is the place where David distinguishes the "unreal" within himself. Drenched in suggestive terminology, Giovanni's room is reminiscent of a closet: "We passed the vestibule and the elevator into a short, dark corridor which led to his room" (63); "the room was not large enough for two. [...] Giovanni had obscured the window panes with a heavy, white cleaning polish" (85). The description of the room resounds like that of a closet. Like a closet or cave, Giovanni's room is small and dark, and it contains a pre-configured amount of space.

For David, the room resembles a closet, and he is a prisoner. Like the prisoners in Plato's allegory, David's hands are figuratively positioned at his sides, and he is forced to gaze at the wall in front of him. David says, "He locked the door behind us [...]. I thought, if I do not open the door at once and get out of here, I am lost. But I knew I could not open the door, I knew it was too late" (86). David's choice of words indicates a sense of powerlessness. The verb "to know" highlights David's awareness of his position; he is simply unable to leave the room when he enters it. David also notes that he "spent a lifetime" in the room with Giovanni (85). Like the prisoners of the parable, the prisoners of Giovanni's room (also) watch shadows on the wall. David notes, "Sometimes strange shapes loomed against [our window]. At such moments, Giovanni, working in the room, or lying in the bed, would stiffen like a hunting dog and remain perfectly still until whatever seemed to threaten our safety had moved away" (86). Due to the white polish on the windows, David and Giovanni are unable to see outside of the realm of the room. As occupants inside the room (or closet), Giovanni and David interpret the shadows and respond with apprehension. Like the occupants of Plato's cave, who are unaware of what the shadows actually represent, Giovanni and David attempt to ascribe meaning to the shadows projected on the walls of the room. Scared of what the shadows really represent, they wait until the shadows are no longer visible in order to feel at ease.

Plato explains that the philosopher (occupant of the cave—in this case, the closet) is like a released prisoner who understands that the shadows on the wall are not constitutive of reality and that true knowledge comes from knowledge of unchanging ideas (Plato 293). When David leaves Giovanni's room, he has a disturbing revelation. David acknowledges, "The beast which Giovanni had awakened in me would never go to sleep again; but one day I would not be with Giovanni anymore. And would I then, like all the others, find myself turning and following all kinds of boys down God knows what dark avenues, into what dark places" (84). As a beast, David is savage, vile, and wild. This "beasting" is David's realization of his homosexuality. His exploits with Giovanni have revived his desire to be with men, and he realizes that his relationship with Giovanni will someday end, thus causing him to pursue other men, and this pursuit is something that can only be done in secret, dark places. David concludes, "With this fearful intimation there opened in me a hatred for Giovanni which was as powerful as my love and which was nourished by the same roots" (84). David's ambivalence stems from the fact that he has fallen in love with Giovanni, but he also hates who (or what) he has become as a result of these intimate acts.

Giovanni's room becomes the place of "life" for David. As place and space, the room as closet becomes the location where David's identity as a homosexual man is birthed. Baldwin writes, "I remember that life in that room seemed to be occurring beneath the sea. Time flowed past indifferently above us; hours and days had no meaning" (75). Here Baldwin engages the sea metaphor to explain the transformation within David, emphasizing the notion that David's identity is not fixed. Reading the room as Plato's cave allows David to be seen as a philosopher who traverses international boundaries to grapple with his identity; recognizing the cave as closet allows for a reading of the text that foregrounds the experiences specific to individuals who are forced to question their identity away from the public eye. The room allows David to interact freely with Giovanni without concern for public contempt, but also to hide his true feelings towards Giovanni. Outside of the room, David is forced to confront the implications of his re-awakened desire. When David emerges from the room, he realizes that he is an "other" due to his sexual identity and the futility of the relationship between him and

Giovanni. In this text, reading through the metaphor of the closet reveals how David learns about his queer subjectivity.

Conclusion

Baldwin's works seek to create safe spaces where the discussion of sexual identity can take place. In "The Outing" Baldwin suggests the notion of closet in depicting a young boy discovering his homosexual desire during a religious excursion. In *Giovanni's Room*, the room itself functions as a closet where secrets are held and contained and where identity is created. Thus, the closet can be seen as a vehicle of expression, a tool through which the subject (as individual) can be examined. Writing from within the closet creates a new narrative space where oppressed identities and oppressed people are visible and audible. Baldwin, in his use of the closet as a metaphor, attempts to shape a silence while breaking it. The silence that he gives voice to is the notion of homosexuality and its associated troubles, trials, and temptations. The closet functions as place of oppression, loneliness, and alienation; it also functions as a space of safety, a space for expression, and a space free from societal prejudices.

Works Cited

Baldwin, James. *Giovanni's Room*. NY: Vintage Books 2013. Print.

_____. "'Go The Way Your Blood Beats': An Interview with James Baldwin." Interview by Richard Goldstein (1984). *James Baldwin: The Last Interview and Other Conversations*. Brooklyn: Melville House, 2014. 56-74. Print.

_____. "The Male Prison." *Nobody Knows My Name: More Notes of a Native Son*. 1961. New York: Dial Press, 1967. 155-62. Print.

_____. "The Outing." 1965. *Going to Meet the Man: Stories*. New York: Vintage Books, 1995. 227-49. Print.

Bowen, Matthew L. "'They Came and Held Him by the Feet and Worshipped Him': Proskynesis before Jesus in Its Biblical and Ancient Near Context." *Studies in the Bible and Antiquity* 5 (2013): 63-89. *EbscoHost*. Web. 6 Dec. 2014.

Brown, Michael P. *Closet Space: Geographies of Metaphor from the Body to the Globe*. Routledge: New York, 2000. Print.

Butler, Judith. "Performative Acts and Gender Constitution: An Essay in Phenomenology and Feminist Theory." *Theatre Journal* 40.4 (1988): 519-31. *JSTOR.* Web. 24 Nov. 2015.

Foucault, Michel. "Sex, Power, and the Politics of Identity." *Ethics: Subjectivity and Truth.* Ed. Paul Rabinow. Trans. Robert Hurley, *et al.* New York: New Press, 1997. 163-74. Print.

Girard, Rene. *Deceit, Desire, and the Novel: Self and Other in Literary Structure.* Trans. Yvonne Freccero. Maryland: John Hopkins UP, 1965. Print.

Harris, David. "The Politics of Otherness." *Radical Otherness: Sociological and Theological Approaches.* Eds. Lisa Isherwood and David Harris. London: Routledge, 2013. 48- 73. Print.

Henderson, Mae G. "James Baldwin's *Giovanni's Room*: Expatriation, 'Racial Drag,' and Homosexual Panic." *Black Queer Studies: A Critical Anthology.* Eds. E. Patrick Johnson and Mae G. Henderson. Durham: Duke UP, 2005. 298-322. Print.

Mansfield, Nick. *Subjectivity: Theories of the Self from Freud to Haraway.* New York: New York UP, 2000. Print.

Miller, D. Quentin. Ed. *Reviewing James Baldwin: Things Not Seen.* Philadelphia: Temple University Press, 2000. Print.

Muñoz, José Esteban. *Disidentifications: Queers Of Color And The Performance Of Politics.* Minneapolis: U of Minnesota P, 1999. Print.

Nelson, Emmanuel. "Critical Deviance: Homophobia and the Reception of James Baldwin's Fiction." *Journal of American Culture* 14.3 (1991): 91-96. *JSTOR.* Web. 9. Mar. 2016.

Plato. *Republic.* Trans. John Lleweyn Davies and David James Vaughan. London: Wordsworth Editions, 1997. Print.

Polchin, James. "The Baldwin of Giovanni's Room." *The Gay & Lesbian Review Worldwide* 21.6. (2014) 31-33. *Gale Literary Index.* Web. 7 Jan. 2016.

Rohy, Valerie. "Displacing Desire: Passing, Nostalgia, and *Giovanni's Room. Passing and the Fictions of Identity.* Ed. Elaine K. Ginsberg. Durham: Duke UP, 1996. 218-33. Print.

Romanet, de Jerome. "Revisiting Madeleine and 'The Outing': James Baldwin's Revision of Gide's Sexual Politics." *MELUS* 22.1 (1997): 3-14. *JSTOR.* Web. 13 Apr. 2014.

Ross, Marlon B. "Beyond the Closet as Raceless Paradigm." *Black Queer Studies: A Critical Anthology.* Ed. E. Patrick Johnson and Mae. G. Henderson. Durham: Duke UP, 2005. 161-89. Print.

Sedgwick, Eve K. *Tendencies.* Durham: Duke UP, 1993. Print.

_____. *The Epistemology of the Closet.* California: U of California P, 1990. Print.

Seidman, Steven. *Beyond the Closet: The Transformation of Gay and Lesbian Life.* New York: Routledge, 2002. Print.

Shin, Andrew, and Barbara Judson. "Beneath the Black Aesthetic: James Baldwin's Primer of Black American Masculinity." *African American Review* 32.2 (1998): 247-61. *JSTOR.* Web. 3 Mar. 2014.

Somerville, Siobhan B. "Feminism, Queer Theory, and the Racial Closet." *Criticism* 52.2 (2010): 191-200. *JSTOR.* Web. 7 Aug. 2014.

_____. *Queering the Colorline: Race and the Invention of Homosexuality in American Culture.* Durham: Duke UP, 2000. Print.

Williams, Kemp. "The Metaphorical Construction of Sexuality in *Giovanni's Room" Literature and Homosexuality.* Ed. Michael Meyer. Amsterdam: Rodopi, 2000. 23-33. Print.

Zondervan NIV Study Bible. Full ref. ed. Kenneth L. Barker, gen. ed. Grand Rapids, MI: Zondervan, 2002. Print.

White Femininity and the Black Female Gaze: Internalized Oppression
Toni Morrison's novel *The Bluest Eye*_____

Julie Prebel

Introduction: Internalized Oppression and Racial Contempt

Toni Morrison, a writer with numerous literary laurels, including a Pulitzer Prize (1988) and a Nobel Prize for Literature (1993), was born Chloe Wofford in 1931 in Lorain, Ohio, the setting for her first novel, *The Bluest Eye*, published in 1970. Morrison has talked about the challenges of writing her first novel, especially in the 1960s when much of the fiction published by black writers was written by men and often focused on themes of black power and the black is beautiful movement—narrative themes that Morrison found inspiring and somewhat limiting. Morrison explains that the "assertion of racial beauty" in the black is beautiful cultural movement of the 1960s was a "reaction . . . against the damaging internalization of assumptions of immutable inferiority originating in an outside gaze" (*The Bluest Eye*, ix; hereafter *TBE*). The "outside gaze" to which Morrison refers is the gaze of the white male or white female, a way of looking at and denigrating African Americans through the perspective of white supremacy. While Morrison appreciated the freedom of no longer "looking through the [white] master's gaze" and instead being able to write from a black perspective, she questioned whether the black is beautiful theme might overlook black female experiences: "And I thought, 'Wait a minute. Before the guys get on the my-beautiful-black-queen wagon, let me tell you what it used to be like before you started that!'" (Bollen 2012). Thus, instead of a novel about black power and beauty, Morrison says she was "interested in reading a kind of book that I had never read before. I didn't know if such a book existed, but I had just never read it in 1964 when I started writing *The Bluest Eye*" (Parker 252).

In *The Bluest Eye*, Morrison focuses on the racial stigmas associated with appearance and beauty—and, more broadly, the contempt of blackness—and shows how the "demonization of an entire race could take root inside the most delicate member of society: a child, the most vulnerable member: a female" (*TBE*, Foreword xi). Morrison's novel depicts the devastating consequences of internalized racism and racist beauty standards primarily through the novel's central figure, eleven-year old Pecola Breedlove, and her desire for blue eyes, which she believes will transform her appearance from ugly to beautiful, her life from one of misery to happiness. Morrison notes that "implicit in [Pecola's] desire [is] racial self-loathing" (*TBE*, Foreword xi), reinforced by Pecola's desire to emulate the images of white womanhood/girlhood deemed beautiful and also by her community who sees her as abjectly black and ugly. Morrison directs the gaze of white supremacy on Pecola to demonstrate that "what racism does is create self-loathing, and it hurts. It can ruin you" (Bollen 2012). The story unfolds in 1941 from the perspective of the novel's main narrator, nine-year old Claudia MacTeer, who attempts to make sense of experiences, with Pecola at the center, that are "difficult to handle" (*TBE* 6). The most difficult of these experiences is Pecola's rape by her father, Cholly, which instead of garnering Pecola empathy from Claudia; Claudia's ten-year old sister, Frieda; or the Lorain community, only reinforces how they see her: as the epitome of ugliness and unacceptability. Ultimately, Claudia and others in the novel blame Pecola for what happens to her, believing that she "deserved our contempt" (*TBE* 205), while Pecola suffers the oppressive consequences of her own self-loathing and her community's disdain through her schizophrenia at the end of the novel.

This chapter will examine the ways that Pecola Breedlove not only internalizes white oppression as she seeks self-validation by trying to emulate whiteness, but she also becomes the embodiment of internalized oppression for those around her. At the end of the novel, deluded into believing she has the blue eyes she desired, Pecola becomes the manifestation of the history of violence and oppression both she and her community experience. In particular, the qualities that discredit and marginalize Pecola—her perceived blackness and ugliness—are qualities those around her seek to deflect, expel from the community, or make less visible in the construction of their own identities. Although Pecola's story compels the narrative, the novel also focuses on how other characters experience racial self-loathing brought about by the internalization of white oppression. Thus, as I will show in the reading that follows, Pecola's presence is a visual reminder of the white supremacist forms of oppression that she and the other characters internalize or fight against—and that Morrison highlights throughout the novel.

Narratives of White Privilege versus Historicized Oppression

Just as Pecola is simultaneously hyper-visible and unseen in the novel, so, too, is white oppression—in many forms—seen and unseen, or overt and covert. One of the ways that Morrison depicts *and* challenges narratives of white oppression is through her deconstruction of the idealized ideology of family, childhood, and community reflected in the excerpts from the Dick and Jane stories that open the novel and return at key moments throughout. William Elson's and William Gray's Dick and Jane series were early readers or primers (originating in the 1930s and popular in the 1940s) that aimed to teach reading literacy through the repetition of easy-to-learn sight words and simple stories focused on the title characters, Dick and Jane, their family, house, pets, and friends. Many literary critics of *The Bluest Eye* have commented on Morrison's reference to the Dick and Jane stories and noted that Morrison uses them to critique the racialized ideals and assumptions embedded in the Elson-Gray series. In particular, Morrison's Dick and Jane references demonstrate the dissimilarities between the white nuclear family as a nexus of American white privilege and what Debra T. Werrlein calls the "sharply different version of 1940s family and childhood" shown especially through the Breedloves (59). The Dick and Jane stories feature white, middle-class children in socially and economically stable families unaffected by history or present events of the time period, with images of American life that emphasize the seeming innocence and homogeneity of suburban families and communities. Werrlein notes that these stories "equate white privilege with a historyless version of Americanness," a "mythic homogeneity" that obscures the experiences of "poverty . . . and brutal history of racial persecution in the United States" (59-60), the latter of which Morrison reveals through the Breedlove family.

This contrast between the Elson-Gray version of the distinctly white American family and Morrison's emphasis on the history of oppression that shapes black family life can be seen in both her stylistic innovations and content revisions of the Dick and Jane stories. Morrison excerpts parts from the series, as shown in the opening pages of the novel, and presents what appears to be an idyllic description of family life: "Here is the house. It is green and white. It has a red door. It is very pretty. Here is the family. Mother, Father, Dick, and Jane live in the green-and-white house. They are very happy" (*TBE* 3). In contrast to this opening paragraph, which replicates the style and content of the original series, Morrison then disassembles the narrative, removing punctuation, compressing sentences, and squeezing words together in a way that results in a disordered or disjointed text: "Hereisthehouseitisgreenandwhiteit hasareddooritisveryprettyhereisthefamilymotherfatherdickand janeliveinthegreenandwhitehousetheyareveryhappy" (*TBE* 4). As shown in this stylistic contrast, which frames and introduces the novel, Morrison unravels the coherence of the family narrative presented in the Elson-Gray primers, "highlighting the meaninglessness of the Dick and Jane formula" (Werrlein 60) and illustrating the incompatibility of white, middle-class narratives and the experiences of poor blacks.

Morrison uses similarly fragmented phrases as epigraphs (of sorts) in key chapters in the novel, including when she introduces the Breedlove family and where they live, "HEREISTHEFAMILY MOTHERFATHERDICKANDJANETHEYLIVEINTHEGREEN ANDWHITEHOUSETHEYAREVERYH," (*TBE* 38). Instead of a pretty green and white house sheltering a happy, white family within, the Breedloves live in the front section of an abandoned store, in a space that "foists itself on the eye of the passerby in a manner that is both irritating and melancholy" (*TBE* 33). Along with foreclosing the possibility that this space is anything but undesirable, a site of despair, Morrison debunks the myth—implicit in narratives of white privilege like Dick and Jane—that poverty and family dysfunction are either non-existent or the result of easily changeable circumstances. We are told that "the Breedloves did not live in a storefront because they were having temporary difficulty adjusting to the cutbacks at the plant [where Cholly previously worked]," but instead "they lived there because they were poor and black, and they stayed there because they believed they were ugly" (*TBE* 38). In presenting the Breedloves in this way, Morrison not only disputes narratives of ideal families with possibilities of upward mobility, but she also suggests that poverty and race can disenfranchise and disempower families and individuals. The Breedloves internalize these feelings of powerlessness and worthlessness, isolating themselves because they are convinced they are socially undesirable. Morrison leaves no doubt that the Breedloves do not fit into the Dick and Jane model of an ideal family when Claudia describes how the MacTeer family takes in Pecola temporarily after the Breedloves are put "outdoors" when Cholly sets fire to the family's house. This displacement of Pecola and her family from their home is more than simply the inconvenience of needing to find a new place to live; as Claudia describes, to be "outdoors . . . was the real terror of life. . . . Outdoors was the end of something, an irrevocable, physical fact, defining and complementing our metaphysical condition" (*TBE* 17). As explained through Claudia, within the poor black community the "concreteness of being outdoors" reaffirms their social position as "a minority in both caste and class" and deepens the burden of their racial and class oppression (*TBE* 17).

In her appropriation of the Dick and Jane books, which notably "never feature nonwhite Americans," Morrison thus shows the stark contrasts between white narratives of home and family that portray "safe American childhoods that thrive in families that defy . . . hardships with economic and social stability" (Werrlein 56-58) versus the story of the Breedloves, who seem trapped in a racialized system of poverty that keeps them powerless and victimized by intersecting forms of oppression: class, race, and (as will be shown below) gender. In highlighting narratives of whiteness, as she does through her use of the disassembled Dick and Jane text, Morrison shows how the Breedlove family has "emerge[d] from histories of oppression" (Werrlein 61) and she attributes family degeneration and instability to a self-perpetuating structure in American society of racial violence and oppression.

Oppression as Self-Negation: Images of White Femininity and the "Adoring Black Female Gaze"

Morrison's chapter on Pauline Breedlove and her internalization of white ideals begins with another Dick and Jane fragment, "SEEMOTHERMOTHERISVERYNICEMOTHERWILLPLAY WITHJANEMOTHERLAUGHSLAUGHMOTHERLAUGHLA" (*TBE* 110), which highlights the contrast between the "shallow ahistoricism of the white text" (Werrlein 60) and Pauline's experiences of powerlessness. Pauline's sense of her oppression begins in early childhood, when an untreated wound from a rusty nail leaves her with a permanent and somewhat debilitating injury, a "foot that flopped when she walked," inducing her "general feeling of separateness and unworthiness" to take root, her sense that "she never felt at home anywhere, or that she belonged anyplace" (*TBE* 111). Pauline internalizes these feelings, which intensify after she and Cholly marry and move north from Kentucky to Ohio, and she "assigned herself a role in the scheme of things" after the birth of her children, becoming the "ideal servant" for a "well-to-do [white] family whose members were affectionate, appreciative, and generous" (*TBE* 126-127). The Fisher family exemplifies the ideal white familyhood represented in the Dick and Jane stories, living in a house with hot running water, embroidered linens, and well-stocked cupboards, and with a clean and pretty white daughter who is the antithesis of the ugliness Pauline sees in Pecola. As Pauline immerses herself in her work for the Fishers, she neglects her own home and family, redefining herself as the invaluable "Polly" and pushing her family further to the periphery of her existence: "More and more she neglected her house, her children, her man—they were like the afterthoughts one has just before sleep, the early-morning and late-evening edges of her day, the dark edges that made the daily life with the Fishers lighter, more delicate, more lovely" (*TBE*

127). Pauline's work for the Fishers and her attempt to assimilate herself into the "lighter" and whiter world they represent "provides her with the semblance of acceptance and community she cannot find or create in her own home or neighborhood," as Jane Kuenz persuasively argues (425).

In much the same way, Pauline finds it difficult to reconcile the everyday realities of her home life with the idealized images of white domesticity and white womanhood she sees in the movies. Like her retreat to the Fisher home, Hollywood films provide her an escape from the dreariness of her life, as Pauline reflects: "the onliest time I be happy seem like when I was in the picture show. . . . Them pictures gave me a lot of pleasure, but it made coming home hard" (*TBE* 123). Not only does Pauline emulate the experiences of the white female film stars portrayed on the screen, she also tries to alter her appearance to look like them. As many critics of the novel have noted, Pauline's admiration of whiteness on the screen and her internalization of white beauty standards have devastating consequences—both for her and for Pecola. Instead of providing Pauline with an escape from the facts of her existence, ultimately the images she consumes at the movie theater reinforce an idealized life that "she does not now have and which she has little, if any, chance of ever enjoying in any capacity other than that of the 'ideal servant'" (Kuenz 425).

In her analysis of black women and film spectatorship, bell hooks argues that the proliferation of images of white women in film and other media perpetuates a negation of black female subjectivity. hooks explains that often, when black women view conventional Hollywood films, they have to "forget racism" and instead adopt an "adoring black female gaze," a way of looking at the projected images of white womanhood on the screen that brings about both viewing pleasure and self-negation (120). In her reading of *The Bluest Eye*, hooks argues that in Pauline Morrison "constructs a portrait of the black female spectator" whose "gaze is the masochistic look of victimization" (120). In other words, Pauline's pleasure in viewing the images of white womanhood on the screen, and her desire to transform herself into the white women she sees, involves a painful disavowal of her own identity as a black woman. Morrison reinforces this point by describing how Pauline's desire to emulate the images of white beauty she sees on the screen "ended in disillusion"; instead of finding an escape by watching movies, Pauline "collected self-contempt by the heap" (*TBE* 122). In Morrison's novel, Pauline represents the ways that black female spectators "develop looking relations" that "den[y] the 'body' of the black female so as to perpetuate white supremacy" (hooks 118), mainly through narratives and images that reinforce the desirability of whiteness and white womanhood.

Pauline is also complicit in perpetuating this self-contempt and self-negation by projecting onto Pecola her beliefs that physical beauty must conform to white standards or ideals in order to be valued. Even before Pecola is born, Pauline imagines a child—and a childbirth experience—that will be "just like them white women" (*TBE* 125). However, Pauline is instead denigrated at the hospital by racist doctors who insist that "these here [black] women" (*TBE* 124) do not need the same attention or care as white women in labor and is disappointed when she sees her daughter does not have the fair skin and light eyes of her seeming namesake, Peola, from a film Pauline admires, *Imitation of Life*. Pauline grows to despise Pecola, who "looked so different from what [she] thought," with "tangled black puffs of rough wool to comb. . . . Lord she was ugly," in contrast to the fair-haired beauty of the Fisher girl (*TBE* 125-127). Thus, Pauline projects onto Pecola her own internalized feelings and experiences of oppression, while Pecola learns from a young age to recognize her perceived ugliness and to accept Pauline's fantasy that "she might one day wake up blonde and blue-eyed, not ugly and black" (Rosenberg 439).

Whereas Pauline settles down into being ugly in a world that associates beauty with whiteness, Pecola's "mantle" of ugliness acts as a main source of her isolation and oppression: "she hid behind hers. Concealed, veiled, eclipsed—peeping out from behind the shroud very seldom" (*TBE* 39). Pecola seeks validation not just in being seen as beautiful by others, but also in being seen at all; she is simultaneously overlooked and the visual object of disgust when people do notice her. As Morrison describes, when Pecola is subject to the gaze of others, "there is the total absence of human recognition—the glazed separateness" of her from them (*TBE* 49). Pecola internalizes the disinterest and disgust others have for her, associating her apparent ugliness with her blackness. For example, when she goes to the corner store to purchase candy, she sees in the glance of the white, male shop owner a look of "distaste," which she "has seen . . . lurking in the eyes of all white people" (*TBE* 49). Pecola concludes that "the distaste must be for her, her blackness," which she understands as immutable: "her blackness is static and dread" (*TBE* 49). Pecola believes that acquiring blue eyes will enable her to conceal her blackness, to "deflect the racializing scrutiny of white culture" (Berlant 111), and be accepted by whites and her black community.

Like Pauline, Pecola attempts to enact this self- and social transformation by consuming images of whiteness: in this case, quite literally through acts of ingestion. For example, as Pecola unwraps the Mary Jane candies, which are imprinted with the image of a little girl with "smiling white face . . . blond hair [and] blue eyes," she feels her shame brought on by "an awareness of her worth" during her interaction with the shop owner ebb away. Just as Pauline escapes into the images of white womanhood projected on the film screen, Pecola escapes into the "world of clean comfort" symbolized in the image of white girlhood on the candy (*TBE* 50). However, in this case, Pecola does more than simply look at the image in another example of hooks' adoring black female gaze; she consumes this image and, in doing so, intensifies her visual pleasure. Pecola moves from consuming through her gaze to eating the candy, and for her "to eat the candy is somehow to eat the eyes, eat Mary Jane. Love Mary Jane. Be Mary Jane" (*TBE* 50). Pecola wants to do more than to pass herself off as white; by eating the candies, she believes she can become white, complete with the blue eyes she so desires, in an act of "curious transubstantiation" (Kuenz 427) that leaves Pecola with a sexualized feeling that eating the candies "brought her nine lovely orgasms with Mary Jane" (*TBE* 50). In a similar act of consuming images of white girlhood, during her brief stay with the MacTeers, Pecola drinks large amounts of milk from a blue-and-white cup imprinted with the image of white child star, Shirley Temple, popular in films of the mid-1930s. Pecola does not consume large amounts of milk simply out of "greediness" for the milk itself; instead, she "was fond of the Shirley Temple cup and took every opportunity to drink milk out of it just to handle and see sweet Shirley's face" (*TBE* 23). Pecola's acts of drinking the milk from the Shirley Temple cup reaffirm her emulation of images of white, blue-eyed girlhood and her belief that by consuming these images, or by "swallow[ing] its whiteness" (Rosenberg 441), she might effect a self-transformation from black and ugly to white and beautiful.

These acts of gratification come at the expense of Pecola's self-alienation from her own body or, more destructively, a "self-annihilation" (Werrlein 67). Pecola's desire to "be" Mary Jane (or Shirley Temple) reflects her desire not to be seen, at least not in the way others see her, as black and ugly. This desire to "cast off [her] visible body" is a form of self-erasure, a way to make herself disappear in order to take on an "identity [that] might be inhabited safely" (Berlant 111). Pecola's desire to dematerialize her physical body is especially strong during times of violence at home, as she wills her body to disappear, part by part, so she might remove herself from the oppressiveness of her family: "Little parts of her body faded away. . . . Her fingers went, one by one; then her arms disappeared all the way to the elbow . . ." (*TBE* 45). Pecola's attempts to make herself invisible to the violence around her fail, though, because "try as she might . . . could never get her eyes to disappear" (*TBE* 45). Pecola believes that if only "those eyes of hers were different," then her parents would no longer be violent and "do bad things in front of [her]" (*TBE* 46) or *to* her.

The Violence of White Oppression and the Consumption of Blackness

Pecola's loss of selfhood, symbolized in part through her visual and physical acts of consumption, is ultimately irrevocable when Cholly rapes her. Pecola never recovers physically or mentally from being raped; although she loses the pregnancy, one of the physical manifestations of the rape, her schizophrenia at the end of the novel signals her complete subjugation. Although it is difficult to read Cholly's rape of his daughter as anything but horrifically violent, critics of Morrison's novel have noted that his destructive impulses and actions are the result of his internalization of white oppression. For example, Elisabeth Mermann-Jozwiak argues that Cholly's actions reveal the displacement of his experiences of "emasculation and powerlessness" (195) brought on by his history with white men and as the object of a threatening white male gaze. When Cholly's first teenaged sexual encounter with a girl named Darlene is interrupted by two white men with flashlights and guns, he is forced to "simulate" under the threat of violence what was at first an act of pleasure. While the white men shine their lights on and point their guns at the terrified couple, Cholly forces himself through the motions of a sex act, redirecting his shame and fear of white violence towards Darlene: "he hated her. He almost wished he could do it—hard, long, and painfully, he hated her so much" (*TBE* 148). First Darlene, then Pauline, and finally Pecola become the "scapegoat[s] for Cholly's disgust with the female body as well as his own self-hatred and fear of emasculation" (Mermann-Jozwiak 195). As disturbing and abhorrent as his actions are, Cholly's abuse of women, including his own daughter, can thus be read in the context of his own victimization and oppression.

Whereas Pauline and Pecola experience their ugliness through their physical embodiment, Cholly's ugliness, as Morrison suggests, is enacted more through his "behavior" and is the "result of despair, dissipation, and violence" (*TBE* 38). Despite differences in how feelings of powerlessness manifest in these characters, there are some similarities in how they experience and respond to the effects of their internalization of white oppression: especially in terms of tropes of vision and of eating. Morrison juxtaposes Cholly's rape of Pecola with the story of his sexual encounter with Darlene and with his first physical encounter with Pauline, highlighting the intersections between vulnerability, visual spectatorship, and bodily ingestion. When Cholly returns home drunk, he first watches Pecola as she washes dishes, and though initially he "saw her dimly and could not tell what he saw or what he felt," his sight—and his feelings—soon become a confused mixture of "revulsion, guilt, pity, then love" (*TBE* 161). Instead of responding with compassion for Pecola, though, Cholly blames her for his feelings of inadequacy and especially for the revulsion she inspires in him—as he does with Darlene earlier. He reads Pecola's body, "hunched" as if "crouching from a permanent and unrelieved blow," as a physical "accusation" against him, prompting his feelings of "guilt and impotence" (*TBE* 161). These are similar feelings to what he experiences with Darlene, and he has the same reaction to enact violence against Pecola: "he wanted to break her neck—but tenderly" (*TBE* 161). His gesture towards tenderness recalls his first meeting with Pauline, when he took her maimed foot in his hand and "gently nibble[d] . . . on her calf with his teeth" in what he recalls as an act of "tenderness, a protectiveness" (*TBE* 162). Cholly's confused emotions and "mixture of his memories of Pauline" are triggered when he sees Pecola unconsciously scratch her calf with her toe, and his assault of her begins as he "nibbled at the back of her leg. His mouth trembled at the firm sweetness of her flesh" (*TBE* 162).

Just as Pecola experiences a sort of erotic, sexualized pleasure when she eats the Mary Jane candies, here Morrison seems to recall that confused mixture of pleasure and consumption when Cholly rapes Pecola. These acts of consumption highlight eating not as a source of nourishment, but more as a way to mitigate feelings of shame and inadequacy brought on by histories, narratives, and images of white supremacy. In her analysis of narratives and images of white racism in the nineteenth-century, Kyla Wazana Tompkins focuses on "the relationship between eating and racial identity" (1). Although Tompkins' focus is on white consumption of "racist images [depicting] the edible and delicious black subject" (1), her point that the "white relationship to the black body" is often depicted "through the metaphor of consumption" (115) offers another way to interpret acts of ingestion in Morrison's novel. As Tompkins notes, the "mouth" both "reveals vulnerability" and "at other times it is a sign of aggression" (4); this is clearly the case in Cholly's acts of nibbling, especially with Pecola, when his feelings of powerlessness, either to act on his own behalf when he was "small, black, helpless" against "big, white, armed men," or on behalf of his daughter whose "young, helpless, hopeless presence" rouses him to "fury" (*TBE* 151, 161), quickly turn to an act of aggression that destroys his daughter mentally and physically. Cholly has no means of connecting with his daughter—"What could he do for her—ever? What give her? What say to her?" (*TBE* 161)—and so, in what is unquestionably the novel's most violent and horrific act, he attempts to close the gap between himself and Pecola through her flesh. Cholly's acts of ingestion are notably different than Pecola's, as he is not consuming images of whiteness; however, Morrison links his actions, like Pecola's and Pauline's, to the internalization of white oppression. Moreover, when Pauline later finds Pecola unconscious on the kitchen floor, she beats Pecola nearly to death; Pauline's and Cholly's actions demonstrate "that histories of suffering not only debilitate parents, but turn them from nurturers into oppressors" (Werrlein 61-62), as they project the violence of their own internalized oppression onto the racialized female body of their child.

Conclusion: Pecola as Scapegoat and Black Resistance to Oppression

Pecola is thus both singular as a character and representative of the oppression and victimization of her family and her black community. As Mermann-Jozwiak notes, "her body is written on by discourses of power and domination manufactured in a white supremacist society" (189). Morrison depicts other characters in the novel exploiting and abusing Pecola because they cannot "critique the [white] culture that systematically excludes them" (Gillan 285). For example, at the end of the novel, as Claudia reflects on her own complicity in the "damage done" to Pecola, she acknowledges that the community used Pecola as a scapegoat, noting that Pecola represented "all of our waste which we dumped on her and which she absorbed" (*TBE* 204-205). Claudia recognizes that the community's hostility towards Pecola is linked to a sense of collective self-hatred brought on by experiences with "the land of the entire country [which] was hostile" towards them (*TBE* 206). By projecting their internalized oppression onto Pecola, the community deflects the social and cultural circumstances of their subjugation and feels virtuous and beautiful in contrast to the irrevocably damaged Pecola: "All of us . . . felt so wholesome after we cleaned ourselves on her. We were so beautiful when we stood astride her ugliness . . . her guilt sanctified us, her pain made us glow with health. . . . We honed our egos on her, padded our characters with her frailty" (*TBE* 205). At the end of the novel, while the community appears to move on from the tragedy of the Breedloves, Pecola becomes trapped in her mind, deluded that she has the blue eyes she desired, yet hopelessly "beating the air" like a "grounded bird, intent on the blue void it could not reach" (*TBE* 204).

While Morrison's novel highlights the devastation enacted on individuals and communities through the internalization of white oppression, it is important not to overlook instances where Morrison offers the possibility of agentive black personhood. As shown throughout this essay, the novel can be read (as Morrison intends) as a depiction of oppression brought about by the history and continued perpetuation of white supremacy; yet, there are also times when characters act out against such structures by refusing to consume the damaging effects of white narratives or visual images. Claudia, for example, "in marked contrast to Pecola Breedlove's surrender to Western values, refuses to be tamed into conventional behavior" (Rosenberg 440) by accepting narratives and images that privilege white beauty standards. Instead of emulating the image of Shirley Temple, which Pecola consumes eagerly, Claudia's response is an "unsullied hatred for all the Shirley Temples of the world" (*TBE* 19). Claudia's hatred of white images of girlhood-womanhood manifests in her destruction of the white dolls she receives as Christmas gifts; instead of embracing the "blue-eyed, yellow-haired, pink-skinned" white dolls, which "the world had agreed . . . was what every girl child treasured," Claudia "had only one desire: to dismember it" (*TBE* 20). Claudia recognizes that her desire to deconstruct the dolls reflects her refusal to assimilate to the standards of beauty they represent, and she notes that the "truly horrifying thing was the transference of the same impulses to little white girls" (*TBE* 22). This transference suggests Claudia's ability to see whiteness, in images and in reality, as something to be destroyed with "disinterested violence" (*TBE* 23) and to be deconstructed as a damaging mythology.

In her resistance to whiteness, Claudia represents bell hooks' concept of the "oppositional gaze," which, in contrast to the adoring black female gaze (of Pauline and Pecola), is enacted by "black women spectators" who "actively choose not to identify with [an] imaginary [white] subject because such identification was dis-enabling" (hooks 122). Claudia's refusal to take pleasure in looking at white female images positions her as a "critical spectator" who "look[s] from a location that disrupt[s]" the narrative of white supremacy (122). At the end of the novel, Claudia appears to "survive intact," more in "control of her destiny" (Rosenberg 440), which suggests her greater success than Pecola and other characters in resisting the consumption and internalization of white oppression. Claudia's desire to dismember, like the deconstructed Dick and Jane narrative, opens up a reading of the novel as a critical response to white power and supremacy. In *The Bluest Eye*, Toni Morrison thus gives us a multidimensional story of both despair and hope, as she holds out the possibility for black resistance to white oppression.

Works Cited

Berlant, Lauren. "National Brands/National Body: Imitation of Life." *Comparative American Identities: Race, Sex, and Nationality in the Modern Text*, edited by Hortense J. Spillers, Routledge, 1991.

Bollen, Christopher. "Toni Morrison." *Interview Magazine*, 11 May 2012, www.interviewmagazine.com/culture/toni-morrison/.

Gillan, Jennifer. "Focusing on the Wrong Front: Historical Displacement, the Maginot Line, and *The Bluest Eye*." *African American Review*, vol. 36, no. 2 (Summer 2002), pp. 283-298.

Hoby, Hermione. "Toni Morrison: 'I'm Writing for Black People . . . I Don't Have to Apologise'." *The Guardian*, 25 Apr. 2015, www.theguardian.com/books/2015/apr/25/toni-morrison-books-interview-god-help-the-child/.

hooks, bell. *Black Looks: Race and Representation*. Routledge, 2015, www.amazon.com/Black-Looks-Representation-Bell-Hooks/dp/0896084337/.

Kuenz, Jane. "*The Bluest Eye*: Notes on History, Community, and Black Female Subjectivity." *African American Review*, vol. 27, no. 3, 1993, p. 421, doi:10.2307/3041932/.

Mermann-Jozwiak, Elisabeth. "Re-Membering the Body: Body Politics in Toni Morrison's *The Bluest Eye*." *Lit: Literature Interpretation Theory*, vol. 12, no. 2, 2001, pp. 189–203, doi:10.1080/10436920108580287/.

Morrison, Toni. *The Bluest Eye*. Vintage International, 2007.

_____. *Playing in the Dark: Whiteness and the Literary Imagination*. Vintage, 2015.

Parker, Bettye J. "Complexity: Toni Morrison's Women—An Interview Essay." *Sturdy Black Bridges: Visions of Black Women in Literature*, edited by Roseanne P. Bell, Bettye J. Parker, and Beverly Guy-Sheftall, Anchor Books, 1979.

Rosenberg, Ruth. "Seeds in Hard Ground: Black Girlhood in *The Bluest Eye*." *Black American Literature Forum*, vol. 21, no. 4, 1987, p. 435, doi:10.2307/2904114/.

Tompkins, Kyla Wazana. *Racial Indigestion: Eating Bodies in the 19th Century*. NYUP, 2012.

Werrlein, Debra T. "Not So Fast, Dick and Jane: Reimagining Childhood and Nation in *The Bluest Eye*." *MELUS: Multi-Ethnic Literature of the United States*, vol. 30, no. 4, Jan. 2005, pp. 53–72. doi:10.1093/melus/30.4.53/.

Not Just Any Ol' Injun: The (Re)Appropriation and Alteration of Native American Stereotypes
Louise Erdrich's novel *Tracks*_____

Robyn Johnson

> We started dying before the snow, and like the snow, we continued to
> fall. (Erdrich 1)`

Many critics analyze Native American[1] literature through a postcolonial lens, examining the devastation to family and culture as a result of the loss of land, emasculation of Native men, and commoditization of culture. Often Natives Americans are represented as self-destructive victims of postcolonialism, who can only save themselves through finding themselves, as seen through the works of Sherman Alexie and Janet Campbell. The postcolonial lens is justified by the extensive stereotyping and abuse of Native American characters in American media and literature, dating back to around the 1700s.

Born from the political and literary minds of a developing America, the stereotypical images of the Savage and Noble Savage filled a psychological need of colonial Americans. Shari Huhndorf explains that "the self-aggrandizing tales that mainstream America told themselves about the nation's origins—supporting opportunities for Indian-hating" justified "Europe's bloody conquest of the Americas with fictions of Natives peoples' aggression and inherent malevolence" (20). The Savage became an image that created fear in colonists and new Americans, justifying the extermination of Native Americans. While the Savage became a staple of American mythology, it lacked a romantic element. It was one-dimensional, simply a blood-thirsty bestial man who slaughtered and raped indiscriminately. So, in the nineteenth century, American Romantic writers came to believe that it lacked the finesse needed to support the American identity. American Romantics, individuals who preferred emotion and instinct over reason, sought to rewrite history in a manner that made America's conquest less of a bloody battle with the Savages, and more of a rightful inheritance. It was through the creation of the Noble Savage that the American's right to inherit gained momentum. Romantics created the Noble Savage to embody the best qualities of a Native: physical prowess and beauty, adaptability, connection to the land, and a romantic sense of his own extinction. It is the romantic sense of extinction that allows American to "rightfully" inherit America. At the end of numerous Romantic novels,[2] the Noble Savage bows, leaving to die in the wilderness, but not before bestowing his land and rights to the colonists whom he has fought to save. This bestowment grants colonists the rights to America, making them the inheritors. Immediately, the stark contrast between the Savage and the Noble Savage become clear.

Philip Deloria explains that "Savage Indians served Americans as oppositional figures against whom one might imagine a civilized national Self," while the Noble Savage, "[c]oded as freedom . . . proved equally attractive, setting up a "have-the-cake-and-eat-it-too" dialectic of simultaneous desire and repulsion" (3-4). According to Deloria, the Savage served to highlight American's civilized nature. Compared to a murderous, brutal Savage, Americans were educated and controlled, knowing what was right and what was wrong. Deloria continues to explain that the Noble Savage, however, served as a critique of Western society, emphasizing freedom and connecting to the land. While the Savage encouraged conquest, the Noble Savage encouraged inheritance. Through such tactics, a rich and inaccurate belief system grew, claiming that Native men fell into one of two categories, the Savage, who was a threat to women and children, and the Noble Savage, who, although strong and brave, was doomed to extinction.

With the creation of readily available books, film, and television, these stereotypes were further expanded upon to include the stereotypical images of the Authentic Indian, the Indian Princess, the Chief, the Squaw, and the Warrior. Such images were propagated by popular films from the early 1900s, such as *Heart of an Indian* (1912), which "showed Indians as sensitive people"; *The Battle of Elderbrush Gulch* (1914), which "presented the Indians as absolute savages"; *The Vanishing American* (1925); and *Broken Arrow* (1950), which featured "a 'noble savage' stereotype" (*Redface!*). Such media resulted in male Natives becoming labeled as one of four possible stereotypes, but created a belief that female Natives only fell into two categories: the Princess or the Squaw: "She was a dangerous and seductive threat to the white frontiersman, or she was the faceless, dutiful figure tagging along behind her buck with a papoose in tow. . . . The princesses of celluloid fame generally served the white man, fell in love with him and died tragically" (*RedFace!*). Through such films, American media created a patriarchal society with dominate males and submissive, tempting females out of hundreds of tribes, some which were matriarchal.[3] The result is inequality for Natives as they fight the pervasive stereotype which looks them into a fictional past.

Some authors have taken subtle, but important stances on colonialism and the use of Native stereotypes. While white colonists and Americans still possess most of blame for the destruction of Native Americans, a few postmodern authors have begun approaching the conversation with an altered view. Rather than seeing the destruction of Native Americans as solely the fault of whites, some have begun creating fiction that exhibits that the fault lies in both whites and Natives.

Louise Erdrich, renowned Native American author, tackles the issue of colonization in several of her works, focusing on life of the Chippewa people, both on and off the reservation. *Tracks*, the 1988 prequel to several of her fictional books, follows the lives of three Chippewa members. Through the narration of Pauline and Nanapush, the story of Fleur and those she meets is explored. Using hard realism, Erdrich paints a world of starvation, survival, and betrayal with distinct characters. It is these distinct characters that illuminate the unique approach that Erdrich has taken to Native stereotypes and colonialism.[4] Through Pauline and Fleur, Erdrich explores the injustice and inequality that Native, specifically Native women, face. In an unusual approach, Erdrich appropriates the traditionally masculine stereotypes of the Savage and Noble Savage and applies them to Pauline and Fleur. By applying the constructed male stereotypes to women, Erdrich shows that Native stereotypes of American mythology are not naturally occurring, but rather these stereotypes are placed upon and reproduced by Native and white societies.

Pauline's Savagery

Tracks possesses a dual narration, revealing the story of Fleur through the eyes of Nanapush and Pauline. Nanapush, the comic relief, is Fleur's adoptive father figure, known for his humorous and mischievous ways. As both a storyteller and comic relief, Nanapush represents Erdrich's version of the Authentic Indian. Created to represent what "real" Indianness looked like, Authentic Indians are generally old men, who tell stories and maintain the Indian ways. As the Authentic Indian, Nanapush represents the old ways, acting as a teacher and guide to the younger Chippewa. His "authentic-ness" is established within the first two pages of the book. He tells Lulu, his granddaughter,

> I guided the last buffalo hunt. I saw the last bear shot. I trapped the last beaver with a pelt of more than two years' growth. I spoke aloud the words of the government treaty, and refused to sign the settlement papers that would take away our woods and lake. I axed the last birch that was older than I, and I saved the last Pillager. (2)

In this excerpt, Nanapush illustrates his "authentic-ness" by establishing himself as present for the large events in Chippewa history. Due to excessive hunting, animals, like buffalos, bears, and beavers, sacred animals to the Chippewa, have become endangered and extinct. The idea of extinction is continued by the mention of the "last birch" and the "last Pillager," which insinuates that not only was Nanapush alive to see the world when there were many birch trees and the Pillager family flourished, but that he has outlived them all. By referring to these extinct entities, Nanapush tells readers he lived before the colonists took over Chippewa land. It also informs readers that he is a traditional Chippewa man, who is skilled in hunting and trapping, furthering his authenticity. His voiced resistance to United

State government also supports his "Authentic Indian" identity as he resists changes, holding on to the past and old ways.

Through this imagery, Erdrich is quickly and solidly establishing Nanapush as the Authentic Indian. However, Erdrich also uses Nanapush to establish her pattern of appropriation. Instead of being a "pure" version of the Native stereotype, Nanapush is a hybrid of the Authentic Indian and Chippewa trickster, who shares his name. As a trickster character, Nanapush talks incessantly and is sexually suggestive, while simultaneously trying to teach and guide Lulu in the "authentic" ways of the Chippewa. Yet Nanapush's role as Authentic Indian and trickster acts only as a base line to see Erdrich's pattern of appropriation and manipulation. His story and how he came to be such a hybrid is never explored or explained. Yet his narration and presence does significantly add to the development of other Native stereotypes in the text. Despite his efforts to appear as a wise teacher, Nanapush plays an active role in the creation of the "saved" Savage through his unfair treatment of Pauline.

Pauline's role in *Tracks* has been analyzed as an example of Natives who wish to assimilate. Critics have focused on her conversion to Catholicism, her envy of Fleur, and her mixed blood line. Michelle Hessler dedicates her essay, "Catholic Nuns and Ojibwa Shamans: Pauline and Fleur in Louise Erdrich's 'Tracks,'" to discussing the decisions and events that leads to Pauline's radical Catholicism and Fleur's dedication to the Chippewa ways. While Hessler admits that Pauline is treated as an outcast, the main motivation for her conversion is associated with her desire to be "all white." Annette Van Dyke also explores the bloodlines of Pauline and Fleur in her essay, showing how Pauline's bloodline causes her to be treated as an outsider, despite her own spiritual power. It is this outsider status that Daniel Cornell claims makes Pauline not a liar, as many in the book view her, but a character that "takes up a position that in a male authored order belongs solely to men: she demands the equality of a constituting gaze. . . . It is not lies that she constructs but her own right to look" (52).

Cornell's point that Pauline takes on a male position is a point this essay agrees with. However, the male position that Pauline takes up is not one that she necessarily chooses. Rather than just being a symbol of feminine power or assimilation, Pauline represents the Savage Indian, who is "saved" by Catholicism. Due to her obvious outsider status, Pauline faces ridicule and alienation, becoming the "beast" that the people around her already believe she is. Through the events of *Tracks*, Pauline grows from a child to an adult, developing into her role as Savage and later the "saved" Savage because of the inequality she faces from the white and Native societies.

To facilitate Pauline's transformation to the Savage Indian, Erdrich first aligns Pauline with the Savage Indian through basic characteristics. Similar to how Nanapush's age and storytelling aligns him with the Authentic Indian, Pauline's physical appearance ties her to the Savage Indian. On the most basic level, the Savage Indian is a dark, unattractive male, whose physical appearance mirrors his internal evil. While Pauline does not start out as "evil," her natural physical appearance already lies her closer to the Savage Indian than the Noble Savage, who is renowned for physical beauty. During our first introduction to Pauline, she admits, "I wanted to be like my mother, who showed her half-white. I wanted to be like my grandfather, pure Canadian" (14). By saying this, Pauline clearly illustrates her desire to be white. Pauline's mother, readers discover through this confession, has light-colored skin from her father (Pauline's grandfather), who is Canadian, not Chippewa. Instead, Pauline describes herself as dark, dingy, and plain. Her lack of physical beauty makes Pauline "invisible." She says, "I blended into the stained brown walls, a skinny big-nosed girl with staring eyes" (16). Pauline tells readers of her physical plainness and how it made her invisible to the people of Argus. Due to her invisibility, Pauline sees and hears the ugliness of the people around her, until she "knew everything" (16). Her plainness is only emphasized by her close relation to Fleur, who is deemed as a great beauty. Yet despite Pauline's claim that her plainness is useful, she clearly desires to be "whiter" and acknowledged.

This desire is critical to Erdrich's appropriation of Native stereotypes. In addition to his physical unattractiveness, the Savage Indian is a male character who hates the whites and acts in barbaric ways, often killing as many whites as he can. Through Cornell's argument, it is possible to view Pauline as a "masculine" female, allowing for an easier transition of the Savage stereotype to a woman. Yet, Erdrich's manipulation of the Native American stereotype goes beyond simply turning the male role into a female. While using the physical plainness as a starting place, Erdrich creates a female Savage who breaks tradition by resenting her Native blood, allowing Erdrich to claim the stereotype and rewrite it. Part of the rewrite is that instead of being a single dimensional character that only thinks about murdering whites, Erdrich's Savage is emotionally conflicted about race. Despite voicing a deep dislike of her Native blood, there is evidence that Pauline's true feelings are the exact opposite. In several places, Pauline voices a desire to be among the Chippewa people. After she is sent to Argus, Pauline says, "I tried to stop myself from remembering what it was like to have companions, to have my mother and sisters around me, but Fleur came to us that June, I remembered" (15). Despite her belief that she "was made for better," Pauline secretly desires to be among her people, which is why she originally attaches to Fleur. At this point in the story, Pauline is merely a fifteen-year-old girl, rebelling against her family. Her hidden desire to be Chippewa, not white, hints at her Savage stereotype origins and even ensures her descent into savagery when her true desires are never met. In addition, the treatment Pauline receives through the story, proves she will never be accepted as a Chippewa and pushes her towards savage characteristics.

Yet Pauline's savageness is not innate. It comes from the exclusion that she faces both in the white and Chippewa community. According to Hessler, "the white girls in Argus either ridicule or ignore her [Pauline]" (40). The treatment of a Native by whites is nothing new in Native literature, but it is the treatment of Pauline by other Natives that proves Erdrich's belief that stereotypes are supported and furthered by both whites and Natives. The Savage Indian is an image that was created out of fear of the unknown and "unlike." As mentioned before, the Savage is deemed as unattractive, dangerous, and violent to the whites' way of life. Erdrich's Savage, Pauline, represents the same threats, but to whites and Natives.

Pauline's father warns her of other Natives before she goes to Argus. He tells her "You'll fade out there. . . . You won't be an Indian once you return" (14). Initially his words seem to warn Pauline about assimilation, but he is actually warning her of how other Natives will perceive her. Upon her return from Argus, Pauline is met with isolation and abuse. Nanapush continually criticizes and isolates her in the Native community. He voices the communal belief about Pauline's lack of belonging when he says, "She was, to my mind, an unknown mixture of ingredients, like pale bannock that sagged or hardened. We never knew what to call her, or where she fit or how to think when she was around. So, we tried to ignore her . . . " (39). Pauline does not fit into the tribe's idea of Native, but she is also not white. Therefore, she is something that cannot be labeled or placed, which makes her dangerous and unknowable. Nanapush blames, in part, Pauline's inability to fit in with her lack of physical beauty: "Because she was unnoticeable, homely if it must be said, Pauline schemed to gain attention by telling odd tales that created damage" (39). Even though Nanapush is a storyteller himself, he deems the stories that Pauline tells as damaging and dangerous, the result of her need for attention. This passage is important because it emphasizes Pauline's lack of physical beauty as the source of her "badness." Her skin is too dark to be white, but she is too homely to be appreciated as a Chippewa, unlike Fleur. In this instance, Nanapush aligns her internal worth with her external appearance, just as the Savage Indian is. It appears no matter how Pauline tries to be "good," her physical appearance marks her as a "bad person," showing how the Natives, along with the whites, are supporting and furthering the Savage stereotype.

When she first returns to the reservation, Pauline attempts to fit in and be honest. Yet when she is honest, others still do not believe her. Nanapush says, "That is all to say that the only people who believed Pauline's stories were the ones who loved the dirt" (39). Associating Pauline with dirt lowers her status and reliability in the tribe. They view her as less than themselves. While she is Native to the whites, Pauline is white to the Natives: "'Go, go!' he [Nanapush] said. 'You're more and more like the whites who never wash themselves clean!'" (153). As Pauline is punishing herself through physical suffering, Nanapush and many other members of the tribe take this chance to ridicule her. Her physical ugliness continues to reflect their views of her, rather than her internal ugliness. Instead of seeing her actions as a call for help, the Chippewa use it as an excuse to ignore and banish her to the edges of their society.

Pauline is fully aware of her position in the tribe, driving her growing savagery. She first tries to assimilate into the tribe, claiming, "I thought I must get married, must find myself a husband. I thought that the reason I was not wanted was just that I was alone. So, I cast around the village" (72). Desperate for acceptance, Pauline places herself out there in a vulnerable manner, which Napoleon abuses. As an older man, Napoleon takes advantage of Pauline's youth, using her in an inappropriate sexual relationship. This relationship gains Pauline more shame and ridicule, opposite of her desires. Therefore, she continues to try to find a person who would want her. Envious of Eli and Fleur's relationship, she reaches out to Eli and Fleur, only to be rejected as she is by the rest of the tribe. Despite Fleur's usual kindness, Pauline perceives that "Fleur underestimated me, thought so little about me it was almost like being despised" (76). Pauline's resentment to being ignored and rejected grows so that even those who are kind to her, like Fleur, become enemies. When she attempts to seduce Eli and fails, Pauline says, "So I both turned from him and desired him, in hate" (77). Pauline's feelings about Eli reflect her transformation and its roots.

Through her continued abuse, mental and physical, Pauline's sense of affection, justice, and life becomes warped. She desires unhealthy relationships, blaming those who are kind, like Fleur, and turning to violence for attention and retribution. Pauline's behavior becomes increasingly violent and savage as her isolation increases, until she is the Savage Indian, killing both whites and Natives. The external ugliness that the Natives and whites place upon her becomes internalized, and she becomes what they have always viewed her as: a Savage. Erdrich shows how Pauline's forced isolation begins to wear on Pauline's psyche. Starting at fifteen, Pauline begins to internalize the prejudices, and this manifests as an obsession with death. Pauline tells us that "Sometimes in my head I have dreams I could not shake. I saw my sisters and my mother swaying in the branches, buried too high to reach, wrapped in lace I never hooked" (15). This dream shows death metaphorically in several ways. First, Pauline is seeing the death of her Chippewa heritage revealed through her mother and sisters, who would traditionally pass their knowledge on to Pauline. Due to Pauline's life in Argus, Pauline will never learn the Chippewa traditions from her family. Second, Pauline is not among those who are dead, she is an outsider observing the deaths. The fact that she "never hooked the lace," emphasizes her lack of participation in the death ceremony, highlighting her outsider status. In this, Pauline recognizes her own guilt at rejecting her Native blood, but it also the internalization of the rejection she feels from her tribe.

Death becomes Pauline's only method of connecting with the Chippewa tribe. Unable to be accepted as a normal member, Pauline adopts and adapts to the negative view they place upon her and immerses herself in death. She views death as something that makes her different: "I had the merciful scavenger's heart. I became devious and holy, dangerously meek and mild. I wore the nuns' castoffs, followed in Bernadette's tracks, entered each house where death was about to come and then made death welcome" (69). Through comparing her heart to that of a scavenger, Pauline believes she is paying a compliment to herself. Instead, it paints her as bestial figure, feeding on the dead for survival. This bestial image, however, is the one the tribe already began to place upon Pauline and, therefore, shows how eventually people internalize the stereotypes placed upon them.

As Pauline continues to accept the negative traits placed upon her, her desire to belong sours until it turns from affection to hate. Like how her feelings for Eli turned from desire for love to desire for hate, Pauline's feelings about her place among the Chippewa deteriorates. Her obsession with death turns dark as she begins to have murderous and violent episodes that further connect her to the stereotypical Savage Indian. After the rape of Fleur, a great tornado comes. Pauline and her cousin, Russell, find that the men, who raped

Fleur, have found shelter in a freezer. At the age of fifteen, Pauline helps commit murder. She recalls vaguely, "It was Russell, I am sure who first put his arms on the bar. . . . Sometimes, thinking back, I see my arms lift, my hands grasp, see myself dropping the beam into the metal grip" (27). Despite her unclear description, we are led to believe that Pauline either helped or barred the men into the freezer herself. She dreams of the event saying, "Every night when my arms lowered the beam, it was my will that bore the weight, let it drop into place—not Russell's and not Fleur's" (66). Whether or not the action was solely Pauline's, it illuminates her growing violent nature.

Murder, like with all versions of the Savage Indian, becomes a means to an end and justifiable in Pauline's mind. Before she completely abandons her Native heritage, Pauline returns to the lake to find Misshepeshu, the water-demon. She engages him in a violent battle, in which she suffers "stinging blows" and "strung a noose around his neck" (202). After the brutal battle, Pauline emerges victorious to see whom she has actually killed. She says, "Eventually, it took on the physical form of Napoleon Morrissey. . . . I dragged him by the suspenders down a crooked path, into to the woods, and left him in high weeds. They could find him or not for all I cared" (203). Napoleon's murder is critical in Pauline's transformation. Initially, it is a violent and brutal murder for which Pauline feels no remorse. She has become the Savage that everyone has viewed her as. Secondly, the fact that Pauline believes she is murdering Misshepeshu is crucial. Misshepeshu, a powerful deity, represents Chippewa culture. By killing Misshepeshu, Pauline vents the anger and pains she has felt at the hands of the Chippewa, becoming the enemy of the tribe, as they have always labeled her. Finally, by revealing that Misshepeshu is Napoleon, a man who represents the epitome of the physical and emotional abuse that Pauline suffers, Erdrich exhibits how the mistreatment has repercussions. Pauline may be a Savage now, violent and murderous, but she is conditioned by the actions of Napoleon and the other members to become that. Her savagery results not from her own innate viciousness, but from the rejection and abuse she faces. It is no wonder that she turns to radical Catholicism.

Through Pauline, Erdrich exhibits the process by which a Savage Indian is created. Adding to the manipulation of stereotypes, Erdrich "saves" Pauline through Catholicism. However, the violence that Pauline enacts is only increased by her conversion. After facing abuse and rejection for most of her life, Pauline chooses a religion that supports self-punishment. She says, "I was hollow unless pain filled me, empty but for pain . . ." (192). Just as she seeks out unhealthy relationships among whites and Natives, Pauline seeks salvation through savage self-abuse. Even in her "saved" state, Pauline can be viewed as a Savage Indian. Yet Pauline's state of savagery births not from her mind, but from the years of abuse and isolation among whites and Natives. Starting with physical similarity, Erdrich weaves together a highly dislikable character, as Savage Indians always are, in a manner that causes readers to question how people could have allowed it to happen. Through Pauline, Erdrich exemplifies the consequences of ostracizing a person. She challenges the belief that Savage Indians naturally exists and provides the process by which they are created. Additionally, she proves the falsehood of the "saved" Indian by showing Pauline's steep descent into personal abuse through Catholic rules. Yet Pauline is only one representation of many Native stereotypes.

Fleur's Nobleness

The Noble Savage, like the Savage Indian, is normally depicted as a male. He is a male who exhibits the best qualities of a Native and a man. Traditionally, the Noble Savage is heroic, intelligent, and honorable. Physically, he is the perfection of his race, handsome even to non-Natives. Erdrich's use of the Noble Savage in *Tracks* follows these guidelines. Fleur, despite being female, is given a great number of masculine qualities, just like Pauline. After being saved from consumption by Nanapush, Fleur chooses to return to her family's land, despite being the last one alive. Nanapush says, "She returned to Matchimanito and stayed there alone in the cabin that even fire did not want. A young girl had never done such a thing before" (8). Even at seventeen, Fleur does things a young girl usually does not do, insinuating masculinity. Pauline confirms Fleur's masculine tendencies by saying Fleur "dressed like a man" (12). Fleur even plays cards with the men of Argus, even though "[w]omen didn't usually play with men" (18). As with other Noble Savages, Fleur possesses great physical strength. Pauline says, "Kozka hired her [Fleur] for her strength. She could lift a haunch or carry a pole of sausages without stumbling and she soon learned cutting from Fritzie . . ." (16). Even her later husband, Eli initially sees her through a masculine lens. The first time he meets Fleur, she is "gutting with long quick movements, arms bloody and bare" (42). Despite her gender, Fleur becomes an image of masculine strength. Fleur not only dresses like a man, but works, hunts, and protects her family's land as would be expected of a Noble Savage man.

Following the Noble Savage tradition, Fleur is not only physically strong but alluring to all people of opposite gender, no matter race. Pauline states,

> She knew the effect she had on men, even the very youngest of them. She swayed them, sotted them, made them curious about her habits, drew them close with careless ease and cast them off with the same indifference. . . . They never looked into her sly brown eyes or noticed her teeth, strong and sharp and very white. Her legs were bare, and since she padded in beadworked moccasins they never saw that her fifth toes were missing. They never knew she drowned. They were blinded, they were stupid, they only saw in the flesh (16, 18).

Like the male forms of the Noble Savage, Fleur is physically alluring to the men who gaze upon her. Yet like the male Noble Savages, Fleur is merely an object to these men, not a real person.[5] Pauline emphasizes this in the last few lines. She says, "They were blinded...they only saw in the flesh" (18). Just as people only see Pauline as ugly and savage, people only see Fleur as strong and beautiful. They do not acknowledge or see the trauma that Fleur as endured, including frostbite, starvation, and drowning. Fleur's real-life struggles are ignored because they would ruin the perfect image she creates. The beadwork moccasins, therefore, represent this chosen ignorance. Fleur, as the Noble Savage, must represent all the positive aspects of the Chippewa tribe, which means she must know how to sew, do beadwork, and perform other traditional tasks. This perfect Chippewa image, in the form of her moccasins, hides from view the unglamorous and imperfect parts of Fleur: her missing toes.

In addition, Fleur is spiritually connected to the world around her, emphasizing the "savage" part of her stereotype. Joni Adamson Clarke points out that "Fleur Pillager is human; yet, at times she is wolf, water-monster and bear. Indeed, she could be described as a visual pun who disorders the boundaries between human and animal" (28). Nanapush describes Fleur as "wild as a filthy wolf, a big bony girl whose sudden bursts of strength and snarling cries terrified the listening Pukwan" (3) and he continues by saying, "All she had was raw power, and the names of the dead that filled her" (7). Just as the Noble Savage represents the last of a dying race, Fleur is the last of the Pillager family. She represents the end of a line, since her daughter is taken by Nanapush. Her role as the last Pillager allows her to possess great spiritual powers that connects her to the andromorphic past. Like oral traditions in which animals and humans share characteristics, Fleur is more than just human.[6]

Finally, Fleur possesses the trait of honor as the Noble Savage. Throughout the story she cares for those who have been mistreated. Despite Pauline's later resentment, Fleur cares for Pauline in her times of need. Even when Pauline lies to Fleur, Fleur decides not to hold it against the ostracized girl. Rather, Pauline says, "Still, Fleur forgave me . . ." (143). Later, when Nanapush ridicules Pauline for her self-punishment of not bathing, Fleur helps Pauline by washing her. She baths Pauline so that Pauline no longer will face ridicule, and Fleur comforts her by saying, "We are all skinny this year" (153). Even though Pauline causes strife in Fleur's life, Fleur only shows kindness to the girl, providing food and shelter when Pauline has none. Fleur provides strength and support for her mother-in-law, Margret, as well, despite Margret's attempts to sabotage Eli and

Fleur's relationship. After Margret is dishonored by having her head forcibly shaved, Fleur shaves her own head. Nanapush says,

> Margret, you, and I watched, did not say a word to make Fleur stop as she cut her braids off, shaved her own head clean, and put the hair in a quilled skin pouch. She turned to us, still beautiful as before, but now in a frightful way. Then she went out, hunting, didn't even bother to wait for night to cover her tracks. (117)

After shaving her head, Fleur wanders around town to show the dishonor that Clarence and Lazzare committed towards Margret. No matter how Margret treats Fleur, Fleur acts with honor towards her mother-in-law. Margret admits that "[s]he's [Fleur] living in the old days when people had respect" (174).

However, like Pauline, Fleur is not born as the Noble Savage. Through the story of her persona is created by combining her own innate characteristics and the way she is treated by others. Although Fleur is a natural beauty, it is the perception of others that deems her as wildly beautiful and "savage." Told from the perspective of Nanapush and Pauline, we see Fleur as others see her. Even Nanapush, who loves Fleur, continually refers to her wolf smile and wild nature. Just as Pauline becomes a liar and outcast because of how she is treated, Fleur is perceived as an object of wild beauty. Repeatedly, both Nanapush and Pauline refer to Fleur's smile not as her own but that of a Pillager. She has no identity outside of her deceased family. Fleur becomes an object of the Pillager line and of nature.

Jennifer Sergi argues that "[w]hen Fleur returns to Matchimanito from Argus, the townspeople attribute good fishing and no lost boats to Fleur's ability . . ." (281). Pauline supports Sergi's conclusion when she says, "She [Fleur] was the one who closed the door or swung it open. Between the people and the gold-eyed creature in the lake, the spirit which they said was neither good nor bad but simply had an appetite, Fleur was the hinge" (139). Pauline voices the mentality that many share in the tribe. Fleur is the connection to Misshepeshu. Misshepeshu, as a Chippewa deity, represents the traditional beliefs, both good and bad. To a certain degree, Misshepeshu is Chippewa culture. Therefore, Fleur's role as the "hinge" is significant to her role as Noble Savage. She is the physical connection and border between Misshepeshu and the Chippewa. Only through Fleur can Misshepeshu be communicated with, maintained, or controlled. It is a spiritual power so great that it can only be held by the noblest of people. It places Fleur in a position of both awe and fear, emphasizing her role as Noble Savage. Unfortunately, since the narration is provided by Nanapush and Pauline, we can only guess as to how Fleur feels about this.

Both similar and different from Pauline, Fleur finds her objectification leads to isolation. However, Fleur chooses to embrace her isolation by refusing to join Eli's family on their land once they are married and refusing to take up residence with Nanapush as a teenager. While Pauline is ostracized for her mixed blood, Fleur faces isolation because she is both feared and sought after as the Noble Savage is. Therefore, just as the tribe and whites create a Savage in Pauline, they create a Noble Savage in Fleur.

The pressure placed upon Fleur as the Noble Savage is visible when her land is finally taken from her. Nanapush voices the belief of the tribe when he says,

> Fleur had not saved us with her dream, and it now seemed what was happening was so ordinary that it fell beyond her abilities. She had failed too many times, both to rescue us and save her youngest child, who now slept in the branches of bitter oaks. Her dreams lied, her vision was obscured, her helper slept deep in the lake and all her Argus money was long spent. (176-77)

Despite all she does, Fleur is partially blamed for the loss of her own and other Native land. The expectation of the tribe, especially Nanapush, is that her great spiritual powers should have stopped what was coming. Like the Noble Savage, however, Fleur is unable to do this. Nonetheless, unlike the Noble Savage, the events were something that could have been avoided. While blame is placed partially on Fleur, the truth is that the loss of her land resulted from Margret not paying the taxes for the Pillager lots. No matter her spiritual power, Fleur could not have prevented this mistake with magic. In a twisted way, Erdrich is completing the Noble Savage tradition. According to Philip Deloria, "In their dying moments, these Indian figures [Noble Savages] offered up their lands, their blessings, their traditions, and their republican history to those who were, in real life, violent, conquering interlopers" (65). Fleur, as the Noble Savage, loses her land. Erdrich alters this loss so that it is not the will of Fleur, but the result of the whites and other Native's actions. Just as the white and Natives created Fleur into the romanticized Noble Savage, they complete the stereotype by forcing her to vanish. Nanapush attempts to bring back Fleur to her vitality by instructing her to mourn and then take up the fight, but Fleur has reached her breaking point. She says, "I'm tired, old Uncle" and goes back to bed (177).

In her last manipulation of the Noble Savage, Erdrich does have Fleur leave on her own terms. Instead of allowing the whites and Natives she deems as traitorous to befoul her family's land, Fleur orchestrates it so all the trees are cut and waiting to fall. Once the trees fall and all stand in awe of her, Fleur takes her leave. Nanapush concludes,

> When she buckled herself into the traces of the greenwood cart, I said, "Stay with us." I go no answer. There was none that I expected. . . . She looked at me, her fact alight, and then she set out. I stood in the middle of the path. I watched her until the road bend, traveling south to widen, flatten, and eventually in its course meet with government school, depots, stores, the plotted square farms. (224)

Taking up the tradition of the Noble Savage leaving into the sunset, Fleur leaves with a few precious items, never to return. Her last image is beautiful, poetic, and tragically noble. Erdrich creates a character who is forced into the role of Noble Savage, vanishing not because it is necessary, but because she cannot stand to be with her own people anymore.

Through Fleur's role as Noble Savage and Pauline's role as Savage Indian, Erdrich creates a colonial scenario where the enemy of the Chippewa is not only the whites, but the Natives, too. By appropriating and altering the Native stereotypes, Erdrich exerts control over the role of Natives, taking back the power that colonialism often takes from Native Americans. The ending maybe the same, the loss of Native land and culture, but Erdrich's method creates a world in which Natives do have power and are not just victims. Nanapush best illuminates Erdrich's purpose when he says, "Our trouble came from living, from liquor and the dollar bill. We stumbled toward the government bait, never looking down, never noticing how the land was snatched from under us at every step" (4). Through recognizing the shared fault, Erdrich calls attention to the injustice that Native people, especially Native women, face in a colonial and postcolonial society. Her criticism lies on the actions of all ethnicities who buy into the Native stereotypes and Natives who ostracize members of their tribes rather than embracing them.

Notes

1.   The term Native American is controversial for identifying indigenous people of the United States. Some prefer the terms American Indian, Indigenous American, or Aboriginal American. For now, there is no consensus on which term is best. I chose to use Native American because books by Louise Erdrich and other indigenous authors are found under the label Native American literature.

2.   Two examples are James Fenimore Cooper's *Last of the Mohicans* and Lydia Maria Child's *Hobomok*.

3.   Southwest tribes, such as the Pueblos, Hopis, and Acoma, were known for matriarchal structure. While there were several tribes that were patriarchal, the treatment of men and women were much more equally established then the Native American stereotype represents.

4.   Gloria Bird explores evidence of colonialism in *Tracks* in her essay "Searching for Evidence of Colonialism at Work: A Reading of Louise Erdrich's 'Tracks.'"

5.   Christina Judith Hein's essay "'Can the Squaw Bluff?': Negotiations of Vision and Gazes in 'Tracks' and "The Last Report on the Miracles at Little No Horse' by Louise Erdrich" explores in depth the power of gaze and vision, focusing on how the lack of gaze upon Pauline grants her power and how Fleur has power in her gaze.

6.   For more about Fleur's role in oral traditions read Joni Adamson Clarke's "Why Bears are Good to Think and Theory Doesn't Have

to be Murder: Transformation and Oral tradition in Louise Erdrich's *Tracks*."

Works Cited

Bird, Gloria. "Searching for Evidence of Colonialism at Work: A Reading of Louise Erdrich's 'Tracks.'" *Wicazo Sa Review*, vol. 8, no. 2, 1992, pp. 40-7.

Clarke, Joni Adamson. "Why Bears are Good to Think and Theory Doesn't have to be Murder: Transformation and Oral Tradition in Louise Erdrich's *Tracks*." *Studies in American Indian Literatures*, vol. 4, no. 1, 1992, pp. 28-48.

"Common Portrayals of Aboriginal People." *MediaSmarts*, n.d. Accessed 27 Apr. 2016.

Cornell, Daniel. "Woman Looking: Revis(ion)ing Pauline's Subject Position in Louise Erdrich's *Tracks*." *Studies IN American Indian Literatures*, vol. 2, no. 4, 1992, pp. 49-64.

Deloria, Philip. *Playing Indian.* Yale UP, 1998.

Hein, Christina Judith. "'Can the Squaw Bluff?': Negotiations of Vision and Gazes in 'Tracks' and 'The Last Report on the Miracles at Little No Horse' by Louise Erdrich." *American Studies*, vol. 54, no. 1, 2009, pp. 121-42. *JSTOR.* 28 Apr. 2016.

Hessler, Michelle R. "Catholic Nuns and Ojibwa Shamans: Pauline and Fleur in Louise Erdrich's 'Tracks.'" *Wicazo Sa Review*, vol. 11, no. 1, 1995, pp. 40-5.

Huhndorf, Shari M. *Going Native: Indians in American Cultural Imagination.* Cornell UP, 2001.

Indian Country Diaries. Native American Public Telecommunications, 2006. Accessed 27 Apr. 2016.

McLaurin, Virginia A. *Stereotypes of Contemporary Native American Indian Characters in Recent Popular Media.* U of Massachusetts P, 2012.

Redface. Red-Face.us, n.d. Accessed 28 Apr. 2016.

"Savage." *Merriam-Webster.com*, 2016. Accessed 29 Apr. 2016.

Sergi, Jennifer. "Storytelling: Tradition and Preservation in Louise Erdrich's *Tracks*." *World Literature Today*, vol. 66, no. 1, 1992, pp. 279-82.

Van Dyke, Annette. "Questions of the Spirit: Bloodlines in Louise Erdrich's Chipewa Landscape." *Studies in American Indian Literatures*, vol. 2, no. 4, 1992, pp. 14-27. *JSTOR.* Accessed 28 Apr. 2016.

Tracking Wolves: A Metaphor for Cross-border Inequality
Cormac McCarthy's novel *The Crossing*_____

Peter Arnds

El lobo es una cosa incognoscible.

(Cormac McCarthy, *The Crossing* 46)

To what extent international boundaries, migration, ethnicity, and wolves can come together is perhaps nowhere demonstrated better in contemporary literature than in Cormac McCarthy's novel *The Crossing* (1994), which together with *All the Pretty Horses* (1992) and *Cities of the Plain* (1998) forms part of his so-called Border Trilogy. When sixteen-year-old Billy Parham traps an errant pregnant wolf near his home in New Mexico, he decides to take her back to Mexico, from where she has entered the United States, oblivious to any international boundaries. By returning her, Billy is himself trespassing onto foreign ground and is accused by various locals of treating Mexico as if it were a dumping ground for wild animals. This first out of three journeys to Mexico ends with the wolf's death after she has to fight several packs of dogs against which she has been pitted by the locals; Billy ends up having to shoot her. Alienated and disillusioned, he returns to his home in New Mexico where he finds his parents murdered. The only family tie left to him is his younger brother Boyd, with whom he sets out on his second journey to Mexico to find their parents' murderers and retrieve the horses they have stolen. After Boyd is shot through the chest and nursed back to health, he disappears with a local girl. Billy returns to the US again, now at war with Germany. He wants to join the army but fails to be recruited due to a heart murmur. Failing to fit in, he returns to Mexico for the third time, where he learns of his brother's death. He exhumes his remains and returns them to their home soil across the border.

Although wolves are elusive animals and may therefore be unrecognizable, as McCarthy argues, they have served cultures around the world and, through the ages, as a metaphor for human behavior, both good and nefarious. Negative images of the wolf prevail. McCarthy's pregnant wolf trespasses across the border from Mexico into the US and is regarded by farmers as vermin, while Billy Parham recognizes a common bond between himself and the wolf. McCarthy's she-wolf is a metaphor at multiple levels, expressive of violence between humans and animals, for inequality between different social and ethnic groups, the inequality between two regions both known for their shared harshness and potential for violence, and for the boy himself.

This novel deserves renewed attention in light of the politics of im/migration, especially of undocumented individuals. The text is part of a discourse employing the wolf metaphor in the context of migration, which has found increasing use also in the media (e.g., "Donald Trump supporters tell immigrants 'The wolves are coming, you are the hunted'—as race hate fears rise," *The Independent*, 9 Nov. 2016), especially in articles on "lone-wolf" attacks ("We Must Track and Trap Lone Wolf Terrorists," *The Observer*, 25 Nov. 2014). The wolf metaphor in the context of migration, violence, and social and ethnic difference is not a new phenomenon, however. As a figure for the persecution of individuals, the image reaches back to the biopolitical practices of early medieval Northern Europe, when humans abandoned by their communities and condemned to a life of exile and migration were seen as wolves, as expressed in the Old Norse word *vargr*, denoting both "wolf" and "outlaw." This premodern form of expulsion has been discussed extensively by the Italian philosopher Giorgio Agamben in his book on the *homo sacer*, and it had its antecedents in the proscription during antiquity. Emerging from this paradigm of a morally unclean person, usually a murderer, condemned to a life on the run, this image, from the early modern age onward, becomes exploited in the context of gender— women persecuted as she-wolves/witches—race, and colonialism. In the British colonies, for example, the wolf became a metaphor for the colonized Other. In his 1596 publication "A View of the Present

State of Ireland," the poet Edmund Spenser maintained that the Irish all turned into wolves for one year. In the American settlements then, wolves and the indigenous were considered creatures of a godless wilderness, which the colonists had a moral duty to subdue (Fogleman), with the wolf standing in for a frontier phenomenon and the boundary between civilization and wilderness, Europeanness and indigeneity. In Europe itself, the wolf's demonization since the Middle Ages once Christianity moved into Northern Europe evolves over time from a metaphor for expelled criminals into a racist metaphor. Literature reflects this process. Literary texts from the early modern period all the way up to the early twentieth century reflect, for example, how so-called "gypsies" were stereotypically defamed as child-devouring itinerants and marauders, and how Jews—living in the diaspora—were labelled as wolves (e.g., Shakespeare's Shylock to whom Gratiano says: "your vicious dog soul used to belong to a wolf"; act 4, scene 1). The wolf as a metaphor for race and ethnic outsiders in the context of migration persists to this day.

McCarthy's she-wolf is a metaphor in the context of ethnicity, migration, and social inequality, but also of personal development, a catalyst for Billy's own development over his three journeys to Mexico, which reflect his identity in transformation, his increasing loneliness and loss of a place in the world. The novel explores the premature disillusionment of a young man who has not even come of age—in that sense, it is a unique kind of *Anti-Bildungsroman*— by way of a series of episodes highlighting man's cruelty towards creatures, human and animal alike. The wolf is a border phenomenon, a border crosser, and oblivious to borders, a key component in this text—the border in a political, personal, and metaphysical sense. It is the border that blurs and disappears, between species, regions, between youth and adulthood, between life and death, the dead being ever present during the journeys of the living.

In crossing from Mexico to the US and back again, the wolf links a series of binaries, including these two countries and their socioeconomic differences, colonization versus indigeneity, but also the gender binary: femininity in a region known for its male cruelty. Moreover, she bridges more abstract binaries, such as myth versus culture, community versus loneliness, home versus loss of home, the protagonist's wanderings across what Gilles Deleuze and Félix Guattari have termed the "striated space" of the nation state encroaching upon the "smooth space" of nomads and the indigenous (Deleuze/Guattari, 20ff). Ultimately, her own lonely wanderings reflect the deep loneliness experienced by the protagonist Billy Parham.

To those forces existing under the pressures of the imagined community, primarily religion and nationalism, on both sides of the border—to ranchers and those trying to establish law and order in a country perceived as lawless, rationalists estranged from all mythical thinking—she is nothing other than the usual pest. Jon Mooallem's argument for species in general,—"the way we see a species, the way we feel about an animal, can impact its standing on the planet more than anything covered in ecology textbooks"— most certainly applies to the way the wolf is seen by the majority of people in this text. Their hatred of the wolf (what I have termed lycophobia), however, clashes with the deeper understanding and respect (lycophilia) for this creature held by a several of McCarthy's typical spectral characters, the indigenous, nomads, gypsies, and other travelers on the margins of society. This controversy about the wolf's status has divided sedentary, agrarian European culture from indigenous and nomadic—i.e., migratory—non-European culture for millennia. The complex relationship between wolves and human migration reaches back to the Stone Age, when nomadic hunters and gatherers first domesticated wolves to assist them with the hunt (Shipman), before the wolf became an enemy as humans became herders. As scholars like Eckhard Fuhr and Erik Zimen point out, nomadic hunting communities tend to see the wolf with greater positivity than agrarian ones. If we turn to storytelling in view of these connections, we need to go back as far as Greek myth. Ancient Greek sheepherders evoke their fear and hatred of the wolf in the myth of Lycaon, the King of Arcadia, whom Jupiter transforms into a wolf and who is expelled to roam the earth for the crime of cannibalism. This is possibly one of the earliest stories featuring the amalgamation of the wolf with exilic wandering:

> Frightened he runs off to the silent fields and howls aloud, attempting speech in vain; foam gathers at the corners of his mouth; he turns his lust for slaughter on the flocks, and mangles them, rejoicing still in blood. His garments now become a shaggy pelt; his arms turn into legs, and he, to wolf while still retaining traces of the man: grayness the same, the same cruel visage, the same cold eyes and bestial appearance. (Ovid 13)

From the perspective of wolf haters, this animal is generally considered to be vermin, the German *Ungeziefer*, a word derived from Old High German *zebar*, the sacrificial animal. *Ungeziefer* has the meaning of an unclean animal not suited for sacrifice, and this is precisely the definition that Agamben gives for the *homo sacer*, the murderer expelled by his community and condemned like Lycaon for a life on the run in the silent fields where his speech will not be heard. Similarly to Kafka, who uses *Ungeziefer* in the first sentence of his *Metamorphosis* (1915) to describe Gregor Samsa's transformation, Agamben has seen this as the fundamental condition of Jewish exile, which, at its most violent extreme, has led to the abandonment of humans in the camps. I would argue that in line with this thinking, the significance of the Lycaon myth and the *homo sacer* are both present in McCarthy's wolf/boy relationship in the context of migration across the US/Mexican border as a principal demarcation line of inequality.

While during the early colonization of North America, the wolf was a metaphor for the frontier between a civilized European world and an unknown wilderness with its indigenous population, that frontier seems to have shifted to the divide between the so-called North and the South with its postcolonial thinking and practices of the former exploiting the latter. The wanderings of McCarthy's wolf reveal the continuity of such colonial power structures at the seam of North/South, Europeanness and indigeneity, especially between the Mexican descendants of the *conquistadores* and their relationship in the state of Sonora with the local native tribe of the Yaqui, whose bloody history of oppression (Folsom) reflects the wolf's own long historical memory of persecution: "Now that the yankees have again betrayed them the Mexicans are eager to reclaim their indian blood. But we do not want them. Most particularly the Yaqui. The Yaqui have long memories." (McCarthy 385)

Those owning the land and holding the reins of power tend to see the wolf, the indigenous, those "last free remnants . . . like shadowfolk of the nation" (104), and itinerants, in the same light. They see her crossing the international boundary and agrarian land as acts of trespassing. Her presence highlights a strange tension Mexico finds itself caught in. The country's reputation in the US is that of wild wolf country, a place of exile for US outlaws: "There ain't no law in Mexico. It's just a pack of rogues" (McCarthy 176). Both the term "pack" and "rogue" point to the wolf, the latter due to that animal's persistent literary connotation with lawlessness and the devil as rogue in European literature from the medieval bestiaries to the picaresque tradition (*Schelmenroman/rogue novel*) of the early modern age. Across the border, however, in Texas and New Mexico, where agrarian culture has even more intensely placed wilderness under permanent pressure of becoming domesticated, the wolf has even less of a place. Mexico is described as aspiring to becoming such a place of law and order like its neighbor. In a globalizing world economy where the differences between North and South are increasingly being levelled, this is the kind of mimicry Homi K. Bhabha describes for the relationship between the colonizers and the colonized. McCarthy's Mexico finds itself in the throes of various colonial structures. While feeling the colonizing pressures of the United States, it also colonizes its own indigenous populations within. What is left after mimicry, according to Bhabha, is semblance rather than essence, a trace, the impure, the second-hand. Colonial power thus implies originality. Dominant culture is contaminated by the linguistic and racial differences of the native self. The wolf in her wolfishness embodies this threat to those in power in Mexico, themselves wolves in the stereotypical sense of the term, in their collaboration with the US and their mimicry of US culture. This tension between Mexico's image as outlaw terrain and its mimicry of US-style law and order is thrown into stark relief by the wolf's return to Mexican soil.

The wolf symbolically divides Mexican society, a rift that also reveals itself in the *corridos*, the Mexican ballads. They are a reflection of Billy's and the wolf's wandering through this desert landscape, tied to his heroic journeys and forever under threat of losing themselves. "Long voyages often lose themselves. . . . Listen to the corridos of this country" (McCarthy 230). But the corrido is more than that, it

> tells all and it tells nothing. I heard the tale of the guerito years ago. Before your brother was even born. You dont think it tells about him? Yes, it tells about him. It tells what it wishes to tell. It tells what makes the story run. The corrido is the poor man's history. It does not owe its allegiance to the truths of history but to the truths of men. It tells the tale of that solitary man who is all men. (McCarthy 386)

As the song lines running through Mexico, the corridos are as divisive as they are unifying, dividing the rich from the poor and uniting the latter. Vince Brewton has argued,

> Boyd's life and death are absorbed and transformed into the corrido, the ballad of the country side that mythologizes the deep economic divide and political struggle between rich and poor in Mexico. . . . Billy Parham's quest to find his brother and bring him home is thus linked with the larger narrative of class struggle and national identity in Mexico. (137)

The American government is being indicted as an ally to the rich and powerful of Mexico in this class struggle. This happens, for example, in the bar scene where Billy has a sort of "stand-off" with the drunken veteran of the revolution. As Brewton points out, at a deeper level, his gesture of refusing the American whiskey Billy offers him signifies "the collusion of the American government with the despotic Mexican regime" (138).

Billy's and the wolf's rhizomatic travel, their shared suffering, is such a corrido telling a story of oppression and homelessness.

To a large extent, the corrido embodies also what is still untamed about Mexico, as does the wolf. Traveling between the powerful and the oppressed, between dominant European culture and indigenous culture, she is seen as forever threatening dominant power and its domesticizing mission. We see this reflected in some of the characters' reactions to her presence, for example, the rancher's view that the wolves brutalize "the cattle in a way they did not the wild game. As if the cows evoked in them some anger. As if they were offended by some violation of an old order. Old ceremonies. Old protocols" (McCarthy 25), or in various Mexicans' subconscious denial of the wolf's true nature, reducing her to a dog: "He looked at the wolf. 'Es buena cazadora su perra?' The boy looked at the wolf. 'Si,' he said. 'Mejor no hay.' 'Es feroz?' 'A veces'" (75). In both cases, wilderness clashes with domestication, outlawry with law and order, a boundary that runs deep across McCarthy's relentless landscape on both sides of the international border, a land "undifferentiated in its terrain from the country they quit and yet wholly alien and wholly strange" (74).

The novel thus constructs tension between those who show no empathy for the wolf and the respect for the wolf in those who identify with her migratory and homeless nature. Her ancient position of outlaw culminates in the scene where having to fight a consistently renewable pack of dogs, the wolf finds herself in the middle of the battle between wild untamed nature and the forces of domesticity designed to eradicate her. Her Sisyphean fight to the death reflects her position traditionally occupied by the *homo sacer*. In medieval terms, the *homo sacer* or *Friedlos*—that is, man without peace—was what, in German, used to be called *wolfsfrei*, as free as a wolf but, in the end, free to be killed by wolves.

The real wolves in McCarthy's novel and in the superstitious sense of the concept of the wolf are those who suppress indigeneity, the colonizers and their sovereign power. Their bond with the she-wolf is as intimate as that of Billy Parham, but in a different way. While Billy Parham identifies with the wolf as *homo sacer*, those with sovereign power are at the opposite end of the *homo sacer* but tied to him/her through lawlessness. In being expelled to a life outside of communal law, the *homo sacer* is uniquely tied to the sovereign whose power to abandon individuals equally positions him outside of the law. This symmetry between the sovereign beast and the persecuted wolf reflects the animal's dual perception of the powerful hunter versus the hunted pest. Sovereignty is inextricably linked to abjection, a fact noted also by Jacques Derrida in his lecture series *Séminaire: La bête et le souverain* (*The Beast & the Sovereign*), where the French philosopher equates the sovereign above the law with the wolf. El lobo es incognoscible, and yet in the end, when, empathetic with the suffering creature, Billy Parham watches her die, she stands in for the forces of inequality, violence, and injustice in the world's power systems. Mexico, I would argue, in this instance becomes a *pars pro toto* for the world at large.

In such a hostile world, Billy and the wolf form a symbiosis that is primarily defined through their shared mobility. One of the differences between human wandering and animal wandering is that humans tend to travel with some kind of ID in order to cross international boundaries. If they do not, they have acquired the status of undocumented migrant, which is the position Billy finds himself in as he enters Mexico:

> "De donde viene?" he said.
> "America."
> He nodded. He looked out across the river. He leaned and spat. "Sus documentos," he said.
> "Documentos?"
> "Si. Documentos."
> "No tengo ningunos documentos."
> The man watched him for a while.
> "Que es su nombre," he said.
> "Billy Parham". . . .
> "Pasaporte?"
> "Nada." (McCarthy 95)

This scene in particular moves the novel close to the current debates about undocumented immigrants. What is different, however, is the direction of travel. While the debate is generally about undocumented Mexicans illegally entering the US, here is a US citizen who illegally enters Mexico and with a wolf in tow at that. In American literature and film there is a widespread romantic stigma attached to US citizens making off to Mexico, which in the popular imagination is a land of unfettered freedom and exile for outlaws. To an extent McCarthy's text plays with this motif, and yet it quickly also debunks this myth:

> "You think that this country is some country you can come here and do what you like." "I never thought that. I never thought about this country one way or another. . . . We was just passin through, the boy said. We wasn't botherin nobody. Queríamos pasar. No más." "Pasar or traspasar?" The boy turned and spat into the dirt. He could feel the wolf lean against his leg. He said that the tracks of the wolf had led out of Mexico. He said the wolf knew nothing of boundaries. . . . The boy only said that if he were allowed to go he would return with the wolf to America and that he would pay whatever fine he had incurred but the hacendado [rancher] shook his head. He said that it was too late for that and that anyway the alguacil [sheriff] had taken the wolf into custody and it was forfeit in lieu of the portazgo [toll]. When the boy said that he had not known that he would be required to pay in order to pass through the country the hacendado said that then he was in much the same situation as the wolf. (McCarthy 119)

Billy and the wolf share the act of trespassing, but a great deal more than that. McCarthy's wolf is a victim of a "country not for old men"—nor for women either—but in final analysis, her loneliness also reflects Billy Parham's own boyhood loneliness, his Lycaon-like journey into wilderness, exile and loss of a place in this world, running through "the silent fields" (Ovid 13). The growing bond between the pregnant wolf and the sixteen-year-old orphan becomes the driving force of the entire plot, drawing on the tension between the wolf's traditional role as nurturer and her perception as destroyer.

McCarthy exploits this mythical figure of the nurturing she-wolf in contrast to a violent male world: "Men with torches . . . were dragging the wolf from her stall by her chain and she . . . tried to keep low to the ground to protect her underbelly" (McCarthy 112).

In final analysis, the wolf is an archetype and as such also functions as a metaphorical representation of that archetypal Mexican mother,

> this old woman of Mexico, her sons long dead in that blood and violence which her prayers and her prostrations seemed powerless to appease. Her frail form was a constant in that land, her silent anguishings . . . what direr histories yet against which could be counted at last nothing more than her small figure bent and mumbling, her crone hand clutching her beads of fruitseed. (McCarthy 390)

Billy is located between both, the wolf as nurturer—"He tried to see the world the wolf saw" (McCarthy 51)—and the world he comes from, which sees her as vermin. The nurturing side of the pregnant wolf is that element that has gone missing in Billy's life, orphaned and thrust into the world as lone wolf. "He told the boy that although he was huérfano still he must cease his wanderings and make for himself some place in the world because to wander in this way would become for him a passion and by this passion he would become estranged from men and so ultimately from himself" (McCarthy 134). Billy is the *homo sacer* outside the community of men, outside his national community, which has no place for him in its army but which also looks upon his wolfish freedom with the traditional feelings of both hatred and reverence: "Ragged, dirty, hungry in eye and belly. Totally unspoken for. In that outlandish figure they beheld what they envied most and what they most reviled. If their hearts went out to him it was yet true that for very small cause they might also have killed him" (170). In this ambivalence of reverence and hate lies his identity as a "lone wolf" and true inner bond with the she-wolf.

Although the wolf may be unrecognizable and generally misunderstood as a pest and outlaw on both sides of the border, those groups who are oppressed, colonized or guided by superstition and long memories (like the Yaqui) and wisdom show respect for her, for wolves in general. To such individuals or groups the she-wolf as archetype is a mythical being representing a world order:

El lobo es una cosa incognoscible, he said. Lo que se tiene en la trampa no es mas que dientes y forro. El lobo propio no se puede conocer. Lobo o lo que sabe el lobo. Tan como preguntar lo que saben las piedras. Los arboles, El mundo. . . . He said that the wolf is a being of great order and that it knows what men do not. . . . The wolf is like the copo de nieve. Snowflake (45) . . . Escúchame, joven. . . . The wolf is made the way the world is made. You cannot touch the world. (McCarthy 46)

Such lycophilia extends to an awareness of the wolf's beneficial role within the eco system, the balance between all species sharing this planet, and extends to the harmony between non-human species as much as to the context of undocumented migration, evoking the ideal of Kant's *Weltfrieden* (1795). "Deer and hare and dove and groundvole all richly empanelled on the air for her delight, all nations of the possible world ordained by God of which she was one and not separate from" (Kant 127).

McCarthy's wolf is a catalyst revealing the inequality between individuals, social and ethnic groups, in terms of lycophobia versus lycophilia. In the end, however, she also embodies the idea of levelling all differences and social violence. That this idea is an illusion, however, is shown in her dismal end, being killed by dogs, in itself an interesting detail, as the wolf representing wilderness and freedom from all boundaries is getting killed by an animal standing in for the idea of domestication. Ownership of land, human territorialism, conquest, and colonialism are the forces she is pitted against. As she is being crushed by these forces, so is her human double Billy Parham, whose inability to fit into the domesticated world reaches its climax in that typically McCarthean finale filled with despair, disillusionment, and the destruction of youth. It is this domesticated animal, a dog in its demise, which reflects Billy's own complete and final loss in the world in the final scenes of the book. His own regression rather than progress in the habitual sense of a coming-of-age story/*Bildungsroman* manifests in his reluctance to help the dog, much in contrast with his initial eagerness to help the wolf.

In this novel, as in so many others by McCarthy, the land with all its harshness, social violence, and injustice has, once again, become a winner over the human emotional landscape and its potential of love and compassion. Billy travels across a field of tension between compassion and violence, between life and death. From the moment he sets out to return the wolf to Mexico, death travels with him. Although alive, and holding new life inside herself, the wolf embodies death. Her presence and wandering points to the oppressed strata of Mexican society, to all those undocumented migrants running like Lycaon in the silent fields. On a deeply personal level, she also points to a symbolic bond with the brother whose remains Billy Parham brings home, as her death in Mexico is followed by Boyd's. The wolf is that shadow creature, condemned by humanity to the nocturnal side of life, the shadow of Boyd and ultimately also Billy. While one brother dies in body, the other one does in spirit. In the words of a gypsy, whom Billy encounters south of the border, "journeys involving the company of the dead were notorious for their difficulty but that in truth every journey was so accompanied" (McCarthy 413). Billy's final reaction to the dog seeking help from him reflects this death of his spirit, and as once again the "godmade sun" rises over the American Southwest, there seems to exist no more difference in the struggles and plights of all creatures, as "for all and without distinction" (426) death, that great equalizer, reigns supreme.

Works Cited

Agamben, Giorgio. *Homo sacer: Sovereign Power and Bare Life*. Stanford UP, 1995.

Bhabha, Homi K. "Of mimicry and man: The ambivalence of colonial discourse." *The Location of Culture*. Routledge, 1994, pp. 85-92.

Brewton, Vince. "The Changing Landscape of Violence in Cormac McCarthy's Early Novels and the Border Trilogy." *The Southern Literary Journal*, vol. 37, no. 1, Fall 2004, pp. 121-143.

Deleuze, Gilles, and Félix Guattari. *A Thousand Plateaus. Capitalism and Schizophrenia*. Translated by Brian Massumi, U of Minnesota P, 1987.

Derrida, Jacques. *The Beast and the Sovereign*, vol. 1 and 2. Translated by Geoffrey Bennington, U of Chicago P, 2009.

_____. *Séminaire: La bête et le souverain.* Galilée, 2008.

Fogleman, Valerie M. "American Attitudes towards Wolves: A History of Misperception." *Environmental Review.* 13 (1989): 63-94.

Folsom, Raphael Brewster. *The Yaquis and the Empire: Violence, Spanish Imperial Power, and the Native Resilience in Colonial Mexico.* Yale UP, 2014.

Fuhr, Eckhard. *Rückkehr der Wölfe. Wie ein Heimkehrer unser Leben verändert.* Goldmann, 2016.

Hall, Wade, and Rick Wallach, editors. *Sacred Violence: A Reader's Companion to Cormac McCarthy.* Texas Western P, 1995.

Kant, Immanuel. *Zum ewigen Frieden.* 1795. (Mit den Passagen zum Völkerrecht und Weltbürgerrecht aus Kants Rechtslehre.) Kommentar von Oliver Eberl und Peter Niesen. Suhrkamp, 2011.

McCarthy, Cormac. *The Crossing.* Knopf, 1994.

Mooallem, Jon. "How the Teddy Bear Taught Us Compassion." *TED*, 2014, www.ted.com/talks/jon_mooallem_the_strange_story_of_the_teddy_bear_and_what_it_reveals_about_our_relationship_to_animals/transcript/. Accessed 2 Apr. 2018.

_____. *Wild Ones. A Sometime Dismaying, Weirdly Reassuring Story about Looking at People Looking at Animals in America.* Penguin Press, 2013. Ovid. *Metamorphoses.* Norton, 2010.

Shipman, Pat. *The Invaders. How Humans and Their Dogs Drove Neanderthals to Extinction.* Harvard UP, 2015.

Zimen, Erik. *Der Wolf: Verhalten, Ökologie und Mythos.* Goldmann, 1993.

Historical Trauma and the Haunting of "Comfort Women"

Nora Okja Keller's novel *Comfort Woman* and Yong Soon Min's Art Works_____

Ji Nang Kim

This chapter explores global gender inequality by discussing the works of Korean American female writers and artists, who deal with the subject of comfort women. Especially focusing on Nora Okja Keller's novel *Comfort Woman* and Yong Soon Min's sculptural installations, *deCOLONIZATION* (1991) and *Remembering Jungshindae* (1993), this study examines how Keller and Min reconstruct the silenced history of Korean comfort women by portraying female bodies as "haunted" or "haunting" space where historical trauma is inscribed and remembered. This chapter argues that Keller and Min provide meaningful postmortem communication by foregrounding spectral female bodies as a focus of such representation, remembering, and identification.

Comfort women were victims of sexual slavery by the Imperial Japanese military during World War II. Beginning in 1932, an estimated 80,000 to 280,000 Asian women from ages twelve to early twenties were coerced, deceptively recruited, or sold into sexual slavery for the imperial Japanese military (Korean Research Institute). While comfort women were from various Asian colonies occupied by Japan, 80 to 90 percent of them were Koreans, especially young, unmarried Korean women from socially marginalized groups. During their slavery, the comfort women suffered from constant rape, beating, burning, stabbing, and venereal disease, and many of them were abandoned or killed on the battlefield by retreating Japanese forces at the end of war. Many of the surviving comfort women, despite their survival, could not return home and continued their lives in exile because they feared rejection by a Korean society that considered them promiscuous women whose bodies had been contaminated by foreigners.

The memory of Korean comfort women had been "forgotten" for a half-century in national histories of South Korea and Japan. That is, this female history had been doubly silenced by colonizers and the colonized under Japanese and South Korean patriarchy, colonialism, and nationalism. After World War II, the Japanese government, which for fifty-five years was dominated by the conservative Liberal Democratic Party (LDP), conducted an organized, strategic "forgetting" of the comfort women's history. Especially for the LPD, which supported ex-military officers, the comfort women were obstacles to the construction of heroic narratives of the war as national memory. Similarly, the newly established Korean government was reluctant to make the comfort women a diplomatic issue that might damage national regeneration projects related to Japan and the US. Some conservative nationalists conflated this national regeneration with a break with uncomfortable memories of colonization, including memories of comfort women. Under a patriarchal nationalist regime that emphasized purity and homogeneity as foundations of a burgeoning Korean nationhood, comfort women's bodies as symbols of national shame were kept in a tightly-closed closet. In this sociopolitical context in Japan and South Korea, the term "comfort women" and these women's histories have been totally absent from history books in both nations; their governments expressed no official concerns about the issue until the mid-1990s. Jodi Kim explains this silence long-imposed on the comfort women as, in Homi K. Bhabha's words, "To be obliged to forget—in the construction of the national present" to totalize the people of a nation-state to imagine "unifying the national will" (qtd. in Kim 72). In this national amnesia, the body of the comfort woman—as a symbol of shameful raped woman or of institutionalized sexual violence—becomes an unfavorable subject that disturbs masculinist ideologies imbedded in Japanese and Korean conservative nationalism (Kim 68).

It is since the early 1990s that the issue of comfort women has grabbed the diasporic imagination, especially the imagination of Korean American female writers and artists. Annie Fukushima in *Encyclopedia of Asian American Issues Today* identifies various female diasporic responses to the issue: international exhibits such as the *Quest for Justice* and *Comfort Women—Now and Then—from Exploration to Empowerment*; two comfort women novels, Nora Okja Keller's *Comfort Woman* (1997) and Therese Park's *A Gift of the Emperor* (1997); Soo Jin Kim's experimental video work, *Comfort Women*; Yong Soon Min's sculptural installations *deCOLONIZATION* (1991) and *Remembering Jungshindae* (1993); Miran Kim's paintings, *Comfort Woman* (1995–1998); Sasha Y. Lee's photographs on the issue of comfort women; Dai Sil Kim-Gibson's documentary film, *Silence Broken: Korean Comfort Women* (1999); Hein Seok's documentary films, *The House of Sharing* (2007) and *63 Years On* (2008). Marianne Hirsch refers to these writers and artists as the second generation—"those who are deeply affected by the events they themselves did not experience but whose memory they inherited" (76). She defines their cultural production as a belated act—a form of "retrospective witnessing"—the "postmemory" triggered by the next generation's adoption of the former generation's traumatic experiences (76). These cultural producers' acts of adoption involve "identification and projection that can include the transmission of the bodily memory of trauma" (Hirsch 77). In fact, the female body serves as a focal point in their literary and artistic representations as the body is integral to remembering and narrating traumas.

Korean American activist and visual artist Yong Soon Min expressed Korean women's colonial histories and traumas through a series of reproduced Korean traditional dress—hanbok—as an empty dress where colonial women's bodies are lost and displaced, but leave their spectral traces. In her sculptural installation, *deCOLONIZATION*, Min represents colonized women's spectral bodies by creating a white, translucent hanbok that floats from the ceiling, looking over the space. This mourning work is her version of a history text that visualizes the haunting of traumatic colonial memory: she materializes the colonial female's ghostly body through her own dead mother's dress that floats over a postcolonial present when decolonization is not yet completed.

Figure 1. Yong Soon Min, *deCOLONIZATION* (1991),
from *Yongsoonmin.com.* Copyright © 2012 by Yong Soon Min

The comfort women's haunting bodies are more clearly represented in *Remembering Jungshindae* in which Min represents the comfort woman's bodiless body that haunts the black mourning dress.

Figure 2. Yong Soon Min, *Remembering Jungshindae* (1993),
from *Yongsoonmin.com.*

Min's work gives an impression that the comfort woman's specter comes out of an improper burial place and stands firm in front of audience, revealing her dusty, rotten body. As Elaine H. Kim describes, its "rigid structure" and "textured surface" symbolize "the severity of the comfort woman's history," signifying how comfort women's bodies are exploited, murdered, and improperly buried during the war atrocities (qtd. in Kang 35). Min also attempts to materialize the bloody phantom wounds as a trace of the specter's body by placing glowing red wire mesh screen inside of the dress. These bloody wounds that glow from inside of the dress speak to the audience as the posted Korean script translates: "Your story will not be forgotten." Here, the wounded phantom body becomes a historical text that "opens a deep and painful connection between present and past," conjuring absent memories into the present (Slattery 41).

Like Min's visual art works, Keller's *Comfort Woman* is the diasporic author's mourning work that offers the site for colonial female ghostsess. These bloody wounds come out from the imposed silence. While Min's works offer the multisensorial experience of colonial female ghost by visualizing spectral bodies with images, materials, and colors, Keller's novel makes this bodily remembering speakable through language that adds flesh and blood to this phantom subject. Keller arranges traumatic bodily memories into her story, employing the body as a means of conveying self-contained traumatic psyche and memories. Here, the body not only functions as a marker of traumatic memories, but also assumes a powerful agency in historical narratives that resist the deliberate "forgetting."

In various interviews, Keller mentions that her novel was initiated by her own experience of haunting after she met a former comfort woman, Keum Ja Hwang, who told her survival story at a human rights symposium at the University of Hawaii in 1993 (Hong). Keller, as a witness of Hwang's body and testimony, "felt so haunted" by the images of the dead comfort women's traumatized bodies (Hong). Keller, whose "dreams were haunted . . . filled with images of war and women, of blood and birth," concludes that "the only way I could exorcise these images was through writing" ("Author Questions" 6). While describing her writing routine, she depicts herself "as a shaman": "I really felt that sometimes I entered a type of trance, that I was really connected to something higher [than] myself . . . I was almost like a medium" (Cinader).

In *Comfort Woman*, Keller creates "the novel's double story of haunting" that reflects her "authorial haunting" by dramatizing the haunting or haunted moments of the two female narrators—the former comfort woman, Soon Hyo/Akiko, and her half-American and half-Korean daughter, Beccah (Brogan 153). By juxtaposing the first-person narratives of the dead mother, Soon Hyo/Akiko, and surviving daughter, Beccah, Keller produces a fiction that oscillates between the narratives of the dead and the living, and the past and present. This doubling effectively demonstrates the conflicts and reconciliations between the ancestral ghosts and their daughters, revealing the ways in which their bodies pass down "unclaimed" historical traumas from generation to generation. Keller attempts to create an alternative archive of postcolonial history by dramatizing how these silenced but un-dead bodies deliver their collective traumas of colonialism as a form of history.

Soon Hyo/Akiko, who speaks in the chapters entitled "Akiko" or "Soon Hyo," is a liminal character, neither living nor dead. As Soon Hyo/Akiko's daughter Beccah announces at the end of the first chapter that "[m]y mother is dead," Soon Hyo/Akiko is narrating as a living character in her chapters, but her narratives are haunting Beccah's chapters as the voice of the dead (Keller, *Comfort* 13). Soon Hyo/Akiko's phantomness is a traumatic effect of patriarchy and colonialism that reduces her body to a mere object that is subject to control and exploitation. Twelve-year-old orphaned Soon Hyo is "sold like one of the cows before and after [her]" into the Japanese military camp as her eldest sister's dowry (15). In the Japanese camp, Soon Hyo is forced to become Akiko #41, a comfort woman, whose body only functions as a "disposable commodity" ready to be killed or abandoned if they stop their functioning. Japanese soldiers justify their controls of the colonized female bodies, arguing that Korean women's bodies are naturally "promiscuous" and "base . . . almost like animals" that should be subjected to dominant males (22). Under this colonial rule, which is tightly imbued with racism and sexism, Soon Hyo/ Akiko's body is disciplined only to respond to the colonial orders, "close mouth" and "open legs" and her virginity is "auctioned off to the highest bidder. After that it was a free-for-all" (16, 21). Dehumanized by gendered control and violence, Soon Hyo/Akiko sees herself as a ghost whose identity and existence are denied and rejected. Under repeated sexual violations and the forced abortions, Soon Hyo/Akiko's body becomes "bruised and battered," and as the Japanese doctor describes, "impossible to properly heal" (15). Soon Hyo/Akiko describes these traumatic moments as that of her death—"when I was twelve, I was murdered" (15). She becomes a living dead—"a dead girl's body"—who undergoes a state in which her spirit was murdered but her "body moved on" (15).

Keller dramatizes how Soon Hyo/Akiko becomes a living ghost whose body serves as a site of multiple traumas of colonial/ patriarchal exploitation, but she also reveals how the same body provides a focal point for surviving. First, Soon Hyo/Akiko employs the body as a female language through which she is connected to other colonized female victims. At the military camp, Soon Hyo/ Akiko learns how to use the language of the body as an alternative means of communication and survival. Soon Hyo/Akiko remembers: "We taught ourselves to communicate through eye movements, body posture, tilts of the head, or—when we could not see each other— through rhythmic rustles between our stalls" (Keller, *Comfort* 16). Soon Hyo/Akiko sees the body as the only language that she shares with the comfort women when they are "forbidden to speak" (16). For her, this language of the body is the means of survival by which "we could speak" and "we kept our sanity" (16).

Portraying the colonized female body as a meaningful communicative mode, Keller dramatizes how Soon Hyo/Akiko ultimately exerts her historical agency by transforming her traumatized "empty body" into a dwelling place for the ghosts, in Beccah's words, by "[lending] her body to the spirits" (Keller, *Comfort* 162). As a shaman, Soon Hyo/Akiko delivers the spectral voice of Induk, a major ghost that inhabits her body. Induk is the former comfort woman Akiko #40 whom Soon Hyo/Akiko replaces at the camps after her brutal death. Induk resists the colonial command, "shut the mouth" and "open legs," by speaking out against the Japanese "invasion" of the female body and of Korea: "I am Korea, I am a woman, I am alive. I am seventeen, I had a family just like you do, I am a daughter, I am a sister" (20). This statement is her manifesto as a human being who has national and personal histories. Her statement is her act of resistance against colonial dehumanization that makes her body a mere object of masculinist sexual desire. As a result of her transgression, however, Induk is brutally murdered and her body is symbolically "skewered from her vagina to her mouth" as a colonial lesson to the rest of the comfort women, "warning [them] into silence" (20–1). Induk's ghost haunts the narrator as a symbol of female resistance as well as a figure of historical trauma.

The other ghost that haunts Soon Hyo/Akiko is that of her mother. Soon Hyo/Akiko's mother is also a victim/survivor of the Japanese massacre during the Korean independence movement of March 1, 1919. She survives by pretending to be a dead body "underneath the dead boy," her lover (Keller, *Comfort* 178). Her family reports her death and arranges for her marriage to a stranger to avoid persecution by the Japanese colonial regime. After the death of the husband, she also dies, only leaving her last words, "how tired she was" (180). The mother is a colonized victim, but Soon Hyo/Akiko understands that despite her tragic life, she is also a survivor who raises four daughters. As a survivor, the mother bequeaths her memory and history to her daughter through her "special box" that includes her "past and future" (183). Through the mother's hidden memory that the box delivers, Soon Hyo/Akiko understands her mother: "She was a princess. She was a student. She was a revolutionary. She was a wife who knew her duty. And a mother who loved her daughter, but not to stay or to take them with her"(182).

Jody Kim considers Induk and the mother as "patriotic martyred ghosts" that "haunt Keller's narrative to offer us a counter-history through the voices of the historically dominated" (65). The ghostly characteristics of these female ancestors embody the invisible history of colonized women, revealing the nation's symptomatic failure to deal with such history. Soon Hyo/Akiko repeatedly sees a vision in which Induk's ghostly body is divided, or merged into her mother's and that of her ancestral ghosts as "the boundaries between them melted, blending their features, merging their spirits" (Keller, *Comfort* 36). She witnesses scenes in which Induk's form "would blur until it doubled, then quadrupled, and she would become Induk and my mother, and in turn my mother's mother and an old woman dressed in the formal top'o of the olden days" (53). These spectral bodies haunt their female descendants, requiring them to remember the communal past that has been excluded from national and colonial history. Soon Hyo/Akiko learns the collective past of colonial women through Induk's lamenting or accusing voice that cries out that nobody remembers her "special death" and nobody performs proper rituals for her dead body.

Induk's ghost demands that Soon Hyo/Akiko redress Induk's traumatic life and death; she does so by letting Soon Hyo/Akiko "see" the spectral body. In looking at the spectral body, Soon Hyo/Akiko witnesses a materialized form of colonial trauma that she shares with the ghost:

> See me, she said as she stood up. See me as I am now. I looked and saw: hair tangled through and around maggoty eye sockets and nostrils. Gnawed arms ripped from the body but still dangled from hands to the skewering pole...I forced myself to look, to linger over details of her body. I found her beautiful...I grabbed her, and my fingers slipped into bloated flesh. I kissed it and offered her my own hands, my eyes, my skin. She offered me salvation. (Keller, *Comfort* 96)

Induk's ghost insists that Soon Hyo/Akiko see its deteriorating body, which is skewered by a pole. By "seeing" Induk's spectral flesh and blood in her trance, Soon Hyo/Akiko shares the same historical trauma with Induk's ghost. As Soon Hyo/Akiko admits, "[Induk's corpse] was Akiko 41; it was me" (Keller, *Comfort* 21). In this haunting moment, Soon Hyo/Akiko willingly provides her "empty body" to Induk as a dwelling place for the ghost. She shares "one body, one flesh" with Induk, and gains a new birth, what she calls "salvation" (96-7). For her, Induk's resistant "special death" is a sacrificial act that redeems her sin as one of survivors who remained silent about her death and left her body (96). Through Induk's pseudo-atonement, Soon Hyo/Akiko feels released from her guilt, fear and pain involved with her trauma. Her salvation means her healing from historical traumas by memorializing the silenced ghostly bodies.

By sharing one body with Induk's ghost, Soon Hyo/Akiko also achieves the double agency of the living and the dead and therefore becomes able to produce a traumatic narrative of the dead and the living, in Cathy Caruth's terms, "a double telling, the oscillation between a crisis of death and the correlative crisis of life" (7). Through this "double telling," the ghost's silenced trauma bursts with Soon Hyo/Akiko's shamanic storytelling—her ritual songs and dances that express the "unbearable nature" of Induk's death and life and her victimization and survival. This double telling also serves as a means for Soon Hyo/Akiko's own witnessing. By inviting Induk's ghost to her body, Soon Hyo/Akiko acquires a witness to her own trauma who can speak for her. Feeling that Induk fills her body, Soon Hyo/Akiko confesses: "[Induk] spoke for me: No one performed the proper rites of the dead. For me. For you. Who was there to cry for us in kok, announcing our death? Or to fulfill the duties of yum: bathing and dressing our bodies, combing our hairs, trimming our nails, laying us out?" (38). As each other's witnesses, the ghost and Soon Hyo/Akiko open their traumas to each other, circulating memories to regenerate the silenced history of the comfort women. This is the very moment of postmortem communication when the ghost and Soon Hyo/Akiko speak their traumas.

While the "Akiko" chapters deliver Soon Hyo/Akiko's haunting narratives that bring back her ghostly voice and memory, the "Beccah" chapters are the narratives of Soon Hyo/Akiko's daughter Beccah, who strives to reconstruct her dead mother's history through her traumatized childhood memories. Beccah is a hybrid character who is born and raised between an American missionary father and a Korean shaman mother. Beccah's hybrid body becomes the battleground where her cultural, historical, and spiritual inheritances clash and are reconciled. While Beccah's father Richard tries to inscribe his linguistic rules of his languages—German, English, Korean, and Japanese—by teaching those languages to her, her mother exerts the language of the body by communicating with her via motherly touches: "I touch my child in the same way now; this is the language she understands: the cool caresses of my fingers across her tiny eyelids, her smooth tummy, her fat toes" (Keller, *Comfort* 18). By touching her newborn daughter's body in the same way she touched her dead mother, Soon Hyo/Akiko conveys the language of the body, a "language I know is true," that opens a meaningful communication between her daughter and herself.

After Richard's death, Beccah's cultural and spiritual struggle occurs between her Korean mother's shamanic world and mainstream American society. For example, while Beccah's school teacher understands Beccah's first menstruation as a part of biological knowledge that she should learn from the educational video "The Time of Your Life, in fifth-grade health," Soon Hyo/Akiko understands the menstruation as "the blood of a lost spirit"—the trace by which the lost ghosts attempt to invade her daughter's body (Keller, *Comfort* 185-7). Similarly, for Soon Hyo/Akiko, her daughter's hybrid body is vulnerable because it is continuously attacked by harmful ghosts and evil energy that come from both her Korean home and American society. To protect her daughter, Soon Hyo/Akiko often performs a shamanic ritual, as Beccah remembers: "she peeled the blankets from my body, stripping me naked. When I shivered, she placed each of the seven strips of bed sheet . . . on my body . . . She ran her hands down my face, throat, arms, torso, legs, and when she touched my feet, her hands vibrated" (79). Beccah refuses her mother's shamanic protection by saying, "I wished the sal [evil energy] had killed me outright so that I would not have had to endure my mother's protection" (73). Instead, she seeks comfort in mainstream American cultural values, which offer her logical explanations for her body that is consistent with a typical American childhood.

Beccah, with her hybrid biological and cultural background, sees the "foreignness" and "similarity" between her mother's body and her own (Keller, *Comfort* 209). For Beccah, her mother's body is the subject that she identifies with and, at the same time, she feels alienated from. The bodily "similarity" gives Beccah the feeling of connection between mother and daughter. Just as Soon Hyo/Akiko communicates with her newborn daughter via motherly touches, Beccah experiences the sensation that her body is united with her mother's while massaging her mother's body: "I felt my arms disappear up to the elbows, my body reabsorbed by hers. In those moments, I knew I was truly my mother's daughter that nursed her with my light (85). However, most of the time, Beccah perceives "foreignness" in her mother's body. This "foreignness" is manifested through the mother's "singing and dancing" body, through which she communicates with the ghosts. Whenever Beccah witnesses her mother dancing in her trances, "holding in her arms raw meat—chicken, or pig's feet, or a pig's head—calling, 'Saja, Saja,' in a singing voice," she feels abandoned and discarded. Soon Hyo/Akiko's foreignness also means shame for Beccah as a mark of her mother's "insanity," "weakness" and "vulnerability" (5). This foreignness becomes clearly visible when Soon Hyo/Akiko visits her daughter's school for an exorcism (86). Beccah witnesses her mother's foreignness in her foreign body when she is surrounded by her classmates who yell at her "crazy" mother. The "insanity" and "vulnerability" of Soon Hyo/Akiko's foreign body is evidenced in her appearance as "the frail, wild-haired lady in pajamas"(86). Beccah can't take any action because she feels "ashamed" of her mother. Struggling between her ambivalent feelings of pity and shame toward her mother, Beccah "slipped away," refusing to claim Soon Hyo/Akiko's foreign body as her mother's body (89).

Soon Hyo/Akiko's sudden death enables Beccah to reconsider her mother's life. Realizing that she does not have "the facts for even the most basic, skeletal obituary" about her mother, Beccah attempts to find the clues to restore her mother's history (Keller, *Comfort* 26). The cassette tape that Soon Hyo/Akiko had left for Beccah delivers her mother's ghostly voice singing out "prayers for justice": "The women left to be picked over like fruit to be tasted, consumed, the pits spit out as Chongsindea, where we rotted under the body of orders from the Emperor of Japan" (193). For Beccah, the mother's recorded song is a song of trauma in which Soon Hyo/Akiko sings out how the colonial female bodies were exploited under Japanese imperial rule. Beccah tries to add her own voice to her mother's song as her gesture to understand and share her mother's trauma: "Chongshindae. I fit the words into my mouth, syllable by syllable, and flipped through my Korean-English dictionary, sounding out a rough, possible translation: Battalion slave" (193). Beccah realizes that her mother is a victim, as one of the comfort women, but at the same time, she also sees her mother as a survivor. Overwhelmed by the impact of her mother's ghostly voice, Beccah says, "I could not imagine her surviving what she described, for I cannot imagine myself surviving" (194).

As a witness to her mother's trauma, Beccah emerges as a new subject of remembrance. Beccah remembers her childhood when Soon Hyo/Akiko said to her, "Dance . . . Free your spirit, Beccah-chan, let it loose" as Soon Hyo/Akiko herself was "dancing and singing a song with no words" for the ghosts (Keller, *Comfort* 190). After her mother's death, Beccah performs a Korean death ritual by imitating her mother's dancing and singing "without knowing the words" (208). In this ritual, Soon Hyo/Akiko's and Beccah's bodies serve as the spaces where their traumas are inscribed and recorded: "I looked now, fighting my shame, taking her body piece by piece . . . until I could see her in her entirety, without guilt or judgment . . . I fit my hands against my mother's, palm to palm, fingertip to fingertip, mirror images . . . my hand had become my mother's"(209). Beccah's touch is reminiscent of the language of the body that Soon Hyo/Akiko employs to initiate her daughter into their collective matrilineage. By mimicking the mother's language of the body, Beccah overcomes the "shame" and "guilt" that she had for her mother's foreign body. Finally, she can identify with her mother, finding the mirror image between two female bodies, ready to share one body with the mother's ghost. Beccah begins "speaking to [her] mother" by carrying her mother's ghost in her body, "[f]eeling my mother's arms around my waist" (197). As a final part of her ritual, Beccah eats her mother's ashes while sprinkling them over the river. During this ritual, Beccah, like Soon Hyo/Akiko, claims her mother's spectral body as her own: "Your body in mine" (212). By eating the ash of the mother's body, Beccah internalizes the traumatic memories of the maternal body and becomes a surviving matrilineal descendant whose body itself represents their forgotten history.

Beccah becomes a powerful historical agent by transforming her body into a spectral body that can access her ancestors' unspeakable traumas. Keller metaphorically dramatizes Beccah's transformation through her traumatic dreams of drowning in which her mother and Induk continue to haunt her. Previously, this repeated dream represented Beccah's frustration about Soon Hyo/Akiko's and the ghost's incomprehensible "foreignness," ending with her drowning caused by her mother's "[wrapping] around her leg, holding on to [her]" (Keller, *Comfort* 141). However, in the final dream scene, Beccah "swam for hours, for weeks, for years" with her dancing mother in the river (213). She embraced her mother's ghostly body and "opened [her] mouth to drown. . . . Instead, [she] breathed in air, clear and blue . . . [she] swam through sky, higher and higher, until dizzy with the freedom of light and air (213). This dream scene indicates Beccah's rebirth and empowerment as a subversive spectral agent. Her diasporic body becomes, in Ian Baucom's term, an "intimate, intra-uterine space" in which her memory of colonial female ancestors float back-and-forth between homeland and hostland and between then, now, and yet-to-be. She knows her mother's spectral existence in her hybrid body as "a small seed planted by my mother, waiting to be born" (213).

Beccah's journey to find her own voice and subjectivity reflects that of Min in her two sculptural installations, *deCOLONIZATION* and *Remembering Jungshindae*. For Min, her deceased mother, whose story has been silenced in both her homeland and America, becomes a source of inspiration that retells the history of colonization. Just as her dead mother's hanbok floats in the air and comes out of its deserted tomb, her inherited traumatic past haunts the Korean

American daughter in postcolonial space and time, demanding them to speak for the dead. Beccah, Keller, and Min, the second generation of Korean diaspora, insert their colonial ancestors' ghostly memories into the archive of American history. These Korean American daughters' belated construction of her female ancestor's trauma opens a possibility of an alternative postcolonial history by rewriting Korean national and Japanese colonial history.

Works Cited

Baucom, Ian. "Charting the Black Atlantic." Postmodern Culture, vol. 8, no.1, 1997. *Project Muse*, muse.jhu.edu/article/27632.

Brogan, Kathleen. *Cultural Haunting: Ghosts and Ethnicity in Recent American Literature.* UP of Virginia, 1988.

Caruth, Cathy. *Unclaimed Experience: Trauma, Narrative, and History.* Johns Hopkins UP, 1996.

Cinader, Martha. "Nora Okja Keller, June 1997." *American Authors Unplugged.* Cinasphere, 2015.

Fukushima, Annie. "Comfort Women." *Encyclopedia of Asian American Issues Today*, vol. 1, edited by Wen-Chu Chen and Grace J. Yoo, Greenwood P, 2009, pp. 759-770.

Hirsch, Marianne. "Marked by Memory: Feminist Reflections on Trauma and Transmission." *Extremities: Trauma, Testimony, Community*, edited by Nancy K. Miller and Jason Tougaw, U of Illinois P, 2002, pp. 71 759.

Hong, Terry. "The Dual Lives of Nora Okja Keller," *Asianweek.com*, 5 Apr. 2002, www.asianweek.com/2002_04_05/keller.htm/.

Kang, Hyun Yi, "Conjuring 'Comfort Women': Mediated Affiliations and Disciplined Subjects in Korean/American Transnationality." *Journal of Asian American Studies*, vol.6, no.1, 2003, pp.25-55.

Keller, Nora Okja. *Comfort Woman.* Viking, 1997.

_____. "Author's Questions." *Comfort Woman.* Penguin, 1998.

Kim, Elaine H., "Dangerous Affinities: Korean American Feminisms (En)counter Gendered Korean and Racialized U.S. Nationalist Narratives." *Hitting Critical Mass*, vol. 6, no. 1, 1999, pp. 1-12.

Kim, Jodi. "Haunting History: Violence, Trauma, and the Politics of Memory in Nora Okja Keller's *Comfort Woman.*" *Hitting Critical Mass: A Journal of Asian American Cultural Criticism*, vol. 6, no. 1, 1999, pp. 61-78.

Korean Research Institute for Jungshindae. "Grandmother, What Is Military 'Comfort Women.'" Hankyeore Shinmunsa, 2000.

Min, Young Soon. *deCOLONIZATION. Yongsoonmin.com*, 1991, www.yongsoonmin.com/art/decolonization/.

_____. *Remembering Jungshindae.* Yongsoonmin.com, 1992, www.yongsoonmin.com/art/remembering-jungsindae/.

Slattery, Dennis Patrick. *The Wounded Body: Remembering the Markings of Flesh.* State U of New York P, 2000.

Dwelling in Time: The Representation of Poverty on Film
Pedro Costa's film series *Letters from Fontainhas*_____
Andrew Bingham

I. Representation and Form

Portuguese director Pedro Costa's films *Ossos* (1997), *In Vanda's Room* (2000), and *Colossal Youth* (2006)—produced together in the Criterion Collection as *Letters from Fontainhas* in 2010—stand as a remarkable achievement in contemporary European cinema. Coming out of Costa's decade-long engagement with the impoverished community of Fontainhas on the outskirts of Lisbon, Portugal, and informed by the filmmaker's steadfast directedness towards something real, the films present a few of Fontainhas' residents in the grim light of their own lives—desperate, derelict, perpetually close to death, and yet moving with life in ways that refuse to come to an end. In these films, we experience individuals dwelling, coping with the persistent troubles of their time and place, and we see the ruinous buildings in which they dwell (both as time-bound structures and as something "out of step" with what Costa's audiences may know as contemporary reality)—but with the inner and outer ruin of person and building maintaining a kind of desperate coherence, strangely dignified in its refusal of all that is not its own. Finally, in *Colossal Youth*—which, in an accompanying dialogue, Costa tells Jean-Pierre Gorin with a "violent cry" that "this is condemned [. . .] this world is over"—we see the new residences into which the people of Fontainhas are placed following the demolition of their old quarters by the government as a means of social progression. These new residences do not fit with the spirit of their new inhabitants: they are whitewashed spaces that are somehow uglier than poverty, antiseptic to the point of estrangement—for as its displaced inhabitants tell Costa, "[t]hese walls will tell nothing about us," for they are "losing" the place-bound "memory, tradition, history" of their old homes, their meaning "going blank." From this troubled ground, on which we as viewers "feel that something isn't right,"[1] I posit that a central issue conditioning Costa's trilogy is the question of fitting *representational form*, or the struggle to give some shape to one's life or (filmic) work in a way that neither obscures its truth in time and of place nor mars its authentic ethos as it proceeds to develop or to decay in time. This issue is especially significant for Costa's films, which offer an ethical standard for how to depict impoverished people and environments to an audience that almost inevitably comes from a different, higher socioeconomic reality.

In these films, Costa's techniques demand one thing in particular of his audience: the patience to dwell with the real people "who are very close to the things they represent" (not professional actors) and to whom the simple production, with its lack of artificial lighting and sound stages, offers a unique starkness. The films are blends of documentary and creative narration. I call them works of a participative maker—one who makes a work by participating in some part of life and striving to give it an aesthetic form that is appropriate to both itself and its maker's spiritual vision. In Costa's 2001 film on the filmmakers Jean-Marie Straub and Danielle Huillet—*Where does your hidden smile lie?*—Costa records Straub stating that an artwork proceeds from a general *idea* to a choice of *matter* or *material*, which is then given *form* by the artist. In his magisterial *Notes on the Cinematograph* (1986), Robert Bresson sharpens our sense of the depth of form when he writes "[f]orms that resemble ideas. Treat them as actual ideas" (22). In what follows, I will consider how Costa bears out these ideas in his trilogy: for the question of form, which is the last but also the most difficult, essential part of a good work, finally determines whether the work is authentic and will endure, or whether it is a product of kitsch replete with counterfeit sentiments and spiritual manipulation of what is new and different. It is fruitful to note here the sense of kitsch that the Austrian novelist Hermann Broch elaborates on in his brilliant and little-known essay "Evil in the Value-System of Art" (1933). He writes that kitsch is an enclosed value-system, the ends of which are self-contained and thus without any higher purpose or any interest in a different way of thinking and thus cut off from any context or relation through which it could grow or deep in 'dialogue' with something else; kitsch always disregards ethical matters and may be figured in terms of "art for art's sake" or "business for business' sake." Kitsch is a dead-end, not a road somewhere—even if at first it masquerades as such. Cinematic kitsch is a particularly nefarious instance of this false quality. First, with acting, it deals with counterfeit feelings and sentiments—it fakes what is most precious in real life. Second, cinematic kitsch, completely wrapped in layers of pretense and falseness, nevertheless wants to be successful on its own terms. This means that it must be spiritually manipulating, to convince spectators to "buy into" its counterfeit world and to find this pretense entertaining. This latter point Costa terms "the business of selling feelings," which he defines as "practically all the films that are being made today in America." For Costa, when films are "in the business of selling feelings" rather than works of art with ethical ends, they become part of the host of "unjust deals" happening in "our society," "deals which are not right in both senses of the word, not right in the sense of social injustice, and in the sense of being out of key, out of tune." Justice, similar to being "in key" or "in tune," designates a condition of something fitting with something else, of a mutually befitting measure being taken or applied.

This way of thinking about representational form and its effects involves a certain sense of apprehension, comprehension, and relation with another person or thing. First, *apprehension*— for all forms and formative actions are ways of knowing someone or something. By this I mean that our choice of, say, disinterested repetition; distant recording; dialogue; or silent, close witness will condition what we know about something or someone and will inform our ongoing interaction with them, or even allow them to be themselves and not just a figment of our own imagination. As we will see, this is a central concern in Costa's work. To speak aesthetically, a poem, novel, or play 'knows' its subject-matter each in its own way; and further, different genres of poetry, similar to different kinds of film, each know something differently from other aesthetic forms in turn. So far, this is an arguably neutral point— that different forms allow us to know something in different ways—

and to stay on this level of so-called neutral aesthetics has held an important and finally, to my mind, ruinous place in twentieth-century theories of artistic production, as if questions of aesthetics are reducible to form alone. So we must get around this (potential) stalling point by recognizing further that the process of knowing something is conditioned not only by our own approach but also by the desire to *comprehend* something different than us, something that has its own essence or integrity—its own solidity and ground. In this sense, our forms of knowing are not only chosen by us, but are elicited or demanded by that which we are seeking to know, and at this point, the question of form becomes an ethical question. Costa himself notes that beginning with *Ossos*, he sought to make his Fontainhas films "morally and cinematically interesting," having in mind that being a "good craftsman" is "conditioned" by "a good ethical position" in relation to other people and the world in general.

This sensibility is evident in Costa's trilogy, the cinematic forms of which shift from film to film. But to clarify this for ourselves, we need to ask: do our particular forms of knowing treat what we seek to know with respect for its integrity—its own inherent sense—or do they seek to impose our own values and ideas—our own preconceptions and assumptions of reality—onto it in order to make it "safe" and allow us to remain comfortable, with no need to adjust our views or change our lives through a new understanding of things? When we work to know something—to apprehend it and comprehend it—are we doing it justice, or are we diminishing it due to our own ideas of how it ought to look and be? If Bresson instructs us to be "[p]assionate for the appropriate" (14), how "appropriate"— in the sense of getting to the essence of something, not in the sense of decorum or simple adherence to established rules—is our form of knowing something, and what does this imply for our ongoing relationship with it, our future closeness with or distance from the person or thing? These matters are of the deepest ethical and aesthetic significance for Costa, who holds that

> [g]ood and evil don't exist in heaven or hell, they exist between people. The cinema exists for showing that, too. It exists so we

can see what's not working, where the evil lies between you and I, between me and somebody else, so we can see the evil in society and, so we can search for the good.

These are and must necessarily remain open and personal questions, for there is not just one fitting form that encompasses the plenitude of life—although one could, I believe, argue that there are certain fundamental forms of aesthetic and ethical sensibility that, in general, are superior to other, in the sense that they leave room for the represented persons, things, and ideas to express themselves to the greatest extent possible in a work. Costa's approach to filming impoverished lives is one such example.

II. Participative Making

In his set of very interesting seminar notes titled "A Closed Door That Leaves Us Guessing," Costa writes at some length about the art of film—what he loves and appreciates, what he sees as its sense and purpose, and what it does best. He writes:

> I believe that film is an art that can fight against excess, against inflation, against the excess of things, whether it be the excess of money, images, or effects. Instead, it should be less, less and less. Here, I'm not speaking about minimalism, but that you must find within yourselves the right feeling, something essential, perhaps very subtle, but for that you must look quite deep inside yourself, in order not to get lost and trapped by inflation.

Costa speaks on a few different levels here: first, perhaps not uniquely, but at least in particular, film can fight against "inflation." This is both an analysis of the general condition of the modern world as well as an aesthetic matter—for "inflation" is a critical term, first. Costa here means something akin to what Broch means in "The Style of the Mythical Age" (1947) when he states that "[i]f art can or may exist further, it has to set itself the task of striving for the essential, of becoming a counterbalance to the hypertrophic calamity of the world," a social condition to which the artist responds with "the style of the essential" (111). Similar to Broch, Costa's response to inflation is both aesthetic and, more crucially, ethical—for while he is not prescribing a kind of "minimalism," he advocates a stance of refusal to engage with the inflated forms offered by the world, a refusal of excess based on ethical grounds, on which the artist "cast[s] away everything that is superficial" and works to "get at something more fundamental" to human life and interpersonal relations. Finally, for Costa, the proper approach to filmmaking is not theoretical, but includes "the right feeling, something essential" found within the soul of the artist, a genuine regard for things that resist being enchanted by the reigning environment of excess that Costa sees all over the place in Western culture and, in particular, in Hollywood films (which he likens to a "McDonalds," which is "always open"). These forms of inflation or excess threaten our cultural life—the very ways in which we think and speak and make—and alongside the novelist Broch, Costa wants to posit some integral "feeling," "something essential" through which familiar and unfamiliar aspects of world may be comprehended. This matter is particularly pressing when considering poverty, for what could be more ethically obscene than spending thousands, even millions of dollars to represent impoverished life and market it to well-fed people as entertainment?

Given that throughout its brief artistic history film has struggled—perhaps due to its very method of production—with representing real poverty without some sense of inflation (of sentiment or imagery) or exploitation (because of the amounts of money and all the degrees of manipulation involved), Costa has set himself an enormous task with the Fontainhas project—for he is working to film real poor people, in real ruinous slums, without requiring that they adhere to some image he has of them. In this sense of his art, he has a few fellow filmmakers, I think. Like the great French filmmaker Robert Bresson, he is interested in "documentary"—not so much in the sense of filming new facts or events to convey hitherto unknown information, but in the sense that he is interested in real, personal responses to a certain scene or situation that he has helped to organize. In his *Notes*, Bresson writes that "[t]o create is not to deform or invent persons and things. It is to tie new relationships between persons and things which are, and *as they are*," a register of reality that Bresson qualifies as "feelings," the filmmaker's recording of which is "to be as *documentary* as possible" (13). Costa, too, wants genuine feeling and response—which, despite his claim that "cinema is made above all with feelings," remain very rare in an art form that relies in the main on professional actors and scripted actions, which Bresson critically calls "photographed theatre" (47). And like the enigmatic French film-essayist and social activist Chris Marker in films like *A Grin Without a Cat* (1977) or *Sans Soleil* (1982), Costa is interested in providing a subtle and creative narrative structure around a series of real and possible events, which both guides perceptibly and yet lets the filmed people and objects "speak for themselves" within that guiding framework. To this end, often over the course of the trilogy—especially with *In Vanda's Room*—Costa sets his camera somewhere and, for long stretches, lets his people (Vanda, Ventura, Clotilde, etc.) just be for a while, talking and moving or not talking and not moving, dwelling in familiar places and with familiar people, not behaving differently because of the camera set to record them.

I am not sure about Bresson, whose work is beyond any appellation, but Chris Marker and Pedro Costa both are what I call "participative makers." This type of "maker"—and I am using the ancient term for those individuals that "make something," that work to give some form to their concrete or cultural environment—is "participative," for this way of being recognizes explicitly that in order to know something or someone through creative form, some involvement or participation is needed. This desire for participation is one of the fundamental forms of aesthetic-ethical sensibility that, to my mind, is ethically compelling. It suggests that to really understand something, it is not enough to listen or observe or think, but that alongside these things, one must participate—somehow, to some extent—in the event, situation, condition, or tradition that one is striving to understand. One could call it an immersive, embodied form of knowledge, opposed to any abstractions, which emphasizes one's empathetic presence. The notion of participative making includes both the sense that one must participate in something before one can make a work to do with that thing and also that what one makes—the forms one produces—must participate in that thing (event, condition, idea) somehow. Participation is essential to aesthetics and ethics—to our ways of apprehending, comprehending, and relating to something or someone.

So for Costa to come to the point where he could be peacefully present in Fontainhas and film aspects of the lives of Vanda, Ventura, and the others, he slowly became familiar and friendly with them. This took some time, by his own account; it was at least a year before he could take out his camera and begin filming without feeling like he was exploiting them and without their feeling ill at ease, used, or exploited as objects by an artist from a very different cultural, economic, and educational world. Costa accomplished this difficult task (set by himself) by filming the people in their our environment, recording dialogue that both he and they—especially Vanda and Ventura—helped to shape, and allowing some room for their own sense of what is important to show. In this way, although the overall vision of the films is, of course, Costa's own, the greatness of this vision lies in his insistence that it include other voices that he could neither wholly predict nor predetermine prior to recording them with video camera and microphone. In these films, and especially in *In Vanda's Room*, the characters' own truths emerge through their voices, filtered only through camera and microphone. In this way, characters *participate* in the making of the film in an extraordinary way and to an extraordinary degree.

III. Opening

With film, to participate in something one must be interested in it and begin to feel what one sees represented on screen; that is, one must feel pulled towards it in a way that inspires a responsive action. But interested participation is not enchanted enthrallment; it is not a surrendering to what pulls one in. This is why Costa states that "one of the cornerstones of filmmaking is resistance, resisting everything"—for only by a resolute form of resistance to what is overtly attractive (and thus perhaps illusory) is one able to preserve what he calls "the right feeling, something essential" located "deep inside yourself." Only by claiming this as an unshakeable ground is one able to resist the temptation to inflation or excess, even given the material Costa works with in these films: elements of a very sad prosaic-epic story of general ruin and increasingly muffled voices echoing blankly in an increasingly cold social world. Only a great artist could accomplish this without some kind of inflation—without seeking a sentimental response or manipulating, even with decent intentions, one's emotional comprehension of the filmed persons and their stories.

In *Ossos*, *In Vanda's Room*, and *Colossal Youth* resistance is found not only in the artist's intention, however. The characters also resist—resist Costa, resist outsiders to the community, resist each other. Because so much of the strength of *Letters from Fontainhas* lies in the distinctive voices of its characters and the way they are juxtaposed with each other, with their environment, and with Costa's filmmaking approach, it feels appropriate to resist and refrain from describing scenes from films like *Letters from Fontainhas*, as to describe them drily would seem to be ethically in poor taste—to risk putting the story in one's own voice, so to speak. With that caveat, let me offer two images that speak to the characters' open resistance within the film. First, in the middle of *Colossal Youth*, a government agent is trying to convince old Ventura that an apartment in the new housing development is perfect for him and his large family. He wanders into a room, exclaiming about the benefits of the unit, and as Ventura hesitates and lags behind, somewhere in his own world of memory and dream, the spring-mounted door closes behind him, and the agent continues talking, unaware that Ventura is not only not with him in the room but almost certainly somewhere very far away inside, a place that the agent will never see nor be able to comprehend. The "somewhere else" of Ventura's soul in this scene is never really touched by Costa either, or at least he does not indicate that this is the case, despite saying to Gorin that "Ventura was our prophet."

This intuition of open distance is given stark form at the beginning of the same film—*Colossal Youth*—when we suddenly see a woman at the bottom of a ladder, on the floor below, looking up at the camera, with a knife in her hand to hold the camera at bay, telling a story of her youth, and then when she's done her story, knife still aloft, she backs away into the darkness, resistant to any continuation of stories or filming. These images are both startling and pull us in, and yet we are or become aware that it does not work well to describe these things in isolation, as if a single image of a person's life suffices to let us into the story of that life. Single images may express something, but they do not suffice in any sense of aesthetic wholeness as isolated events. This may seem paradoxical, but while a single camera shot or image may have a certain wholeness or fullness, this whole or full quality emerges only through relation. This is what film may do: by putting an image into relation with other images, it lets the first image be whole. Costa addresses the concentration possible in a cinematic image when he writes that "all the feelings of life must pass through your shot" and inwardly form the filmic image. The fullness or wholeness of an image is set against its own "inflation" and any inappropriate submission to the strength of the other images with which it is set in relation by the filmmaker.

This is what Costa means when he writes that "[i]n films, we resist. It is the material itself that resists. You see it in the clips. There are things that resist in relation to other things, one image another, one sound resists another." The strength of a singular cinematic image—one which pulls us in—may be further clarified through two of Bresson's *Notes*. Considering the matter of beauty, he writes that a "film's beauty will not be in the images," an approach he characterizes as "postcardism" (76). Unlike a postcard, which deals entirely with trite, meretricious beauty, for Bresson, a film ought to include "[n]ot beautiful photography, not beautiful images, but necessary images and photography" (56). Images are "necessary" when they are integral to the various sets of relations of which the film is comprised, and as these images take root in the film and strengthen in relation to other images, they may attain a kind of beauty of their own. But beauty can never be the goal from the start, it cannot define the grounds on which the film stands. This is the region of kitsch, and all that kitsch brings with it.

To give something a fitting form in order to know it, to participate in something in order to understand in a way that allows for creation and making, to feel the tension of interest and resistance and to maintain both—all of these are involved in the process of becoming close to something, which I think is another of those fundamental movements in life. It is a kind of deep desire that is prompted by a generally abstract but sometimes particularly concrete love for the world and for the person in the world that I think is a significant part of human nature. And so having watched these films, I feel sometimes that I have grown closer, that I love Vanda and Ventura in some way—and, of course, I am wrong: I do not love them; I cannot love them, except at a "distance," as Costa notes. But this is the final form of resistance that is needed: the resistance of the audience to the temptation of identification, in two senses: the first and most basic sense is to resist the urge to identify with the characters on the screen. To give in to this form of identification is to forget the idea that proper closeness is impossible without some form of concrete interaction and intimacy, and identification, in this case, inevitably ends with the spectator projecting something onto the filmed person. To this situation, Costa responds: "[i]t's absolutely necessary that you [the audience] must be outside, not on the screen. Never cry or suffer with the character who suffers on the screen, never."

The second sense of identification one must resist is the conflation of the filmed person with the person in real life (and of course, this only pertains to films such as Costa's which deal with real people and not with actors; to do this with Hollywood films would be senseless). To do this is to forget that depiction never exhausts and that illumination is never complete or final at once and that "something on the screen resists" the viewer, inevitably, for one person can never come to the end of another person. And that, indeed, may be a fair description of what Costa accomplishes with these three great films: he shows us something real, but never comes to its end, never assumes or pretends he has control of the whole person and story. In essence, he shows that "a film doesn't hold a complete truth, a film is for making us think, and to have different ideas about things." Reality, even the most prosaic, quotidian existence, is inexhaustible and never "completed." Costa's work always opens up rather than closes down, but this opening does not preclude the persons and things in the work from keeping some things close, or from closing certain doors of their own: "[t]hat's life, opening and closing doors," Costa states. This is to say that Costa's films open certain characters (real persons) to us and open our eyes to certain characters, who even when and as they resist all identification and summation, begin to show us part of themselves. But to show is also to conceal—it is to say this and not that, or to pull away even as one pulls towards—and so when we are talking about people who exist beyond any script or recorded extemporization, we need to keep in mind that as open as they may be or seem, they are also in a way closed to us, a "closed door" through which we may not burst. When a film manages to convey this state of things, Costa writes, it is due to "directors who hide things, who close the doors," and yet through the depth of the film "you can open them, sometimes. Yet, to open the doors of such films is difficult, dangerous—it's work." It is work, for "a film that slightly closes the door," that neither gives nor withholds everything, requires that one meet it half-way, on mutual ground, and demands one's efforts: "it tells you that you can feel pain, but not everything, and so that suggests a bit of trouble." Pain is not neutral territory, but pain felt is mutual territory—one must be alive, as a good film is alive—not closed off from reality.

IV. Closing—the Genuine at the Center of the Work
When a film includes a closed or partly closed door, then it partakes of life's quality of being partially clear. Not everything in life is open, and not everything is closed, but the tension and balance that emerge through the opening and closing make life interesting. This is figured in a film when, in Bresson's words, an image occurs "[w]here not everything is present, but each word, each look, each movement has things underlying" (18). When a film includes real people, as do Bresson's films and Costa's *Letters from Fontainhas*, the "things underlying" are unavailable even to the director, and occur or sway things "*[e]ven in contradiction with what [the director] had imagined*" (*Notes* 52). When this happens, even the director does not "control" the people in the film, in the sense of deciding how and what they will show and conceal. On this ground, our encounters with filmed individuals resembles more clearly our

encounters in daily life, except, perhaps, through the cinema we become more aware of the various ways in which we may tend to succumb to projection or manipulation. In this sense, Costa states that "the cinema is made for concentrating our vision" of things and other persons; despite its technical apparatus, a film is able to give us something genuine and teach us how to see it as genuine. Costa's *Letters from Fontainhas* represent (re-present, make present again) the impoverished lives of a few inhabitants of Fontainhas. He gives us genuine images, and if we do his films justice—if we see them in a manner and with a vision befitting their images—we encounter them as they are, both opening and closing to us and to others. Costa's trilogy shows us how someone is in time, and he accomplishes this by eschewing all condescension to what he films and for whom he films. He eschews all inflation, all excuse, all explanation, and instead seeks, in so far as this is possible, to depict some things and some people as they are and in terms of their own essential reality in a way which augments or renews our understanding of them. In "A Closed Door," Costa reflects on this relationship of art to life: "[c]inema is not exactly life," he writes, but "it works with the ingredients of life and you organise, construct these ingredients in a manner different from life," through an appropriate cinematic form that fits with their reality and does them justice, and in this way, one is "going to see them in a different light."

V. What Remains: Dwelling in Time and Fire

The "different light" a film gives to things "concentrates our vision" of the reality we face in life and on film and reminds us that like events in one's life, "a film doesn't hold a complete truth" but rather is good "for making us think" and keeps our minds supple "with different ideas about things." In films like Costa's Fontainhas trilogy, we find an aesthetic-ethic of representation focused on genuine encounters and on how a person dwells in place and time and belongs there. To respect this dwelling, the filmmaker must work to establish and then remain true to the manner in which one is able to participate—to whatever degree—in this and to give it form and then to demonstrate how one's chosen form is fitting for the work and the ends at which one aims, which must include letting the persons, things, and relationships of one film belong both in their own dwelling places and in the film. On this ground, the "ingredients of life" the filmmaker uses form a cinematic composition—a composition of filmic images that *com-poses*, which places and arranges things with other things in order that something real is felt and seen to be vital, interesting, and worthy of one's time and attention.

I write above "in films like Costa's trilogy," but, of course, no one good or great film is like another good or great film in any significant way. Are there filmmakers close to Costa—his familiars, so to speak? I brought up Straub and Huillet, Bresson, and Marker already, to which one could, I suppose, add Béla Tarr. These filmmakers are by no means identical or even similar in product, but some of their concerns may converge, in a certain light. Even in this esteemed group of great filmmakers, though, Costa's accomplishment with *Ossos*, *In Vanda's Room*, and *Colossal Youth* stands out. For in this work, Costa was able to give filmic form to certain real people, to illuminate—even if all too briefly—how they live, what remains of their lives, and the remains in which they continue to live. Most significantly, Costa shows us how a few inhabitants of Fontainhas were able to maintain some integrity, some wholeness in their lives, through the basic stance of resistance—resistance towards Costa, towards each other, towards us as film viewers, towards the wealthy who disdain them, and towards the government who condescends to them. This basic stance means "to resist fear, to resist death," Costa states in "A Closed Door," and he elaborates:

> [w]hen I say 'resist,' it's a fight. This is not violence . . . yes, there is some violence, but it's not the violence that we impose on ourselves. That needs to be made clear. There's a form of violence that exists in the world, that comes from the beginning of the world, from fire. The other, social, violence must be resisted as strongly as possible, and by the cinema too.

If Costa is concerned with this latter, destructive violence—violence that colonizes the existences of Vanda and Ventura—he fights it not by direct opposition (which all too often only reinforces how things are) in his films but by showing us the kind of vital human fire it extinguishes. In this matter, Costa harkens back to Cézanne and Straub:

> [a]s Cézanne says, we need to see the fire that's hidden in a person or in a landscape. We must strive for what Jean-Marie Straub describes: if there's no fire in the shot, if there's nothing burning in your shot, then it's worthless. Somewhere in the shot, something must be on fire.

In Costa's filmed Fontainhas, Vanda and Ventura are on fire. The films are "letters" addressed to us from Fontainhas, which through Costa's work make our lives richer, more difficult and complex, and more interesting as an ongoing result. The film-letters are made of people whose voices and faces remain with us, whom we keep encountering and hearing in new contexts in our own dwelling in time and place.

Note

1. Unless otherwise noted, quotations in this chapter are from Costa's address "A Closed Door That Leaves Us Guessing," n.p.

Works Cited

Bresson, Robert. *Notes on the Cinematograph*. Translated by Jonathan Griffin, NYRB, 1986.

Broch, Hermann. "Evil in the Value-System of Art." *Geist and Zeitgeist: The Spirit in an Unspiritual Age*, edited and translated by John Hargraves, Counterpoint, 2002.

_____. "The Style of the Mythical Age." *Geist and Zeitgeist: The Spirit in an Unspiritual Age*, edited and translated by John Hargraves, Counterpoint, 2002.

Costa, Pedro. "A Closed Door That Leaves Us Guessing." *Rouge*. Translated by Downing Roberts, 2005, www.rouge.com.au/10/costa_seminar.html/. Accessed 4 Dec. 2017.

_____. *Letters from Fontainhas*. Criterion Collection, 2010.

_____. *Where does your hidden smile lie?* AMIP/CONTRACOSTA/Arte France/INA, 2001.

Immigrants, Nationalism, and Xenophobia in London
Anders Lustgarten's play *A Day at the Racists*_____

Önder Çakırtaş

Introduction

After the First and Second World Wars, ethnic and racial formations began to increase on the axis of nationalism. Indeed, the movement of nationalism, which was effective in the disintegration of states such as the Ottoman Empire and the Soviet Union, led to the formation of states determined to an extent by ethnic population. However, nationalism is not such a recent concept. In introduction to *Nationalism*, John Hutchinson and Anthony D. Smith state that "as an ideology and movement, nationalism exerted a strong influence in the American and French Revolutions, yet it did not become the subject of historical enquiry until the middle of the nineteenth century, nor of social scientific analysis until the early twentieth century" (3). Nevertheless, when historical analysis is made, it is observed that this concept has begun to be adopted, especially after the First World War, when nation states have begun to emerge. "The conception of the national state which was embodied in nineteenth century nationalism attained its highest point in 1919 and the following years," writes Alfred Cobban, who continues, "but it was a mistake to suppose that this was the end of its history" (250). The ideology of nationalism has maintained its existence over the years, but with different characteristics.

In the current century, we see the various permutations of nationalism. It is not a farfetched idea that wars and national traumas, such as those we have seen in the past eighteen years, push nations together and result in immigration. This contact creates and reignites ideological and political discourses, among them, discourses of nationhood and nationalism. Nationalization and national identity are always a threat for immigrants. Immigrants are forced to leave their home countries and to adapt to the identity of the country to which they migrate. Moreover, they are often forced into economically difficult situations, causing nationalists in their new country to accuse them of harming the national economy. For these reasons, they are always foreigners and always exposed to xenophobia.

Such xenophobic attitudes and behaviors in the context of British nationalism are what Anders Lustgarten portrays in *A Day at the Racists*. The ideology of nationalism is the core of Lustgarten's play, in which he explores immigration in Britain, its most imperative issue in the twenty-first century; at the same time, the play participates in a satirical dialogue about how fears of foreigners affect people in psychosocial and socioeconomic terms. *A Day at the Racists* is a political drama that endeavors to comprehend why working-class individuals might feel drawn to the British National Party (hereafter BNP) and also detects the unseen grounds of that psychology: the political neglect of and disloyalty toward the working class by New Labour. Though Lustgarten introduces the play with the words "This play is written in testament to the (forgotten) history of British working-class activism" (253), my main focus in this paper will be on the pejorative approach to the "unwanted different races" and "sinful immigrants" within contemporary London, the setting of the play. I will first explain London's change in identity from multicultural to "nationalist" and "racist," and then I will focus on the core of the play: the desire to define the concept of Britishness as against all other ethnic and cultural identities, despite the multicultural identity of London. The concepts of immigration, race, nationalism, and economic class will be discussed around the concept of Britishness.

London: From a Multicultural Identity to an Unequal One

In *A Day at the Racists*, Lustgarten gives a very realistic dramatization of present-day London, given that London's population has changed dramatically over the last decade. Basically, London is a huge city that tolerates the existence of various kinds of people within its crowded community. So much so that the first act of the play introduces us to the Arabs, Poles,

Blacks and local people in the neighborhood. London rapidly became a destination for migrants after the expansionist policies of England, and eventually it became one of the most overpopulated and cosmopolitan cities in the world. This idea is explained in the following words by Candice Goucher and Linda Walton:

> Industrial and commercial enterprises sought labour, markets and resources and transported all of them for the maximization of profit. Industrialization, wherever it occurred, furthered the migration of capital and labourers, while creating world markets. This was particularly true for industries such as mining and manufacturing. The expansion of empires accelerated migration. The colonial enterprise relied on taxation and forced the colonized to seek wage labour opportunities. [. . .] Postcolonial migrations have continues to pull the populations of the former colonies back to metropoles such as Paris and London, where economic and educational advantages are sought—but not always received—by the immigrants. (670)

These migrations are creating noticeable change in London's population, which is reshaping its identity. The newcomers continue to be the foremost reason for this change since the very beginning of 2010, when this play was written and performed. The reasons for migration vary: there are economic, political, social factors as well as conflicts in Middle Eastern, African, and Caribbean countries. To Shamit Saggar, "Within living memory two waves of migration (postwar, postcolonial and following the accession of the eastern European nations to the EU) have transformed the nature of the capital" (167). In a research project on migration into London that covers the years between 2001 and 2011, on the other hand, Kerwin Datu categorizes the migrants as the poor and the rich. In the category of poor countries, he counts EU post-2001 member states, European countries not in the EU, North America and Caribbean (pre-1980), Central and South America, Middle East, Africa, and Asia (14), and he states that:

> Much debate about migration into London—whether in politics, in the tabloids, on social media or elsewhere—tends to focus on

migrants moving from poorer countries to London to find economic opportunities not available in their countries of origin. (Datu 11)

Datu, who outlines a map of the distribution of immigrants in London, expresses their distribution with the words "ghettoisation in the countryside" to underline what happens to the locations they choose for their settlements and observes that economy is the main concern of many immigrants who originate from poor countries. In fact, immigration to London is a kind of "British Dream" for people in poor countries because they are longing for economic prosperity, peace, freedom, and human rights. To Jonathan Portes, who has done some research on the impacts of migration on the UK economy, there are "broader questions about the dynamic effects on the economy, which economists expect to be substantially more important" (117) as more work is done on them; he suggests that

> [m]igration wasn't really a big issue in this country politically from about the late 1970s to about 1997, as it had been in the late 1960s and early 1970s. At that time, it was not framed as an economic issue but it was primarily about race and the social issues that result from that. As a consequence, there were relatively few economists in this country working in this field, and very little quantitative analysis. (117)

The fact that immigration was seen first as a "racial" problem caused a number of other problems to be ignored. Therefore, the fact that immigrants had economic and political influences for a long time was ignored.

The consequences of immigration in London are also diverse. The most prominent issues occur in business and housing crises. To Christine Whitehead, "Housing is one of the most important factors generating tension between migrants and local populations" (143) in London "because migrants are seen as taking away one of the scarcest resources from those with prior rights" (143). Whitehead also points out that the resulting demand for housing has caused a serious rise in housing prices, along with increasing housing problems. This, of course, causes more conflict between immigrants and the local people.

There is no doubt that immigration influences politics, too. Large numbers of new residents can cause changes to the city's demographics. For example, previous residents may decide they need to relocate. As expressed by Saggar:

> Forty years ago, migrants were too few in number, struggled to enter the mainstream and were marginal to political leadership. Much of that has changed dramatically. Liberal markets and social trends have driven an intake of additional numbers on a large scale. Demographic twists have occurred with the younger migrant age structures being concentrated in the optimal years for child bearing and rearing. Settled migrant communities have started to navigate— some more successfully than others—opportunity structures in education, housing and employment. Significant gains for some have resulted, but with patterns of disadvantage for others. But the scale of population growth and churn has overwhelmed parts of the city and with it the capacity for public bodies to cope. Long-standing, white Londoners (and some black and brown ones too) have left the capital in disproportionate numbers, in part fuelled by fears about the pace of change. (167-68)

The changing sociocultural structure, the increase of different ethnic identities, and a lot of political turmoil have led to the emergence of a new "nationalist" threat to the "others" in Europe. Karen Wren suggests a view in this direction:

> While European integration is creating a Europe without internal borders, there has been growing tension around the concepts of 'race' and nation, as the nation state loses some of its functions, and suffers from a crisis of legitimacy. This has manifested in different ways, with some nation states experiencing a resurgence of separatist nationalism, while others attempt to unify the crumbling nation state by relying on powerful ideologies of nationalism, strengthening national identity through the projection of cultural homogeneity, and asserting the boundedness of culture and exclusion of 'others.' (141)

The emergence of race as the point of tension in the changes the EU was making has led to Britain's recent willingness to leave the EU. As a result of last year's referendum, British Prime Minister Theresa May triggered the two-year process of leaving the EU on March 29, 2017. My study examines one representation of immigrants trying to survive in a nationalist, xenophobic London. I analyze ideological and political sentiments using psychoanalytic methods. London is a British city that resists multiculturalism. That's why one of the main themes of the play is Britishness.

Racism and Xenophobia on Londoners' Stage: *A Day at the Racists*

Alexander J. Motyl argues that "Imperial expansion was critical to the self-definition of the British as a people." He continues, "In a highly complex discourse that included literature, political tracts, religious ephemera, and fiction, the British propagated the idea that the spread of the British Empire was critical for the spread of civilization throughout the globe" (Motyl 62).[1]

In an inversion of this imperialism, as Pete Case complains, his country now suffers its own invasion. In the play, such immigration-based problems as economic imbalances, asylum problems, racial and cultural complications are expressed via a satirical song that is uninterruptedly repeated by immigrant characters: "'Oh I've got a brand new leather jacket and a brand new mobile phone/Brits they live in cardboard boxes while we get furnished homes/Legal aid, driving lessons, central heating and free bills/Oh we get all the benefits and you get all the bills" (Lustgarten 259-260; 263; 268).

In his introduction to the play, Lustgarten quotes a famous dictum of Malcolm X, "Racism is like a Cadillac. There's a new model every year" (253), through which he builds his understanding of British racist and nationalist boundaries as exemplified through his challenging characters. *Merriam-Webster's Collegiate Dictionary* defines nationalism as "exalting one nation above all others and placing primary emphasis on promotion of its culture and interests as opposed to those of other nations or supranational groups," while it defines racism as "a belief that race is the primary determinant of human traits and capacities and that racial differences produce an inherent superiority of a particular race." The overlap of these definitions is the focal point of this play, whose first act features foreigners who are seen as a disruption of a cosmopolitan society. These foreigners in the play are the Africans, the Arabs, the Poles, and the Russians, among some other less visible groups. The resulting confrontations are also sources of intergenerational friction.

Early on, the playwright foregrounds the play's nationalist and racist themes, because Pete Case, the antihero, is "a *white* man in his fifties" (Lustgarten 259). A former leading Labour Party organizer in the local car factories, Pete Case now barely survives as a painter and decorator for his friend's company because immigrant workers often undercut him. Pete is the main character in whom Lustgarten deposits the idea of British nationalism and Britishness as racist-leaning. While doing this, Lustgarten, quite intentionally, gives Pete's words an ironic interpretation. When, for instance, Pete says "Where's it gone, the energy, the confidence, the belief we used to have in this country? The only people who's got it now are the immigrants" (274), Lustgarten emphasizes that British patriotism places high precedence upon the stability of Britain's ethno-racial accumulation and its central phenotypes. While insisting that the British people in his country should endeavor to ensure Britain's national self-protection, Pete is very angry that the country's laws do not take measures against those who migrate from the outside, and he refuses to support them. For this reason, he is confused about how the ruling parties in Britain have perceived the immigration issue and related problems. And he finds it really hard to conceive that the government—though this is believed to be a consequence of multiculturalism strategies—is open to providing housing to the non-British, who are here to earn their livings. That's why he tells Gina:

> My son, right, born and raised in this area, and I went down the social and they've got *nothing* for him, it's all gone to these immigrants on the basis of greater need. And maybe they have got needs, those people, and good luck to 'em, but *so do we*. And we was here first. Nothing against them but we was here first and more than that, we put

our shift in. I've paid my taxes and I put a shift in and I want what's coming. Not to me, because I'm a worn out old bugger. (Lustgarten 277)

Pete's son Mark can't acquire an occupation or get onto the housing list. No one, from his Labour MP to his granddaughter's teacher, gives him the impression they are concerned with this. Pete says, "The only way you can get your son on the housing list is to make him homeless" (Lustgarten 274). Then he comes across an unanticipated proposal that is offered by Gina White, "a young, well-dressed, Asian-looking woman" (Lustgarten 275) standing for Parliament on a platform of serving the local society. She is supporting the British National Party (BNP) and tries to convince Pete to join the BNP. Pete does not want this because he has been a part of the Labour Party, though he has been surprised by what the Labour Party has done. Pete thinks that "we made the Labour Party, do you know what I mean? Froze our bollocks off on picket lines, went on strike and lived off fresh air and fuck all for six months at a time. And now we've turned to dust in their eyes, ain't we? We're the fucking *problem* now. . ." (269-70). In the play, the most comprehensive talk on nationalism and racism is between these two. For instance,

> **Pete:** I'm not a *fascist*, Gina, I'm not a racist!
> **Gina:** Do you think we should cut back on the number of immigrants in this country, who undercut British workers and put them out of jobs?
> **Pete:** I don't have a problem with people trying to feed their—
> **Gina:** Do you think we should cut back on the number of immigrants—
> **Pete:** Yes, I do, I do, alright. (Lustgarten 278-79)

These beliefs are, in fact, a kind of xenophobia. As expressed by Önder Çakırtaş, "Racist behavior brings with it fear and the feeling of exclusion from society that leads a person to psychologically group himself as 'other.' In psychology, fear of the 'others' is termed xenophobia" (14). The playwright emphasizes this by naming one of the characters Zenobia, "a young, middle-class black woman" (Lustgarten 279), who represents such kind of pejorative approach of the British people to an outsider. In Britain, as the play discloses, the British people intend to keep immigrants out of their hometowns. Lustgarten thus establishes a bridge with British past and constantly reminds us the consciousness in the British history in this play. For instance, when Pete comes across Mark's mixed-raced daughter's teacher Zenobia, they talk about the curriculum of the courses, though Zenobia insists she doesn't "set the curriculum" (280). However, Pete's remarks reflect something great part of British nationalism in which "It is usually the case that the teaching of national history is at the centre of school history courses" (Beer 2).

> **Zenobia:** That was an Asian festival. This is Black History Month.
> **Pete:** OK. Fair enough. *(He looks around.)* Lot of . . . lot of ethnic stuff she is getting at the minute.
> **Mark:** It's Black History Month, Dad.
> **Zenobia:** It's the time of year. Come back at Christmas or Easter, it'll be different.
> **Pete:** Other made-up stuff, you mean?
> **Zenobia:** Pardon?
> **Pete:** When does she study the rest of it?
> **Zenobia:** The rest of what?
> **Pete:** Her heritage. British history.
> **Zenobia:** This is part of British history.
> **Pete:** Part of, yes. And I can understand that, why you want to give her all this lot, it's something your generation probably never got. (Lustgarten 280)

Black History Month, adopted in the UK over thirty years ago and observed in October, is considered an important historical reminder in the UK. Paraphrasing Abul Pitre and others, in fact, Black History Month is considered important and celebrated each year because it is a reaction against the ignored or downplayed contributions of the Black community in British and American history. Black History Month proposes to redress this wrong by displaying the accomplishments and aids of the black community over the years (16-18). Thus the statements of Pete Case seem intended to be

---

disgraceful, signalling that he is far from seeing the black community as a whole and, more specifically, Zenobia as part of British history.

Angry Young Men and Anders Lustgarten

Since capitalism is an important theme of the play, *Angry Young Men*, on which Lustgarten bases his work, needs to be addressed as well. Lustgarten opens the play with the introductory words of Trevor Griffiths, "You start from the presumption that only you are intelligent and sensitive enough to see how bad capitalist society is" (253), through which he uncovers the problems of working-class society and the burdens brought by a capitalist society. Here, it is very obvious that Lustgarten draws on the ideas of a well-known group preceding him, a group of mostly working- and middle-class British playwrights and novelists who became prominent in the 1950s. Susan Brook notes that the term "Angry Young Men"

> was coined in the 1950s to describe both authors and dramatists such as John Osborne, John Braine, Alan Sillitoe, Colin Wilson, and Arnold Wesker, and the protagonists of their texts—the disaffected, alienated, lower-middle class, or working class young men typified by Jimmy Porter in Osborne's *Look Back in Anger* (1956), or Joe Lampton in Braine's *Room at the Top* (1957). (19)

In their work, these Angry Young Men protested against a wasteful and extravagant culture as well as wealthy persons' abnormal values and their characteristics. They aimed to emphasize the rights of the working-class community. As suggested by Walter G. Moss, the Angry Young Men and the Beat Generation confronted society with "their common 'existentialism,' their realization of the anxiety of the modern life, their belief that 'long-term goals have lost their relevance,' and that in the atomic age it was necessary to live in the 'moment'" (219).

In this play, Pete embodies an Angry Young Man protesting against the values of conventional consumerist society in England. As Pete's anger and misery slowly conquer his time-honored hatred of the BNP, Pete experiences various psychological weaknesses arising from Gina's campaign. This causes him to move in an unbearable political direction that puts him in opposition to his long-held thinking and newborn endeavors. He is a working-class activist who did not reach his ideals; instead, he is forced to obey the rules of the capitalist society. Pete, just like John Osborne's characters in *Look Back in Anger*, is coming from lower-class English society, and his resentment is aimed mainly at the Labour Party, in which he previously believed, for its support of immigrants. In his dialogues with Gina, for instance, Pete almost vomits his hatred against the politics of the Labour Party:

> **Pete:** But to the people who's important to me. And you look at who's in charge nowadays, the *contempt* they have for working-class people, taking away pensions and healthcare that people've been paying for decades and then bang, just like that, privatised, gone. . . . And you can take it from scum like the Tories cos they've always been that way, but from the Labour Party. . . .
> *He hesitates for a moment.*
> **Gina:** Carry on.
> **Pete:** Cos we made the Labour Party, do you know what I mean? Froze our bullocks off on picket lines, went on strike and lived off fresh air and fuck all for six months at a time. And now we've turned to dust in their eyes, ain't we? We're the fucking *problem* now: chav scum. ASBO meat. A source of *laughter*. Prime time TV entertainment. I hate them for it. I bloody hate them for it. (*Pause.*) Sorry. Sorry. (Lustgarten 277-78)

This is the most obvious statement that Pete wants to leave the Labour Party, to which he has loyally devoted a large part of his life. In fact, this is also a symbol of a tragic collapse, since Pete's loss from a psychosocial perspective is that he has to leave a political party that he associates with his identity.

Pete is angry, and this is the problem of the psychology of alienation. Brook uses the phrase "angry texts" to express "significant differences in the class backgrounds and political allegiances of the protagonists" (20), and to her, "the emphasis on the political significance of these 'angry texts' can be seen in their initial reception during the 1950s and early 1960s" (20) when "[. . .] these texts were identifying political problems and representing authentic experience [. . .]" (22). When considering this theatrical work as an "angry text"—as a "text which seems to have been most strongly associated with political rebellion" (Brook 22)—we can understand Pete as a character forcibly reshaped in terms of politics and economics and about to be displaced from the political party he had belonged to, something he has resisted until the last moment. It is thus Pete's own shift in political allegiance that makes him so angry.

In this play, Lustgarten introduces the history and the fiction in the context of "interpretation of the facts" and "story told about them" that Hayden White proposes in his study of *Historical Emplotment and the Problem of Truth* (39). In his play, Lustgarten presents competing interpretations of the facts of British history. He presents nationalist and racist ideology to his audience through characters reacting to the presence of immigrants in London. At the same time, he brings us together with those who have endless economic struggles so that we can understand that they are angry because they are in economic collapse. They believe that Britishness must be the focal point that makes them "more equal than" the others. Pete wants this. But he fails.

Note

1. As suggested by Bärbel Völkel, "After the collapse of the old orders during the European revolutionary movements in the eighteenth and nineteenth centuries, the modern state developed in part from the necessity to adjust the power relationships between people and to ensure the functional differentiation of society by providing a legal system" (31).

Works Cited

Brook, Susan. "Engendering Rebellion: The Angry Young Man, Class and Masculinity." *Posting the Male: Masculinities in Post-War and Contemporary British Literature*, edited by Daniel Lea and Berthold Schoene, Rodopi, 2003.

Cobban, Alfred. "The Rise of the Nation-State System." *Nationalism*, edited by John Hutchinson and Anthony D. Smith, Oxford UP, 1994.

Çakırtaş, Önder. "Double Portrayed: Tituba, Racism And Politics." *International Journal of Language Academy*, vol. 1, no. 1, Winter 2013, pp. 13, 22.

Datu, Kerwin. "Settlement patterns of migrants from rich and poor countries into the London metropolitan region since 2001." *Migration and London's growth: final report of LSE London's HEIF 5 project on Migration and the Transformation of London*, edited by Ben Kochan, LSE London, 2014.

Goucher, Candice, and Linda Walton. *World History: Journeys from Past to Present*—vol. 2, from 1500 CE to the present, Routledge, 2003.

Low-Beer, Ann. "School History, National History and the Issue of National Identity." *International Journal of Historical Learning, Teaching and Research*, volume 3, no. 1, Jan. 2003.

Lustgarten, Anders. *A Day At The Racists*. Bloomsbury, 2015.

Moss, Walter G. *An Age of Progress?: Clashing Twentieth Century Global Forces*. Anthem Press, 2008.

Pitre, Abul, Ruth Ray, and Esrom Pitre. *The Struggle for Black History: Foundations for a Critical Black Pedagogy in Education*. UP of America, 2008.

Portes, Jonathan. "Immigration and the UK economy: interaction between policy and economic research since the mid-1990s" *Migration and London's growth: final report of LSE London's HEIF 5 project on Migration and the Transformation of London*, edited by Ben Kochan, LSE London, 2014.

Saggar, Shamit. "London as a migration city in the context of UK politics" *Migration and London's growth: final report of LSE London's HEIF 5 project on Migration and the Transformation of London*, edited by Ben Kochan, LSE London, 2014.

Völkel, Bärbel. "Nationalism–Ethnicity–Racism? Thinking History in a World of Nations." *Review of History and Political Science*, vol. 2, no. 1, March 2014, pp. 29-50.

Whitehead, Christine. "The impact of migration on London's housing" *Migration and London's growth: final report of LSE London's HEIF 5 project on Migration and the Transformation of London*, edited by Ben Kochan, LSE London, 2014.

White, Hayden. "Historical Emplotment and the Problem of Truth" *Probing the Limits of Representation*, edited by Saul Friedlander, Cambridge UP, 1992.

RESOURCES

Additional Works on the Theme_____

Alexie, Sherman. *Flight*. Black Cat, 2007.

Alvarez, Julia. *How the Garcia Girls Lost Their Accents*. Algonquin Books, 2010.

Anand, Mulk Raj. *Untouchable*. Arnold-Heinmann, 1933.

Anzaldúa, Gloria. *Borderlands, La Frontera: The New Mestiza*. Aunt Lute Books, 1987.

Aristotle. *The Nicomachean Ethics*. Translated by David Ross, Oxford UP, 2009.

Boas, Franz. *Anthropology and Modern Life*. W.W. Norton, 1962.

Brecht, Bertolt. *Brecht on Theatre: The Development of an Aesthetic*. Edited and translated by John Willet. Methuen Drama, 1964.

Céline, Louis-Ferdinand. *Death on the Installment Plan*. Translated by Ralph Manheim, New Directions, 1966.

Cha, Theresa Hak Kyung. *Dictée*. U of California P, 2001.

Chesnutt, Charles. *The House behind the Cedars*. 1900. Modern Library, 2003.

Child, Lydia Maria. *Hobomok and Other Writings on Indians*. Rutgers UP, 1991.

Das, Bhagwan. *In Pursuit of Ambedkar: A Memoir*. Navayana, 2010.

Davenport, Kiana. *Song of the Exile*. Ballantine, 1999.

Dececco, John, and William A. Percy. *Outing: Shattering the Conspiracy of Silence*. Haworth P, 1994.

Dostoevsky, Fyodor M. *Demons*. Translated by Richard Pevear & Larissa Volokhonsky, Vintage, 1995.

_____. *The Devils*. Translated by David Magarshack, Penguin Books, 1971.

_____. *The Gambler: Stories of the 1960s*. Raduga Publishers, 1990.

_____. *The Insulted and the Humiliated*. Raduga Publishers, 1989.

_____. *Notes from the Dead House*. Translated by Guy Cook and Elena Cook, Raduga Publishers, 1989.

_____. *Notes from the Underground*. Translated by Constance Garnett. Dover, 1992.

_____. *Poor Folk*. Boni and Liveright, 1917.

_____. *Winter Notes on Summer Impressions*. Translated by Richard Lee Renfield, McGraw-Hill, 1965.

Du Bois, W. E. B. *The Souls of Black Folk*.

Himes, Chester. *If He Hollers Let Him Go*, 1945.

Huxley, Aldous. *Brave New World*. Chatto and Windus, 1932.

Joseph, Manu. *Serious Men*. Harper Collins, 2010.

Kang, Han. *Human Acts*. Hogarth, 2014.

Kingston, Maxine Hong. *Woman Warrior*.

Lorde, Audre. *Sister Outsider.*

Menchú, Rigoberta. *I, Rigoberta Menchú*.

Moraga, Cherrie, et al. *This Bridge Called My Back: Writings by Radical Women of Color*.

Morrison, Toni. *Beloved*.

_____. *A Mercy*.

_____. *Paradise*.

_____. *Song of Solomon*.

Reed, Peter J., and Marc Leeds, editors. *The Vonnegut Chronicles: Interviews and Essays*. Greenwood, 1996.

Rousseau, Jean-Jacques. *Discourse on the Origin of Inequality*. 1755. Oxford UP, 2009.

Silko, Leslie Marmon. *Ceremony*.

Tolstoi, Alexei. *Aelita*. Lenizdat, 1922.

Twain, Mark. *Puddn'head Wilson*.

Vonnegut, Kurt. *Cat's Cradle*. 1963. Penguin, 1999.

_____. *God Bless You, Mr. Rosewater*. 1965. Vintage, 1992.

_____. *Slapstick, or Lonesome No More*. 1976. Vintage, 2008.

Walker, Alice. *The Color Purple*.

Wells, Herbert. *The Time Machine*. Penguin, 2005.

Wright, Richard. *Native Son*.

X, Malcolm. *Autobiography*.

Zamyatin, Yevgeny. *We*. Garziani, 1924.

Bibliography

Adorno, Theodor. *Aesthetic Theory*. Edited and translated by Robert Hullot-Kentor, Minnesota UP, 1997.

Aleisis, Angela. *Making the White Man's Indian: Native Americans and Hollywood Movies*. Praeger Publishers, 2005.

Altman, Dennis. *Homosexual Oppression and Liberation*. U of Queensland P, 2012.

Anderson, Victor. "Introduction." *Beyond Ontological Blackness: An Essay On African American Religious and Cultural Criticism*. Continuum, 1999.

Andrews, William L. *To Tell a Free Story: The First Century of Afro-American Autobiography, 1760–1865*. U of Illinois P, 1986.

Angus, Ian. *Identity and Justice*. U of Toronto P, 2008.

Anthony, Ronda C. Henry. "What's Love Got to DO With It? James Baldwin, Cross-Racial/Sexual Bond(age)ing, and the Cult of Hegemonic Black Masculinity." *Searching for the New Black Man: Black Masculinity and Women's Bodies*. Mississippi UP, 2013, pp. 99-126.

Anzaldúa, Gloria. *Borderlands, La Frontera: The New Mestiza*. Aunt Lute Books, 1987.

Awkward, Michael. *Inspiriting Influences: Tradition, Revision and the Afro-American Women's Novels*. Columbia UP, 1991.

Bakhtin, Mikhail. *Speech Genres and other late essays*. Translated by Vern W. McGee, U of Texas P, 1986.

Balshaw, Maria. "'Black Was White': Urbanity, Passing, and the Spectacle of Harlem." *Journal of American Studies*, vol. 33, no. 2, Aug. 1999, pp. 307-22, xroads.virginia.edu/~drbr/balshaw.pdf/.

Bell, Bernard. *The Afro-American Novel and Its Tradition*. U of Massachusetts P, 1987.

Bellin, Joshua David. *The Demon of the Continent: Indians and the Shaping of American*. U of Pennsylvania P, 2001.

Berlin, Ira. *Generations of Captivity: A History of African-American Slaves*. Harvard UP, 2003.

Blackmer, Corrine E. "The Veils of the Law: Race and Sexuality in Nella Larsen's *Passing*." *College Literature*, vol. 22, no. 3, Oct. 1995, pp. 50-67, www.jstor.org.proxy01.its.virginia.edu/stable/25112208/.

Blassingame, John W. *The Slave Community: Plantation Life in the Antebellum South*. Oxford UP, 1979.

Blay, Zeba. "Toni Morrison: Fear Of Losing White Privilege Led To Trump's Election." *The Huffington Post*, 21 Nov. 2016, www. huffingtonpost.com/entry/toni-morrison-fear-of-losing-white-privilege-led-to-trumps-election_us_58330ee2e4b058ce7aac0964/.

Bogar, Adam T. "Victims of a Series of Accidents: Attention and Authority in Kurt Vonnegut's The Sirens of Titan." *The Arts of Attention*, edited by Adam T. Bogar et al., Éditions L'Harmattan, 2016, pp. 359-71.

Boix, Carles. *Political Order and Inequality: Their Foundations and Their Consequences for Human Welfare*. Cambridge UP, 2015.

Bordo, Susan. "The Body and the Reproduction of Femininity." *The Norton Anthology of Theory and Criticism*, edited by Vincent B. Leitch, W.W. Norton & Company, 2010, pp. 2240-54.

Bovilsky, L. *Barbarous Play: Race On The English Renaissance Stage*. U Of Minnesota P, 2008.

Bowles, Samuel, Eric Alden Smith, and Monique Borgerhoff Mulder, editors. "Special Section: Intergenerational Wealth Transmission and Inequality in Premodern Societies." [special section] *Current Anthropology*, vol. 51, no. 1, 2010, pp. 7-126. *JSTOR*, www.jstor. org/stable/10.1086/648539/.

Broch, Hermann. *Hugo von Hofmannsthal and his time*, edited and translated by Michael P. Steinberg, U of Chicago P, 1984.

Brody, Jennifer DeVere. "Clare Kendry's 'True' Colors: Race and Class Conflict in Nella Larsen's *Passing*." *Callaloo: A Journal of African-American and African Arts and Letters*, vol. 15, no. 4, Fall 1992, pp. 1053-65, www.jstor.org.proxy01.its.virginia.edu/stable/2931920/.

Bulgakov. Michail. *The Heart of a Dog*. Collins, 1968.

Butler, Judith. "Performative Acts and Gender Constitution: An Essay in Phenomenology and Feminist Theory." *Theatre Journal*, vol. 40, no. 4, 1988, pp. 519-31. *JSTOR*, 24 Nov. 2015.

Calvo Pascual, Mónica. "Kurt Vonnegut's *The Sirens of Titan*: Human Will in a Newtonian Narrative Gone Chaotic." *Bloom's Modern Critical*

Views: Kurt Vonnegut, new ed., edited by Harold Bloom, Infobase, 2009, pp. 53-63.

Casellas, J. "'Race' and the Construction of English National Identity: Spaniards and North Africans in English Seventeenth-Century Drama." *Studies in Philology*, vol. 106, no. 1, 2009, pp. 32-51, www. jstor.org/stable/20464343/.

Casey, Edward S. *Remembering: A Phenomenological Study.* Indiana UP, 2000.

Chapman, Matthieu. *Anti-Black Racism in Early Modern English Drama: The Other "Other".* Routledge, 2017.

Chapman, Roger. "Fyodor Dostoyevsky, Eastern Orthodoxy, and the Crystal Palace." *Historic Engagements with Occidental Cultures, Religions, Powers*, edited by Anne Richard and Iraj Omidvar, Palgrave Macmillan, 2014, pp. 35-55.

Chernyshevsky, Nikolai. *What Is To Be Done?* Translated by Michael R. Katz, Cornell U P, 1989.

Choi, Chungmoo. "Nationalism and Construction of Gender in Korea." *Dangerous Women: Gender and Korean Nationalism*, edited by Elaine H. Kim and C. Choi, Routledge, 1998, pp. 9-32.

Cormier-Hamilton, Patrice. "Black Naturalism and Toni Morrison: The Journey Away from Self-Love in *The Bluest Eye*." *MELUS*, vol. 19, no. 4, Winter 1994, pp. 109-127.

Costo, Rupert and Jeanette Henry. *Indian Treaties: Two Centuries of Dishonor.* Indian Historian P, 1990.

Davis, Charles, and Henry Louis Gates Jr., eds. *The Slave's Narrative.* Oxford UP, 1985.

Deloria, Philip. *Indians in Unexpected Places.* UP of Kansas, 2004.

Derrida, Jacques. *Specters of Marx: The State of the Debt, the Work of Mourning, and the New International.* Translated by Peggy Kamuf, Routledge, 1994.

Dippie, Brian W. *The Vanishing American: White Attitudes and U.S. Indian Policy.* UP of Kansas, 1982.

Doran, Michael, editor. *Conversations with Cézanne.* Translated by Julie Lawrence Cochran, U of California P, 2001.

Drake, Kimberly. "Rape and Resignation: Silencing the Victim in the Novels of Morrison and Wright." *Lit: Literature Interpretation Theory*, vol. 6, no. 1-2, 1995, pp. 63–72, doi:10.1080/10436929508580148/.

_____, and Missy Dehn Kubitschek. "Toni Morrison: A Critical Companion." *African American Review*, vol. 35, no. 2, 2001, p. 333, doi:10.2307/2903273/.

Ehrenreich, Barbara. *Nickel and Dimed: On (Not) Getting By in America*. Picador, 2011.

Ernest, John. *Liberation Historiography: African American Writers and the Challenge of History, 1794–1861*. U of North Carolina P, 2004.

Escott, Paul D. *Slavery Remembered: A Record of Twentieth-Century Slave Narratives*. U of North Carolina P, 1979.

Evans-Pritchard, E. E. *Social Anthropology*. Cohen & West, 1951.

Felman, Shoshana. *The Scandal of the Speaking Body: Don Juan with J. L. Austin, or Seduction in Two Languages*. Stanford UP, 2003.

Fiske, David, Clifford W. Brown, and Rachel Seligman. *Solomon Northup: The Complete Story of the Author of Twelve Years a Slave*. Praeger, 2013.

Fitzgerald, Shelia, editor. "Feodor Mikhailovich Dostoevski." *Short Story Criticism*, vol. 2, Gale, 1989.

Foster, Frances Smith. *Witnessing Slavery: The Development of Antebellum Slave Narratives*. 2nd ed., U of Wisconsin P, 1994.

_____. *Written by Herself: Literary Production by African American Women, 1746–1892*. Indiana U P, 1993.

Foucault, Michel. "Sex, Power, and the Politics of Identity." *Ethics: Subjectivity and Truth*, edited by Paul Rabinow, translated by Robert Hurley, et al., New P, 1997, pp. 163-74.

Frank, Joseph. *Between Religion and Rationality: Essays in Russian Literature and Culture*. Princeton UP, 2010.

_____. *Dostoevsky: The Seeds of Revolt, 1821–1849*. Princeton UP, 1976.

_____. *Dostoevsky: The Stir of Liberation, 1860–1865*. Princeton UP, 1986.

Galbraith, James K. *Inequality: What Everyone Needs to Know*. Oxford UP, 2016.

Gardner, Jared. *Master Plots: Race and the Founding of an American Literature 1787–1845*. Johns Hopkins UP, 1998.

Gates, Henry Louis, Jr., and Anthony Appiah. *Toni Morrison: Critical Perspectives Past and Present*. Amistad, 1993.

Geertz, Clifford. *Works and Lives: The Anthropologist as Author*. Stanford UP, 1988.

Genovese, Eugene. D. *Roll, Jordan, Roll: The World the Slaves Made*. Pantheon, 1974.

Girard, René. *Deceit, Desire, and the Novel*. Translated by Yvonne Freccero, Johns Hopkins UP, 1965.

Gombrowicz, Witold. *Diary*. Translated by Lillian Vallee, Yale UP, 2012.

Gordon, Avery. *Ghostly Matters: Haunting and the Sociological Imagination*. U of Minnesota P, 1997.

Gravlee, Clarence C. "How Race Becomes Biology: Embodiment of Social Inequality." *American Journal of Physical Anthropology*, vol. 139, no. 47–57, 2009, pp. 47-57.

Gross, Theodore. "The World of James Baldwin." *Critique: Studies in Modern Fiction*, vol. 7, 1962, pp. 139-49.

Grusky, David, editor. *Social Stratification: Class, Race and Gender*. Westview P, 2001.

Grusky, David B., and Szonja Szelényi, editors. *The Inequality Reader: Contemporary and Foundational Readings in Race, Class, and Gender*. Westview Press, 2007.

Harper, Michael S., and Robert B. Stepto. *Chant of Saints*. U Illinois P, 1979.

Hartman, Saidiya V. *Scenes of Subjection: Terror, Slavery, Self-Making in Nineteenth-Century*. Oxford UP, 1997.

Hemer, Oscar. "Writing and Methodology: Literary Texts as Ethnographic Data and Creative Writing as a Means of Investigation." *Methodological Reflections on Researching Communication and Social Change*, edited by Norbert Wildermuth and Teke Ngomba, Palgrave, 2016, pp. 161-82.

Hering, Frank. "Sneaking Around: Idealized Domesticity, Identity Politics, and Games of Friendship in Nella Larsen's *Passing*." *Arizona Quarterly: A Journal of American Literature, Culture, and Theory*, vol. 57, no. 1, Spr. 2001, pp. 3560, muse.jhu.edu.proxy01.its.virginia. edu/article/445001/pdf/.

Hicks, George. *The Comfort Women: Japan's Brutal Regime of Enforced Prostitution in the Second World War*. Norton, 1995.

hooks, bell. *Feminist Theory: From Margin to Center*. South End P, 2000.

Huhndorf, Shari M. *Going Native: Indians in American Cultural Imagination*. Cornell UP, 2001.

Isenberg, Nancy. *White Trash: The 400-Year Untold Story of Class in America*. Viking, 2016.

Izumi, Mariko. *Rhetorics of Responsibility: Comfort Women Reparation Debates and the Ethos of Postwar Japan*. U of Minnesota, 2007.

Jackson, Robert Louis. "Polina and Lady Luck in *The Gambler*." *Fyodor Dostoevsky*, edited by Harold Bloom, Chelsea House, 1988, pp. 187-209.

Johnson, E. Patrick. "'Quare' Studies, or (Almost) Everything I know about Queer Studies I Learned from my Grandmother." *Black Queer Studies*, edited by E. Patrick Johnson and Mae G. Henderson, Duke UP, 2005, pp. 124- 60.

Johnson, Walter. *Soul by Soul: Life Inside the Antebellum Slave Market*. Harvard UP, 2000.

Jones, John. "The Possessed." *Fyodor Dostoevsky*, edited by Harold Bloom, Chelsea House, 1988, pp. 237-267.

Justino, Patricia, and Bruno Martorano. "Inequality, Distributive Beliefs and Protests: A Recent Story from Latin America." *HiCN Working Papers*, vol. 218, Households in Conflict Network, 2016.

Kapches, Mima, and John T. Mayhall. "Anthropology: Wampeters, Foma and Granfalloons." *Canadian Review of Physical Anthropology*, vol. 1, no. 1, 1979, pp. 1-4.

Kaye, Peter. *Dostoevsky and English Modernism, 1900–1930*. Cambridge UP, 1999.

Kawash, Samira. *Dislocating the Color Line: Identity, Hybridity, and Singularity in African-American Narrative*. Stanford UP, 1997.

Kenworthy, Lane, and Malami, Melissa. "Gender Inequality in Political Representation: A Worldwide Comparative Analysis." *Social Forces*, vol. 78, no. 1, September 1999, pp. 235-267.

Kilby, Jane. "The Writing of Trauma: Trauma Theory and the Liberty of Reading." *New Formations*, vol. 47, 2002, pp.217–32.

Kim, D. H. & R. R. Sundstrom. "Xenophobia and Racism." *Critical Philosophy of Race*, vol. 2, no. 1, pp. 20-45. Penn State UP, 2014.

Kjettsa, Geir. *Fyodor Dostoyevsky: A Writer's Life*. Fawcett Columbine, 1987.

Klarman, Michael J. *Unfinished Business: Racial Equality in American History*. Oxford UP, 2007.

Klein, Marcus. "James Baldwin: A Question of Identity." *After Alienation: American Novels in Mid-Century*. World Publishing Company, 1962, pp. 180-82.

Lareau, Annette, and Dalton Conley, editors. *Social Class: How Does It Work?* Russell Sage Foundation, 2008.

Leatherbarrow, W. J. *Dostoevskii and Britain*. Berg, 1995.

Lee, So-Hee. "Cultural Citizenship as Subject-Making in Comfort Woman and A Gesture Life." *Feminist Studies in English Literature*, vol. 14, no. 2, 2006, pp. 91–123.

Lévi-Strauss, Claude. *The Elementary Structures of Kinship*. Revised ed., Beacon Press, 1969.

Levinas, Emmanuel. *Ethics and Infinity*. Translated by Richard A. Cohen, Duquesne UP, 1985.

Lewis, Earl, and Heidi Ardizzone, *Love on Trial: An American Scandal in Black and White*. Norton, 2001.

Locke, Alain, editor. *The New Negro*. 1925. Simon & Schuster, 1997.

Lord, Robert. *Dostoyevsky: Essays and Perspectives*. U of California P, 1970.

Mantsios, Gregory. "Class in America—2012" *Race, Class, and Gender in the United States*, edited by Paula S. Rothenberg with Kelly S. Mayhew, Worth Publishers, 2014.

Manza, Jeff, and Michael Sauder, editors. *Inequality and Society: Social Science Perspectives on Social Stratification*. W.W. Norton, 2009.

Marubbio, M. Elise. *Killing the Indian Maiden: Images of Native American Women in Film*. UP of Kentucky, 2006.

Mathews, Roy T., F. Dewitt Platt, and Thomas F. X. Noble. *Experience Humanities*. McGraw-Hill, 2014.

McBride, Dwight A. *Impossible Witnesses: Truth, Abolitionism, and Slave Testimony.* UP, 2001.

McCammack, Brian. "A Fading Old Left Vision: Gospel-Inspired Socialism in Vonnegut's *Rosewater.*" *The Midwest Quarterly*, vol. 49, no. 2, 2008, pp. 161-78.

McKay, Nellie. *Critical Essays on Toni Morrison.* Hall, 1988.

Morrison, Toni. "Unspeakable Things Unspoken." *Within the Circle*, Jan. 2012, pp. 368–398, doi:10.1215/9780822399889-029/.

Moser, Charles A. "The Achievement of Constance Garnett." *American Scholar*, vol. 57, no. 3, Summer 1988, pp. 4311-438.

Myrdal, Gunnar. *An American Dilemma: The Negro Problem and American Democracy.* 8th ed., Harper,1944.

Newey, K. "Racism on the Victorian Stage: Representation of Slavery and the Black Character." *Victorian Review*, vol. 35, no. 1, 2009, pp. 265-267. *Project MUSE*, 2 May 2017.

Nisetich, Rebecca. "Reading Race in Nella Larsen's *Passing* and the Rhinelander Case." *African American Review*, vol. 46, nos. 2-3, Sum.-Fall 2013, pp. 345-61, muse.jhu.edu.proxy01.its.virginia.edu/journals/african_american_review/v046/46.2-3.nisetich.html/.

Nunes, Zita C. "Phantasmic Brazil: Nella Larsen's *Passing*, American Literary Imagination,and Racial Utopianism." *Mixing Race, Mixing Culture: Inter-American Literary Dialogues*, edited by Monika Kaup and Debra J. Rosenthal, U of Pennsylvania P, 2002, pp. 50-61.

Olivelle, Patrick. *The Law Code of Manu.* Oxford UP, 2004.

Pachmuss, Temira. *F. M. Dostoevsky: Dualism and Synthesis of the Soul.* Southern Illinois UP, 1963.

Panichas, George A. *Dostoevsky's Spiritual Art: The Burden of Vision.* Transaction Publishers, 2005.

Parker, Emma. "'Apple Pie' Ideology and the Politics of Appetite in the Novels of Toni Morrison." *Contemporary Literature*, vol. 39, no. 4, 1998, p. 614, doi:10.2307/1208728/.

Pathak, Bindeshwar, and Satyendra Tripathi. *Windows in India. Study of Varanasi and Vrindavan.* Rawat Publications, 2016.

Pestana, Carla G., and Sharon V. Salinger, ed. *Inequality in Early America.* UP of New England, 1999.

Piatote, Beth H. *Domestic Subjects: Gender, Citizenship, and Law in Native American Literature.* Yale UP, 2013.

Powell, Timothy B. "Toni Morrison: The Struggle to Depict the Black Figure on the White Page." *Black American Literature Forum*, vol. 24, no. 4, 1990, p. 747, doi:10.2307/3041800/.

Ross, Marlon B. "Beyond the Closet as Raceless Paradigm." *Black Queer Studies: A Critical Anthology*, edited by E. Patrick Johnson and Mae. G. Henderson, Duke UP, 2005, pp. 161-89.

Roy, Arundhati. *Algebra of Infinite Justice.* Penguin, 2001.

_____. "Come September." Lensic Performing Arts Center, 29 Sept. 2002, Santa Fe, NM. Keynote Address.

_____. *Field Notes on Democracy: Listening to Grasshoppers.* Haymarket Books, 2009.

_____. *In Which Annie Gives It Those Ones: The Original Screenplay.* Penguin, 2003.

_____. "Introduction: The Doctor and the Saint." *Annihilation of Caste*, by B. R Ambedkar, 1936, Verso, 2014, pp. 17-141.

Roy, Arundhati. *Power Politics.* South End P, 2001.

Salih, S. "Can Fiction 'Do' Racism?" *Eighteenth-Century Life*, vol. 34, no. 3, 2010, pp. 48-50.

Savage, Mike. *Social Class in the 21st Century.* Penguin Random House, 2015.

Scarry, Elaine. *The Body in Pain: the Making and Unmaking of the World.* Oxford UP, 1985.

Schalk, Sami. "Transing: Resistance to Eugenic Ideology in Nella Larsen's *Passing*." *Journal of Modern Literature*, vol. 38, no. 3, Spr. 2015, pp. 148-61, muse.jhu.edu.proxy01.its.virginia.edu/article/587567/.

Schneider, Mark Robert. *African Americans in the Jazz Age: A Decade of Struggle and Promise.* Rowman & Littlefield, 2006.

Schultermandl, Silvia. "Writing Rape, Trauma, and Transnationality onto the Female Body: Matrilineal Em-body-ment in Nora Okja Keller's *Comfort Woman*." *Meridians: Feminism, Race, Transnationalism*, vol. 7, no. 2, 2007, pp.71–100.

Sedgwick, Eve K. *The Epistemology of the Closet.* U of California P, 1990.

_____. *Tendencies.* Duke UP, 1993.

Seidman, Steven. *Beyond the Closet: The Transformation of Gay and Lesbian Life*. Routledge, 2002.

Sekora, John, and Darwin T. Turner, editors. *The Art of Slave Narrative: Original Essays in America*. Oxford UP, 1997.

"Settler Colonialism." *Global Social Theory*. Accessed 4/8/2018. https://globalsocialtheory.org/concepts/settler-colonialism/.

Sharpe, Christina. *Monstrous Intimacies: Making Post-Slavery Subjects*. Duke UP, 2010.

Shields, Charles J. *And So It Goes: Kurt Vonnegut, a Life*. Henry Holt and Co, 2011.

Shin, Andrew, and Barbara Judson. "Beneath the Black Aesthetic: James Baldwin's Primer of Black American Masculinity." *African American Review*, vol. 32, no. 2, 1998, pp. 247-61. *JSTOR*, 3 Mar. 2014.

Simmons, Ernest J. *Introduction to Russian Realism*. Indiana UP, 1965.

Sinyavsky, Andrei. *Soviet Civilization: A Cultural History*. Arcade Publishing, 1988.

Slonim, Mark. *An Outline of Russian Literature*. Oxford UP, 1958.

Smith, Andrea. "Heteropatriarchy and the Three Pillars of White Supremacy: Rethinking Women of Color Organizing." In *Color of Violence: the INCITE! Anthology*. Cambridge, MA: South End Press, 2013.

Smith, Andrea, et al. *Color of Violence: the INCITE! Anthology*. Duke UP, 2016.

_____. "Heteropatriarchy and the Three Pillars of White Supremacy." *Color of Violence: the INCITE! Anthology*, edited by Andrea Smith et al., Duke UP, 2016.

Smith, Mark M. *How Race is Made: Slavery, Segregation, and the Senses*. U of North Carolina P, 2006.

Soh, C. Sarah. *The Comfort Women: Sexual Violence and Postcolonial Memory in Korea and Japan*. U of Chicago P, 2009.

Somerville, Siobhan B. "Feminism, Queer Theory, and the Racial Closet." *Criticism*, vol. 52, no. 2, 2010, pp. 191-200. *JSTOR*, 7 Aug. 2014.

_____. *Queering the Colorline: Race and the Invention of Homosexuality in American Culture*. Duke UP, 2000.

Stapledon, Olaf. *The Last and First Men*. Victor Gollancz, 1999.

Stetz, Margaret Diane, and Bonnie B. C. Oh. *Legacies of the Comfort Women of World War II*. M.E. Sharpe, 2001.

Straub, J. M. & D. Huillet. *Writings*, edited and translated by Sally Shafto, Sequence Press, 2016.

Stuckey, Sterling. *Slave Culture*. Oxford UP, 1987.

Suggs, Jon-Christian. *Whispered Consolations: Law and Narrative in African American Life*. U of Michigan P, 2000.

Sumner, Charles. "Humanist Drama in *A Clockwork Orange*." *The Yearbook of English Studies*, vol. 42, 2012, pp. 49-63, doi:10.5699/yearenglstud.42.2012.0049/.

Sundquist, Eric J. *To Wake the Nations: Race in the Making of American Literature*. Harvard UP, 1993.

Suvin, Darko. *Metamorphosis of Science Fiction*. Yale UP, 1979.

_____. *Positions and Presuppositions in Science Fiction*. Kent State UP, 1988.

Tafira, Kenneth. "Is xenophobia racism?" *Anthropology Southern Africa*, vol. 34, nos. 3&4, 2011.

Tally, Robert T., editor. *Critical Insights: Kurt Vonnegut*. Salem Press, 2013.

Tarkovsky, Andrei. *Sculpting in Time*. Translated by Kitty Hunter Blair, U of Texas P, 1987.

_____. *Time within Time: The Diaries 1970–1986*. Translated by Kitty Hunter-Blair, Faber & Faber, 1991.

Tarr, Bela. *Satantango*. Facets Video, 2008.

Toth, Josh. "Deauthenticating Community: The Passing Intrusion of Clare Kendry in Nella Larsen's *Passing*." *MELUS: The Journal of the Society for the Study of the Multi-Ethnic Literature of the United States*, vol. 33, no. 1, Spr. 2008, pp. 55-73, www.jstor.org.proxy01.its.virginia.edu/stable/30029741/.

Wald, Gayle Freda. *Crossing the Line: Racial Passing in Twentieth-Century Literature and Culture*. Duke UP, 2000.

Weiner, Mark S. *Black Trials: Citizenship from the Beginnings of Slavery to the End of Caste*. Alfred Knopf, 2004.

Wells, Joshua. "Vonnegut, Anthropology, and the Cat's Cradle of Human Socio-Politics." *YouTube*, uploaded by Joshua Wells, 11 Nov. 2013, www.youtube.com/watch?v=HItT9IDJGuk/.

White, Deborah Gray. *Ar'n't I a Woman: Female Slaves in the Plantation South*. W.W. Norton, UP, 1979.

Wilson, Mary. "'Working Like a Colored Person': Race, Service, and Identity in Nella Larsen's *Passing*." *Women's Studies: An Interdisciplinary Journal*, vol. 42, no. 8, Dec. 2013, pp. 979-1009, dx.doi.org.proxy01.its.virginia.edu/10.1080/00497878.2013.830541/.

Woodard, Colin. *American Nations: A History of the Eleven Rival Regional Cultures of North America*. Viking, 2011.

Young, James O. *Cultural Appropriation and the Arts*. Blackwell Publishing, 2010.

About the Editor

Kimberly Drake is Associate Professor and directs the writing and rhetoric major at Scripps College, where she teaches creative nonfiction writing and American literature and culture. She received her bachelor's degree and PhD in English at the University of California, Berkeley, where she specialized in protest literature (including African American literature and working-class literature), theories of race and gender, and theories of writing. Her current scholarly interests lie in writing (literary and popular) that seeks to bring attention to social justice issues. Her publications reflect this interest; for the Critical Insights series of Salem Press, she has been volume editor and contributed chapters to *Literature of Protest* (2013), *The Slave Narrative* (2014), and *Paranoia, Fear and Alienation* (2017). She also contributed a chapter on Chester Himes' critical reception to the Critical Insights volume *Social Justice in American Literature* (2018). Her monograph *Subjectivity in the American Protest Novel* (Palgrave Macmillan, 2011) concerns trauma theory, double consciousness, and topological constructions of identity in novels by Richard Wright, Ann Petry, Chester Himes, Tillie Olsen, and Sarah Wright. She also edited the recipes and stories for the collection *Stinging for their Suppers: How Women in Prison Nourish Their Bodies and Souls* (Lulu Press 2013), a collection of women's writing about cooking in prison. Other publications focus on gender-neutral pronouns and writing pedagogy; prison literature; and punk rock music and memoir. Her current projects concern social determinism and intellectual authority in the American detective novel and canine support in the writing conference.

Contributors_____

Professor Peter Arnds has been Head of the German Department and also of the Italian Department and the Director of Comparative Literature at Trinity College Dublin. His publications include monographs on Wilhelm Raabe and Charles Dickens (Peter Lang, 1997), "Representation, Subversion and Eugenics in Günter Grass's *The Tin Drum*" (Camden House, 2004), and 'Lycanthropy in German Literature' (Palgrave Macmillan, 2015); "Translating Holocaust Literature" (Vandenhoeck & Ruprecht, 2015), the translation of Patrick Boltshauser's novel *Stromschnellen* (*Rapids*, Dalkey Archive Press, 2014, nominated for the IMPAC, Dublin International Literary Award), and "A Rare Clear Day" (RedFox Press, 2015), a collection of his poetry and watercolors. His novel *Searching for Alice* will appear with Dalkey Archive Press in 2019. Most recently, he has spent several months as a fellow to JNU, Delhi, and the J.M. Coetzee Centre for Creative Practice at the University of Adelaide to work on prose and a project entitled "Wolves of the World: Myth, Trauma, Literature." He is a member of the PEN Centre for German Writers Abroad.

Andrew Bingham attended Queen's University (PhD, 2018); his thesis is titled "Aspects of Intimacy: Authority and Integrity in the Modernist Novel." He cofounded, coedits, and writes for *Modern Horizons* (modernhorizonsjournal.ca). More of his writing may be found at http://queensu.academia.edu/AndrewBingham.

Adam T. Bogar, born in 1984, holds an MA English Language & Literature degree (2012) and he has been a member of the Kurt Vonnegut Society (blogs.cofc.edu/vonnegut) since 2009. He has been working as an independent scholar and translator for over thirteen years; his recent notable publication credits include coediting the essay collection *The Arts of Attention* (Éditions L'Harmattan-L'Harmattan Press, 2016) and publishing "Books as Metaphors in *The Martian Chronicles* and *Fahrenheit 451*" (in *Critical Insights: Ray Bradbury*, 2017), "Victims of a Series of Accidents: Attention and Authority in Kurt Vonnegut's The Sirens of Titan" (in *The Arts of Attention*, 2016), "Bradbury, Technology, and the Future of Reading" (in *Critical Insights:* Fahrenheit 451, 2014) and

"Can a Machine Be a Gentleman? Machine Ethics and Ethical Machines" (in *Critical Insights: Kurt Vonnegut*, 2013). He has also been publishing his poetry as well as literary translations. He maintains his portfolio at atbogar.wordpress.com/.

Dr. Sonia Mae Brown holds a MA in English with a focus in creative and professional writing from Long Island University and a PhD in English literature with a focus in African American literature from Howard University. Her research areas are eroticism, sexuality, gender, queer theory, and afro-futurism. Her interests include black women's subjectivity, black female sexuality, sex as a discursive act, language, power, and popular culture. As a self-proclaimed "eroticist" or sexual anthropologist, Dr. Brown is dedicated to enriching the current scholarship on "The Erotic" and exploring the potential for eroticism to be seen as a critical lens of textual inquiry. She is currently working on an essay titled "The Sadomasochistic Impulse in James Baldwin's Literature."

Önder Çakırtaş holds his PhD from Süleyman Demirel University, Isparta (2015) and specializes in political drama, comparative drama, and modern Turkish drama. He is the author of *Politics and Drama* (Apostolos Academic Publishing, 2016) and the editor of *Ideological Messaging and the Role of Political Literature* (IGI Global, 2017), and *Literature and Psychology: Writing, Trauma and the Self* (Cambridge Scholars, 2018). Since 2012, he has been publishing a series of articles on drama, dealing with both theory and practice. He has also published articles and translations in various journals of literature. He is currently teaching English literature in the Department of English Language and Literature at Bingol University, Turkey.

Roger Chapman holds a PhD in American culture studies and history from Bowling Green State University. During the 1990s, he lived five years in Russia, mostly in the city of St. Petersburg, and became a student of Dostoyevsky's works. As Professor of History at Palm Beach Atlantic University, Dr. Chapman regularly teaches courses on American history, Russian history, Cold War history, and Western humanities.

Boyarkina Iren got her PhD in English literature from the University of Rome "Tor Vergata" in 2014. Her PhD thesis "Musical Metaphors and Parables in the Narratives by Olaf Stapledon" is dedicated to the works by this great science fiction writer and philosopher. She has also done extensive research in the field of English and American science fiction literature, English and American literature of the nineteenth and twentieth centuries, feminist literature, cognitive linguistics, and translation studies. She has published works dedicated to Olaf Stapledon, Doris Lessing, H. G. Wells, Arthur Clarke, Mary Shelley, Anne Tyler, Henry James, James Joyce, and Edith Wharton, among others.

Lucky Issar has worked in the field of education in India and Denmark. Currently, he is doing research at the Department of English Philology at Free University of Berlin, Germany. He loves reading literature, traveling, and living in Denmark. He is an admirer of the Indian author Arundhati Roy and her works.

Robyn Johnson is a first-year PhD student at the University of California Riverside, focusing on Native American literature and culture. She received her master's in literature from the University of Tennessee Chattanooga and her bachelor's in secondary education English and mathematics from DePaul University. Robyn is interested in Native American literature, traditional stories, how non-Natives represent Native Americans in literature, early American literature, folklore, and pop culture. Robyn has previously published two articles, "I Will Not Bow: Analysis of the Feminine Refusal of Hegel's Master-Slave dialectic in Inuyasha" (2017) in the *International Journal of Comic Art* (IJOCA) and "A World Without Fathers: Patriarchy, Colonialism, and the Male Creator in Northwest Tribal Narratives" (2014) in *American Indian Quarterly*. When not attending school, Robyn travels to literary and interdisciplinary conferences internationally to present and participate in the discussion of Native American and American literature.

Almas Khan is a fellow at Georgetown Law and a recent PhD graduate in English literature from the University of Virginia. Her scholarship concentrates on American literature's interaction with jurisprudence and doctrinal developments in constitutional law, particularly as implicating civil rights after the Civil War. Almas is presently revising her dissertation, "A Fraught Inheritance: Legal Realism, Literary Realism, and the Forging of American Democracy," into a monograph. She has previously published articles in the *Cambridge Journal of Postcolonial Literary Inquiry*, the *English Academy Review*, and the anthology *Social Justice and American Literature* (editors Robert Hauhart and Jeff Birkenstein, Salem Press).

Ji Nang Kim earned her PhD in English from Texas A&M University in 2015 and is currently working at Houston Baptist University. She majored in Asian/Asian diaspora literature and culture with a special interest in postcolonial theory and Asian American studies. Her research investigates the intersections between trauma studies, body/gender studies, and postcolonial/transnational theories with an interdisciplinary methodology that combines visual arts, film, literature, and history. Currently, she is developing her dissertation, *Transnational Spectrality: History, Trauma and Phantom Bodies in Postcolonial Asian Art and Literature*, for book publication. The project especially discusses Nora Okja Keller's *Comfort Woman*, Salman Rushdie's *Midnight's Children*, and Michael Ondaatje's *Anil's Ghost*, along with visual art works that dramatize traumatic Asian histories, such as military sexual slavery during Japanese colonial rule in Korea, the Partition of India and Indo-Pakistani wars, and the Sri Lankan Civil War.

Julie Prebel is Associate Professor of Writing and Rhetoric at Occidental College, where she teaches a range of writing, rhetorical theory, and cultural studies courses that resonate with her wider interests in critical race, gender, and sexuality studies. She has published on nineteenth and early twentieth century women writers, utilizing an intersectional feminist theoretical approach. Although this chapter is Professor Prebel's first publication on Toni Morrison, she has studied and taught Morrison's work for over twenty years and has mentored several student thesis projects focused on Morrison.

Jericho Williams is a Professor of English at Spartanburg Methodist College. His current research interests include American and African American literature as well as education in literature. He has published essays about educational debates in the fiction of Claude McKay and

Wallace Thurman in *Critical Insights: The Harlem Renaissance* (Salem Press, 2015) and environmental education in American slave narratives in *Ecogothic in Nineteenth-Century American Literature* (Routledge, 2017) and in the writings of Henry David Thoreau (The Thoreau Society Newsletter). He is preparing forthcoming essays about African American historical fiction, Nella Larsen, and Zora Neale Hurston.

Index

63 Years On 160
1984 xi, 78, 79, 80, 81, 82, 83, 84, 85, 86, 87, 88, 89, 90, 91, 92, 93, 105

Aboriginal American 141
activism ix, xxvi, 190
Adam and Eve 98
adulthood 56, 146
aesthetics 177, 181
African Americans x, xi, xii, xxiii, 50, 51, 53, 56, 58, 63, 64, 65, 71, 72, 73, 75, 108
Agamben, Giorgio 145
Age of Frustration 82, 83
aggression 119, 120, 124
Ahmed, Sara xxix
Aleksey 23
Alexie, Sherman 124
alienation 101, 105, 117, 129, 199
Alien Land Laws 70
allegory 102, 103
Allegory of the Cave 102
All the Pretty Horses 144
American Anti-Slavery Society 55
American Dream xxxii, 65
American Indian vii, xviii, xix, 141, 142, 143
American mythology 124, 127
American Renaissance period 47
American slavery xvi
Ammu 4, 5, 6, 7, 8, 10, 11, 12, 14, 16
Angry Young Men 198
Animal Farm 80, 93
Anjum 13, 14, 15
anthropology x, 35, 36, 42, 44

Anti-Bildungsroman 146
anticlimax 74
antihero 26, 27, 28, 195
Aristotle 205
Asian immigrants 70
Auld, Hugh xvi, xvii
Auld, Sophia xvi
Authoritarianism 87
Autobiography of an Ex-Colored Man, The 64, 76

Baldwin, James xi, xxiii, 94, 105, 106, 107
barbarism 24, 79
Bates, H. E. 19
Battle of Elderbrush Gulch, The 125
Baucom, Ian 171
Beat Generation 198
Beccah 163, 164, 167, 168, 169, 170, 171, 172
Belinsky, Vissarion 20
Bellew, John 65
Bennett, Arnold 31
Bergeron, George 39
Bhabha, Homi K. 149, 159
Bible, the 22, 105
Big Brother 81, 84
Bildungsroman 146, 155
biopolitics 145
Bird, Gloria 141
black community 73, 112, 116, 120, 197, 198
black Harlem 73
Black History Month 197
Black Lives Matter xxiii
blackness xii, 109, 116

black resistance 122
black subjectivity 119
black women xii, 114, 122
Bluest Eye, The 108, 110, 114, 122, 123
Boas, Franz 43, 45
Border Trilogy 144, 156
Boyd 144, 150, 156
Braine, John 198
Brave New World 92
bravery xviii
Breedlove, Pauline 113
Breedlove, Pecola xii, 109, 121
Bresson, Robert 175, 179
Brian 69, 71, 73, 156
British Dream 192
Broch, Hermann 175
Broken Arrow 126
Brook, Susan 198
Brothers Karamazov, The 30, 31
Brown, Michael P. 94
Buddhism 7
Burch, James H. 52

Campbell, Janet 124
cannibalism 148
capitalism x, xx, 8, 26, 27, 198
Caruth, Cathy 167
Case, Pete 194, 195, 197
caste-hierarchy 4
caste-system ix
catalyst 146, 155
Catholicism 128, 129, 135
cave 102, 103, 104
Chacko 4, 5, 6, 10
Chernyshevsky, Nikolai 25
chiasmus xxix
Child, Lydia Maria 141
Chippewa people 126, 130

Cholly 109, 112, 113, 117, 118, 119, 120
Christianity 7, 24, 146
cisgender xxi, xxii
Cities of the Plain 144
Civil Rights Act of 1964 75
Civil War 47, 54, 63, 75
Clarence 138
Clarke, Joni Adamson 137, 141
class ix, x, xi, xiii, xix, xxii, xxv, xxx, 3, 4, 6, 8, 9, 15, 16, 17, 19, 21, 22, 41, 42, 45, 52, 58, 64, 65, 69, 70, 78, 88, 90, 91, 110, 111, 112, 150, 190, 196, 198, 199
classism 68
Claudia 109, 112, 120, 121, 122
Closed Door, A 178, 186, 187, 188
Closet Space 94, 105
Cobban, Alfred 189
colonialism xii, xiii, xiv, 126, 141, 145, 155, 159, 163
Colossal Youth 174, 182, 187
Comfort Woman 158, 160, 162, 163, 172, 173
communism 32
Communist Manifesto, The 21
Concept of Fiction, The 35
Conrad, Joseph 31
Constant, Malachi 38
consumption xxv, 25, 26, 117, 119, 122, 135
Cooper, James Fenimore 141
Cornell, Daniel 128
Costa, Pedro 174, 180
Crenshaw, Kimberlé xxx
Crime and Punishment ix, 19, 23, 25, 29, 30
Crimestop 82

Crimethought 81
Crossing, The xii, 144, 157
Crystal Palace 24, 25, 26, 27, 29, 32
Cullen, Countee 63
cultural relativism x, 42, 43

Darlene 118, 119
Darwinism 41
Datu, Kerwin 191
Day at the Racists, A 189, 190, 194
Dead Souls 21
Debs, Eugene Victor 45
de Buffon, Count xvii
deCOLONIZATION 158, 160, 161, 171, 173
dehumanization x, 51, 58, 94, 165
Deleuze, Gilles 147
Deloria, Philip 125, 140
Derrida, Jacques 152
despair 80, 111, 118, 122, 155
Devils, The ix, 30, 33
diaspora 71, 146, 172
Dick and Jane 110, 111, 112, 113, 122, 123
difference viii, ix, x, xv, xvi, xvii, xx, xxix, 5, 42, 83, 89, 145, 156
disability xxvi, xxvii, xxviii, xxix, xxxii
disillusionment 146, 155
documentary xiii, 160, 175, 179, 180
domination xiv, xxv, 86, 120
Dostoyevsky, Fyodor 19, 32, 33
Douglass, Frederick xvi, xxxi, 47, 48, 49, 54, 55, 58, 59
drama 190

Draupadi 16
Dualism 27, 33
Du Bois, W. E. B. vii, 63
dwelling 164, 166, 174, 180, 186, 187, 188
dystopia xi, 26, 78

ecology 147
egalitarianism 38, 41, 45
Eli 132, 133, 136, 137, 139
Eliza 50, 51
Elson-Gray readers 110, 111
Elson, William 110
empiricism xxvii
Engels, Friedrich 21
Enlightenment era xxvii
enslavement vii, 50
epistemology 15
equality xi, xv, xvi, xvii, xviii, xix, xxiii, xxvi, xxviii, xxix, 5, 7, 25, 38, 39, 40, 41, 43, 80, 81, 87, 88, 91, 92, 128
Erdrich, Louise 124, 126, 128, 141, 142, 143
Erevelles, Nirmala xxvii
Ernest, John 48, 59, 60
erotic 119
Estha 4, 6, 15
ethics 181
ethnicity 69, 144, 146
eugenics xxviii
evolution 54, 82, 83
existentialism 198
exploitation vii, ix, 9, 56, 163, 164, 179

femininity 146
film viii, x, xiii, xxiv, 114, 115, 116, 125, 153, 160, 174,

175, 176, 177, 178, 179,
180, 181, 182, 183, 184,
185, 186, 187, 188
Fisher family 113
Fleur xii, 126, 127, 128, 129, 130,
131, 132, 133, 134, 135,
136, 137, 138, 139, 140,
141, 142
folk society 43, 44
Fontainhas 174, 177, 179, 181,
182, 185, 186, 187, 188
Ford, William 53
fraternity 25
freedom x, xvii, xix, 25, 27, 40,
47, 48, 49, 50, 51, 58, 91,
108, 125, 153, 154, 155,
171, 192
Freeland, Dave 73
Freeland, Felise 73
Freese, Peter 37
Freud, Sigmund 20
Frieda 109
Fuhr, Eckhard 147
Fukushima, Annie 159

Gabriel 97
Gambler, The 23, 33
Garnett, Constance 30, 33
Garrison, William Lloyd 54, 55
Gee, James xxii
gender inequality 158
gender violence 3, 12, 14
genealogy 14
Gide, Andre 95
Gift of the Emperor, A 160
Gina 195, 196, 198, 199
Giovanni's Room 94, 95, 102, 105,
106, 107
Girard, Rene 99

Glampers, Diana Moon 39, 40
God of Small Things, The ix, 3, 4,
10, 14, 15, 17
Gogol, Nikolai 20
Good Kings Bad Kings xxvi, xxxii
Gorin, Jean-Pierre 174
Gorky, Maxim 32
Goucher, Candice 191
Gratiano 146
Gray, William 110
Great Depression, The 58
Great Migration 71, 76, 77
Greenspan, Alan xx
Griffiths, Trevor 198
Grin Without a Cat, A 180
Guattari, Félix 147, 156

Harlan, John Marshall 63
Harlem Renaissance 64, 76
Harper, Frances E. W. 64
Harrison Bergeron x, 35, 38, 39,
40, 41, 42, 46
Hattenhauer, Darryl 40, 41
Hazel 39, 40
Heart of an Indian 125
hegemony xxv
Hein, Christina Judith 141
Hemer, Oscar 35, 44
Hessler, Michelle 128
Hirsch, Marianne 160
Hobbs, Allyson 68
Hobomok 141
homoeroticism 99
homo sacer 145, 148, 151, 152,
154
homosexuality 95, 104, 105
House of Sharing, The 160
House of the Dead 30, 32
Howells, William Dean xv, 64

Huhndorf, Shari 124
Huillet, Danielle 175
humankind ix, 28, 82
Hussein, Saddam 29
Hutchinson, John 189, 200
Hwang, Keum Ja 162

Icarus 74
identity xi, xiii, xxi, xxii, xxix,
    xxx, 48, 50, 51, 63, 65, 71,
    94, 95, 96, 97, 101, 102,
    104, 105, 115, 117, 119,
    124, 128, 138, 146, 150,
    154, 164, 189, 190, 191,
    193, 199
ideology xvi, xxiii, 41, 88, 110,
    189, 190, 200
illusion 155
imagery xxvi, 128, 179
imagination 153, 159, 176
im/migration 145
Immigration Act of 1924 70
imperialism 194
imprisonment ix, xxi, 87
income redistribution 41
India ix, 3, 5, 7, 8, 9, 11, 13, 14,
    15, 17, 92
indigeneity 146, 148, 151
Indigenous American 141
Induk 164, 165, 166, 167, 171
inequity viii, xv
Ingsoc 79, 82, 83, 88
injustice xii, xv, xxiii, xxiv, 9, 17,
    126, 141, 152, 156, 176
In Vanda's Room 174, 180, 181,
    182, 187
Islam 7
isolation 51, 115, 131, 132, 135,
    139, 183

Jazz Age 63, 75
Jefferson, Thomas xvii, 52
Jesus Christ 99, 105
Jim Crow laws xi, 63, 71, 75, 76
Johnnie 95, 97, 98, 99, 100, 101,
    102
Johnson, James Weldon 64
Jones, Alice 75
Juan José Saer 35
justice xiii, xv, xxvii, xxviii, xxx,
    xxxii, 5, 16, 17, 32, 48, 90,
    92, 132, 169, 177, 186

Kaepernick, Colin xxiv
Kafka, Franz 148
Kalyani 12, 17, 18
Kant, Immanuel 155, 157
Karna 15, 16
Kaurva brothers 15
Kaye, Peter 31
Keller, Nora Okja 158, 160, 172,
    173
Kendry, Clare 64
Kim, Elaine H. 162
Kim-Gibson, Dai Sil 160
Kim, Jodi 159
Kim, Miran 160
Kim, Soo Jin 160
King of Arcadia 147
Korea 159, 165
Korean American 158, 159, 160,
    171, 172
Kozka 136
Krishna 16
Kuenz, Jane 114
Ku Klux Klan 66
Kunti 16

labor vii, ix, xviii, xix, 5, 6, 45,
    48, 51, 52, 53, 54, 56, 57,
    58, 59, 86, 115
Labour Party 195, 196, 199
Lampton, Joe 198
Larsen, Nella 63, 76
Last of the Mohicans 141
Lawrence, D. H. 31
Lazzare 138
Leatherbarrow, W. J. 26
Lee, Sasha Y. 160
Leninism 26, 89
Lenin, Vladimir 26
Letters from Fontainhas 174, 182,
    185, 186, 188
LGBT 10
Liberal Democratic Party 159
liberalism 90
liberty viii, xi, xv, xvii, 25, 74, 88,
    90
life and death 146, 150, 156, 166
literature of inequality vii, x, 48
loneliness 101, 105, 146, 147, 153
Look Back in Anger 198, 199
Lord, Robert 27
lower castes 3, 4, 5, 6, 7, 9, 13, 14
Lustgarten, Anders 189, 190, 198
lycophilia 147, 155
lycophobia 147, 155

MacTeer, Claudia 109
MacTeer family 112
Madeleine 95, 106
Mahabharata 15, 16
Male Prison, The 95, 105
Man Without a Country, A 45, 46
Margret 137, 138, 139
Marker, Chris 180
Marxism 89, 93

Marx, Karl 21
materialism 22, 23, 25, 26, 30, 32
May, Theresa 194
McCarthy, Cormac xii, 144, 156,
    157
McDormand, Frances xxiv
McRuer, Robert xxix
media xxiv, xxv, xxxii, 114, 124,
    126, 145, 191
Mehta, Deepa 17
melancholy 24, 111
Melville, Herman 47
Menchú, Rigoberta 206
Mermann-Jozwiak, Elisabeth 118
Metamorphosis 148
metaphor x, xii, 64, 72, 75, 78, 86,
    94, 95, 96, 97, 99, 101, 104,
    105, 119, 145, 146, 148
Mikhail 20, 22
Mingus, Mia xxviii
Ministry of Utmost Happiness, The
    3, 12, 17
Min, Yong Soon 158, 160, 161
Misshepeshu 134, 138, 139
Moby-Dick 47
Mooallem, Jon 147
Morrison, Pauline 114
Morrison, Toni 108, 122, 123
Morrissey, Napoleon 134
Moss, Walter G. 198
Motyl, Alexander J. 194
multiculturalism 194, 195
multidimensional xxx, 122
Mustazza, Leonard 41
My Bondage and My Freedom 47,
    48, 49, 54, 55, 56, 58, 59
myth of Lycaon 147
mythology 122, 124, 127

Nanapush 126, 127, 128, 129, 131, 132, 135, 137, 138, 139, 140, 141

Narrative of the Life of Frederick Douglass, An American Slave 47, 54, 55, 59

nationalism xiii, 147, 159, 189, 190, 193, 194, 195, 196, 197

Nationalism 189

Native Americans 124, 126, 141

neoliberalism xxi

Newspeak 78, 81, 82, 83, 84, 85

New World Government 89

Noble Savage, The 135

norms xxi, xxii, xxv, xxvii, xxviii, xxix, xxx, 6, 9, 11, 12, 14, 94

North Star, The 55

Northup, Solomon 47, 48, 49, 58

Notes from the Dead House 19, 22, 33

Notes from the Underground ix, 19, 23, 25, 26, 27, 28, 30, 33

novel viii, ix, x, xi, xii, xiii, xxv, xxvi, 3, 4, 6, 8, 9, 10, 12, 13, 14, 15, 16, 20, 22, 23, 25, 26, 27, 30, 31, 32, 35, 37, 38, 44, 45, 63, 64, 65, 66, 67, 68, 69, 70, 71, 73, 74, 75, 78, 79, 80, 82, 83, 85, 86, 87, 88, 89, 90, 94, 95, 102, 108, 109, 110, 111, 114, 115, 118, 119, 120, 121, 122, 124, 144, 145, 146, 149, 151, 152, 156, 158, 162, 163, 176

Nussbaum, Susan xxvi

Odumegwu-Ojukwu, Chukwuemeka 44

Ogden, K. G. 83

oppositional gaze 122

oppression viii, ix, xii, xiv, xix, xxx, 3, 58, 94, 105, 109, 110, 111, 112, 113, 115, 118, 120, 121, 122, 149, 150

optimism 26, 28

Orwell, George xi, 78, 92

Osborne, John 198, 199

Ossos 174, 177, 182, 187

Other viii, xxv, 63, 77, 105, 106, 145, 197

Outing, The 94, 95, 96, 99, 101, 102, 105, 106

Pachmuss, Temira 23

Pandva brothers 15

Paravan 4, 5, 6, 10

Pardee, Shiela 36

Parham, Billy 144, 145, 147, 150, 151, 152, 153, 155, 156

Park, Therese 160

Pascual, Calvo 45

Passing xi, 63, 64, 65, 66, 67, 68, 69, 71, 74, 75, 76, 77, 106

passing novels 64

patriotism 69, 195

Pauline xii, 113, 114, 115, 116, 118, 119, 120, 122, 126, 127, 128, 129, 130, 131, 132, 133, 134, 135, 136, 137, 138, 139, 140, 141, 142

Pavolovna, Vera 25

Pecola xii, 109, 110, 112, 113, 114, 115, 116, 117, 118, 119, 120, 121, 122

Phillips, Wendell 55

Pillager, Fleur 137
Pitre, Abul 197
Plato 102, 103, 104, 106
Plessy 63, 64, 74, 77
Polina 23, 33
Poor Folk 19, 20, 21, 22, 33
Porter, Jimmy 198
Portes, Jonathan 192
Possessed, The 30, 31, 33
postcolonialism 124
postmemory 160
postmortem 158, 167
poverty xii, xxi, 7, 8, 21, 24, 55,
    80, 111, 112, 174, 179
Price, Margaret xxvii
privilege ix, xvi, xix, xxii, 110,
    112, 121
Proletariat (prole) 79, 81, 84, 86,
    90
protest xxiv, xxxi
psychology 190, 196, 199

queer xi, xxi, 12, 13, 94, 96, 105
Quest for Justice 160

racial inequality vii, xvii
racial injustice xxiii, xxiv
racial passing 68, 76
racism xii, xxiv, 69, 71, 72, 109,
    114, 119, 164, 194, 196
Rahel 4, 6, 8, 11, 15
rape 14, 109, 118, 133, 158
Raskolnikov, Rodion Romanovich
    29
rationalism 27, 28
Raven, Philip 82
realism 19, 126
rebellion vii, xii, 58, 200
Redfield, Irene 65, 69

Redfield, Robert 36, 43
Redwine, C. Horner 37
Remembering Jungshindae 158,
    160, 161, 171, 173
representation xxvi, 102, 135, 154,
    158, 186, 194
resistance vii, viii, xii, 54, 89, 122,
    127, 165, 181, 182, 184, 187
Rhinelander, Leonard 75
Richard 32, 45, 105, 168
romanticism 19
Room at the Top 198
Roy, Arundhati ix, 3, 17
ruin 109, 136, 174, 182
Rumfoord, Winston Niles 38, 41
Russell 133, 134
Russian socialism 26
Ryder, Guy xx

Saggar, Shamit 191
Samsa, Gregor 148
Sans Soleil 180
Satan 97
Savage Indian, the 129, 131, 132,
    134, 135
schizophrenia 109, 118
Science fiction 78
Seok, Hein 160
Sergi, Jennifer 138
Settler colonialism xiv
sexism 69, 164
sexual identity 94, 95, 101, 102,
    104, 105
sexuality viii, xiv, xxvii, xxx, 69,
    94, 95
sexual rights 10
Shakespeare, William 146
Shape of Things to Come, The 79,
    82, 83, 88, 89, 93

Shylock 146
Silence Broken: Korean Comfort Women 160
Sillitoe, Alan 198
Simmons, Ernest 24
Sinyavsky, Andrei 31
Sirens of Titan, The x, 35, 37, 38, 40, 41, 42, 45, 46
Slaughterhouse-Five 35, 46
slave narratives x, 47, 48, 49, 50, 52, 54
slavery x, xiii, xvi, xvii, 47, 48, 49, 50, 51, 52, 53, 54, 55, 56, 57, 58, 158
Slavophile 22, 32
Smith, Anthony D. 189, 200
Smith, James McCune 55
social change xxiv, xxv, xxix
social equality xxvi
social inequality xiv, xxiii, 37, 42, 146
social injustice xii, 176
socialism ix, xi, 22, 26, 27, 30, 78, 82, 88, 89
Sollors, Werner 67, 77
Solzhenitsyn, Alexander 32
Soon Hyo/Akiko 163, 164, 165, 166, 167, 168, 169, 170, 171
Souls of Black Folk, The vii, 63, 76
Spade, Dean xxvii, xxxi
spatiality xi, 63, 65, 68, 71, 72, 74
Spenser, Edmund 146
spirituality ix
Stalin, Joseph 88, 93
Stapledon, Olaf 92
stereotypes viii, xii, xiii, 125, 126, 127, 128, 129, 130, 133, 135, 140, 141

Stewart, Duncan xxiv
Stone Age 147
Straub, Jean-Marie 175, 188
subgenre vii, x, 48
subjectivity 95, 102, 103, 105, 114, 171
Sweet, Ossian 63
Sylvia 95, 97, 99, 100, 101

Tarr, Béla 187
Temple, Shirley 117, 121
territorialism 155
Thoreau, Henry David 47
thoughtcrime 81, 82, 85
Thought Police 81, 90
time xv, xxi, xxii, xxv, xxvi, 7, 15, 20, 21, 31, 32, 37, 40, 42, 53, 56, 65, 66, 69, 71, 78, 82, 85, 88, 101, 110, 114, 136, 144, 146, 169, 170, 172, 174, 175, 181, 186, 187, 188, 190, 192, 196, 197, 198, 199, 200
Tim, Tiny xxvi
Tolstoy, Leo 31
Tompkins, Kyla Wazana 119
Tracks xii, 124, 126, 127, 128, 129, 135, 141, 142
tragic mulatta 73
transformation xi, xiii, xxix, 65, 104, 116, 117, 129, 132, 134, 146, 148, 171
transgender xxi, xxiv
Trauma 158, 159, 161, 163, 165, 167, 169, 171, 172, 173
Treaty of Versailles 83
Triangulation of Desire 100
Trump, Donald 145
Tsarist autocracy 21

Tsarist Russia 19
Turgenev, Ivan 31
Twain, Mark 64
Twelve Years a Slave x, 47, 48, 49, 58, 59
tyranny vii

underground man 27, 28
Ungeziefer 148
Untouchables 3, 6, 7, 10, 13, 17
utilitarianism 27
Utopianism 88

Vanda 174, 180, 181, 182, 184, 187, 188
Van Dyke, Annette 128
Vanishing American, The 126
Velutha 4, 5, 6, 9, 10, 11, 14, 16
Ventura 180, 181, 182, 184, 187, 188
victimization 114, 118, 120, 167
Vince Brewton 150
violence vii, viii, xii, xiii, xxi, xxii, xxv, xxvi, 3, 11, 12, 13, 14, 15, 16, 53, 57, 79, 86, 87, 89, 109, 113, 117, 118, 119, 120, 122, 132, 135, 145, 152, 154, 155, 156, 159, 164, 187
Völkel, Bärbel 200, 201
Vonnegut, Kurt x, 35, 45, 46

Walker, David 75, 77
Walton, Linda 191, 201
Warren, Kenneth 51
Water 17
wealth xx, xxi, xxii, xxvii, xxxii, 3, 19, 29, 32, 41, 58, 91, 92

wedlock 16
Wells, H. G. 79, 88, 92
Weltfrieden 155
Werrlein, Debra T. 110
Wesker, Arnold 198
white abolitionist movement 55
White, Hayden 200
Whitehead, Christine 192
white racism 119
white standards (beauty) xi, xii, 115
white supremacy xii, 108, 109, 115, 119, 121, 122
Wilson, Colin 198
Wilson, David 49
Wingfield, Laura xxvi
Winter Notes on Summer Impressions ix, 19, 23, 24, 25, 32
Wofford, Chloe 108
wolves xii, 144, 145, 146, 147, 149, 151, 154
womanhood 109, 114, 115, 116, 121
Woolf, Virginia 31
World War I 64
World War II xiii, 36, 64, 158, 159
Wren, Karen 193

xenophobia 190, 196
X, Malcolm 194

youth ix, 102, 132, 146, 155, 183

Zenobia 196, 197, 198
Zimen, Erik 147